Withdrawn

THE CONCISE ENCYCLOPAEDIA
ENCYCLOPAEDIA
AND
1992 PRICE GUIDE TO
GOSS CHINA

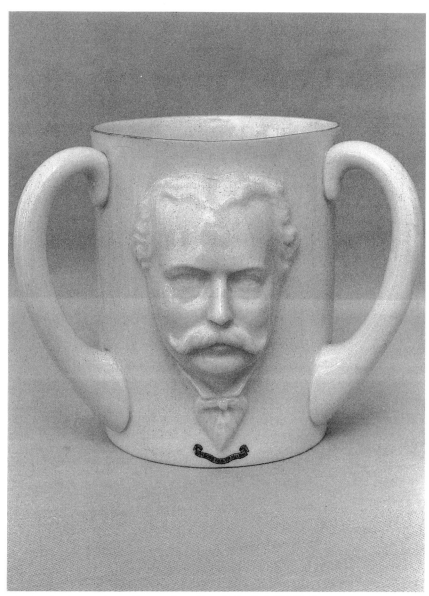

Three handled Loving Cup, 110mm with profile in high relief of W.H. Goss
Inscribed in the banner ribbon W.H. GOSS F.G.S. F.R.MET.SOC.

THE CONCISE ENCYCLOPAEDIA

AND

1992 PRICE GUIDE TO GOSS CHINA

Nicholas Pine

**Edited by
Norman Pratten**

MILESTONE
PUBLICATIONS

Published by
Milestone Publications
Goss & Crested China Ltd.,
62 Murray Road, Horndean,
Waterlooville, Hampshire PO8 9JL.

Edited by Lt. Cdr. N.H. Pratten RD, FCIS, RNR (Ret'd.).
Photography by Michael Edwards Studio, Havant, and
Images, Waterlooville.

Typeset by Fareham Media, Bishops Waltham, Hampshire.
Printed and bound in Great Britain by
Bath Press, Bath, Avon.

First printed 1978
Revised 1981, 1984, 1986, 1992

British Library Cataloguing in Publication Data
The concise encyclopaedia and price guide to goss china 1992
1. Goss porcelain. Prices - Lists
338.4373827

ISBN 1-85265-119-9

Contents

Acknowledgements

I wish to thank the following who have been kind enough to notify me of new pieces, or provided information concerning alterations and amendments, inscriptions and descriptions, dimensions and variations, in order that this book might be updated. F.R.J. Basket, Birmingham City Public Libraries Department, C.R. Browne, J.A. Cornelius, W. Cover, H. Crooks, W.J. Davenport, A. Davies, R. Davies, W. Elkington, R.L. Evans, J. Farrell, D.G. Fitchett, J. and R. Fitzer, G.F. Flett, J. Garrard, J. and E. Gatenby, P. Gibson, S.K. Godly, H.E. Gordon, R.Gough, N. Griffin, I. Hay, R. Hay, L. Harris, D. Hazle, Dr. P. Herley, B. Holmes, T. Hood, House of Commons Public Information Office, G. Hunt, M. Keown, J.D. Kershaw, L. Killick, C. and K. Lewis-Hall, P. Lomax, P. Mercer, D. Mills, E. Miskelly, B. Morris, A. Munday, S. Munday, C. Murten, R. Nevitt, J. Nicholls, B. and M. Osborne, F. and C. Owen, Palace of Westminster Curator of Works of Art, C. Pugh, K.J. Ramage, M. Regnard, R. and P. Riley, E. and R. Smith, R. Smith, W. Smith, B. and J. Spaulding, E. Stansmore, Stoke-on-Trent City Museum and Art Gallery, P. Tasker, D. Taylor, G. Thomas, J. Till, P. Tillbrook, P. Tranter, Trenton (USA) New Jersey State Library, E. Tull, J. Tunmore, N. Tzimas, T. Usher, J. Varley, G. Walder, B. Waller, C. Waller, F. Ward, B. Warren, M. Welland, T. Wellings, J. Whipp, K. Whitcombe, J. Willis, M.J. Willis—Fear, D. Wiscombe, M. Woods, J. Wright, A Young.

Norman Pratten, assisted by his wife Grace, has contributed far more than that normally contributed by an editor, and his diligence, expert advice, meticulous attention to detail and depth of knowledge in the field of Goss heraldic Porcelain is of incalculable value and I thank him sincerely.

I also wish to thank members of the Goss family for their assistance; in particular, Major W.R. Goss and also Dorothy and Harold Goss, Clara Goss, Louise Goss and Valentine Taggart.

John Galpin was instrumental in compiling the first Price Guide to Goss China, and his meticulous measuring and recording has been invaluable. I thank him for his willing assistance to Goss Collectors for over 20 years.

In addition, I wish to thank The Leicester Mercury for kindly allowing me to use their photographs of the Goss factory and surrounds.

Special thanks are due to Alan Glover for his contribution to the work, particularly for his knowledge and guidance on the Winchester theme, and for contributing a history of Goss in Winchester which was prepared especially for this book.

Without the knowledge and support of my wife, Lynda, this book would be incomplete. I thank her together with my fellow directors and staff of Goss & Crested China Ltd who constantly record new models and suggest improvements.

John Magee will always merit a credit in any book about Goss China. He set Goss China on its present popular course and even now in his retirement from the world of Goss, his wisdom and advice are still as positive as ever.

7

Introduction

This sixth edition of *The Concise Encyclopaedia and Price Guide to Goss China*, includes details of over 600 new pieces and variations which have been discovered since publication of the 1989 guide. Numerous detail corrections and improvements have been made and the height or other main dimensions of virtually every piece has been stated. Full inscriptions in italic type for each inscribed piece, as introduced for the first time in the last edition, have been continued and extended in this edition. There is no inscription if none is stated.

The author has divided the wares produced by the Goss Factory into three periods as follows:

The First Period	1858-1887
The Second Period	1881-1934
The Third Period	1930-1939

The First Period covers ware manufactured by William Henry Goss whilst he owned and ran the factory. The Second Period spans the stewardship of his sons Adolphus, Victor and William Huntley Goss. The Third Period embraces wares made by other factories, but which carry the Goss mark.

The guide has been structured to divide the products of The House of Goss into the three periods. The First Period covers ware produced from the start of the firm in 1858 to 1887 and incudes the early Victorian unglazed figurines, together with a series of famous portrait busts and terracotta wares.

The earliest crested models were made towards the end of the First Period, and the reader's attention is drawn to the introductory comments in each chapter in order to be able to differentiate between the wares of one period from another. In particular, the First Period ornamental ware chapter introduction establishes the distinguishing features of the early crested wares which will enable such pieces to be accurately identified.

The Second Period from 1881-1934 encompasses the introduction of heraldic china, the bulk of which was mass produced and comprises historic models and special shapes, ornamental and domestic wares. The pieces that were also produced during the First Period have the symbol [1] after their respective entries, but as the models and shapes were also made for many years during the Second Period, and it would be confusing to have chapters on both historic models and special shapes in two periods, they are all catalogued in one chapter in the Second Period. Also included are dolls, miniatures, cottages, crosses, fonts and animals, all under separate headings due to their importance.

The first of the named models appeared around 1881 and were of an uneven, heavy, creamy consistency with mould lines clearly visible down both sides. The gilding had to be fired at exactly the right temperature in order for

The carved stone Goshawk set high in the wall of the Goss factory. This building was completed in 1906

The Goss Ovens pictured in 1984. Since this photograph was taken, all the original outbuildings have been cleared and a large warehouse now abuts the rear of the ovens

it to be permanent. However, the factory was unable to perfect this until approximately 1885-1890, hence the poor or complete lack of gilding to be found on the majority of First Period pieces, but which nevertheless does not affect values.

Another characteristic of these early wares is the somewhat diluted, patchy or pastel-like appearance of the colours used for the coats of arms.

The titles of these models were also printed in large capitals on the base and the inscriptions were shorter. Early domestic shapes were also slightly indented on the base and glazed underneath.

From about 1887 onwards, production techniques improved dramatically. The porcelain mix became thinner, more delicate and more perfectly formed. The gilding was better, brighter and permanent. Coats of arms were painted with richer colours and more detailed. The type-size used for the transfer of descriptions to be affixed to the base was smaller and the descriptions lengthier. Various sizes of shield for the arms were introduced in order to suit the proportions of the shape or model. The first models on the production line were of the larger size, but it soon became evident that the general public were more appreciative of the smaller shapes: perhaps because they were prettier, or easier to carry home, and, as collectors today find, more can be fitted into a china cabinet.

Separate chapters are included on domestic, utility and ornamental wares, so as to assist the reader to locate pieces more easily. The tiny domestic items not made for daily use have been classified as ornamental and are re-named Fairy Shapes, as this is how they were originally known. Each piece is catalogued according to the 8th, 9th and War editions of *The Goss Record*, and page references are given. These books were published originally between 1913 and 1921. They have been reprinted by Milestone and give the flavour of Goss collecting at the time, as well as having a full description of the history and origin of most of the originals from which the Goss models were made.

Although the last member of the Goss family to own the pottery sold out in 1929, heraldic souvenir china continued to be made in the same way until 1934. Therefore, the date given for the end of the Second Period is 1934 when the firm went into receivership.

The Third Period, from 1930-1939 covers the heavier and more colourful ranges of pottery introduced to revitalise flagging sales. Although the coats of arms still continued to appear on a range of vases, utility shapes, comical animals and buildings, they are very different from those of the previous period and values are generally lower. Not all of these have the mark W.H. Goss England, but the heavier, duller quality and more garish colours used in the decoration are easily distinguished. Also in this section are the brightly coloured Toby Jugs, Flower Girls, the beige pottery Royal Buff tea sets, and the Cottage Pottery domestic ware attractively shaped as thatched cottages. This beige pottery is comparatively fine with a quite noticeable resonance.

Information on *The Goss Record*, Postcards, the League of Goss Collectors, Cabinets and Leaflets are contained in the earlier chapters, thereby providing

The inside of one of the bottle ovens.

Ashfield Lodge, formerly the home of W.H. Goss, which stands next to the main factory building.

the reader with as much information as possible.

The Goss pottery was ahead of its time and a market leader. The difficult times shared by the pottery industry in England in the last century led the other three hundred or so local potbanks to copy Goss's successful heraldic lines before the turn of the century, and they capitalized on the serious flavour of Goss models by producing generally more light-hearted and amusing shapes. All known crested china made by these other firms is contained, along with their values, in *The Price Guide to Crested China* by Nicholas Pine.

It should be noted that the values indicated in this guide are for shapes only and do not take into account the value of any arms or decorations. Exceptions to this are the League models and the historic models bearing matching arms. Prices are given for both matching and non-matching where both exist, and the correct matching arms are listed. Elsewhere, the additional premium is given for matching arms. For all other additional crest and decoration values, the companion volume to this guide, viz: *The Price Guide to Arms and Decorations on Goss China* by the same author, lists and values some 10,000 different decorations to be found on Goss porcelain.

Therefore, to find the value of any given piece, first look it up in the Price Guide, then add any plusage for the motif or decoration as given in the companion volume.

This edition contains additional illustrations, especially of First Period wares, all of which are now over 100 years old. As for previous editions, the improvement and updating of the listings will be ongoing, and the author will be very pleased to hear about any item of Goss which has not yet been catalogued.

Prices quoted in this guide are for pieces in perfect condition. Worn gilding, faded coats of arms, chips, cracks and bad firing flaws will all affect values substantially. A small crack could easily halve the value, whilst a cottage worth £100 would probably only be worth £25 with a chimney missing.

Although it is always possible to get a damaged piece restored, it is easy to detect restoration. Where the value of a restored item would be greater than that of the same piece in a damaged state, then restoration would be worthwhile. However, inexpensive, sub-standard pieces have always been popular, thus making it possible for those with limited resources to obtain the rarest specimens. Indeed, damaged Goss has risen in value proportionately more than perfect Goss in recent years.

A faded coat of arms devalues a piece considerably. Fading is caused by prolonged exposure to sunlight and is irreversible. The colours most likely to be affected in this way are blue and black. Fading should not be confused with oxidization, which often occurs in the case of pieces stored in newspaper for many years. Oxygen in the air reacts with the surface of the coat of arms and causes a brown metallic film to spread over the enamel, mostly on yellows and reds. A little moistened detergent gently applied will remove this oxidized film and reveal the arms as perfect. Do not forget to thoroughly rinse off the detergent. It is important to note that oxidization will not render a piece sub-standard, whereas fading would. Over the last few years, the majority of prices have increased steadily. The cheaper ranges have enjoyed higher percentage rises than pieces over, say, £70-£100.

When the first edition of this guide was published in 1978, the name Goss was still relatively unknown in the antique world. Now nearly all collecting authorities are aware of Goss china and now appreciate its quality. It is now accepted as being as important as the products of many of the more well-known manufacturers.

Prices herein are drawn from twenty years of experience in buying and selling Goss china, and for the majority of that period making an orderly market in this ware and researching the subject. Auctions have never been a good source of price information, as such outlets often tend to be used as clearing houses for sub-standard and inferior wares. No auction house as yet really understands or cares about Goss china and this often results in as many bargains as rogue pieces being knocked down. Auction houses are, in the author's experience, potential minefields for the unwary, and there really can be no substitute for knowledge.

Value Added Tax has always been a problem, in that it is included as part of the normal retail selling price by Goss & Crested China Ltd, the leading dealers, but not apparently by many others. Indeed, it has often been found that minor unregistered dealers have been charging the same prices as this company and in so doing have in effect been overcharging by some 17½%.

In order, therefore, that prices in this guide should be directly comparable with those quoted elsewhere, VAT has not been included in the value of items under 100 years old which attract this tax.

The leading forum for buying and selling is *Goss & Crested China*, a 32 page illustrated monthly catalogue published by Goss & Crested China Ltd. See the final pages in this book for further details.

Each edition contains examples of pieces from every period of the factory and is available by annual subscription.

There are three clubs for Collectors of Goss china. The Goss and Crested China Club publishes a monthly catalogue, holds regular open days, values pieces, answers collectors queries and provides many other services. See the final pages in this book for further details. The Goss Collectors' Club publishes a monthly magazine, holds regular regional meetings and occasional Goss fairs. The Crested Circle publishes a quarterly magazine and holds specialist crested china fairs.

The W.H. Goss prizewinning entry in the International Exhibition, London 1862

1. A History of the Goss Factory

The production of porcelain at the firm of W H Goss of Stoke-on-Trent spanned four reigns and some 70 years from 1858 to 1929. The family-run firm was headed by William Henry Goss, who was born in 1833, and who had learned his trade and gained a sound grounding in chemistry under the personal guidance of Alderman Copeland of the Copeland Works, also at Stoke. It was a small business in the early days when the founder's children were all young, and the total workforce numbered less than twenty. The Falcon Works was one of 120 potteries struggling to survive in the smoke, dirt and grime of the area known as The Potteries in Staffordshire. The pottery towns include Burslem, Hanley, Lane End, Shelton, Fenton, Tunstall, Longport (Longton) as well as Stoke. These towns had sprung up along the same turnpike road in an area where coal, water power, canals, lime-stone and raw clay were all available or easily accessible.

In a line of business where masters notoriously ill-treated their work force and used child labour (children down the mines at this time fared better), William Henry Goss, along with other enlightened potters, including Minton, Copeland and Wedgwood, campaigned for better working conditions and treated his own staff generously.

When Goss was an impressionable young man of thirteen (he married at sixteen!) the first parian was produced at the Copeland Works by John Mountford in 1846. This was quickly followed by a similar material at Minton, and very soon all the major factories were using this medium to produce elegant classically styled figures, portrait busts of politicians, notable dignitaries of the day, royalty, poets, authors and musicians. Eventually Goss became chief artist and designer at Copeland, and continued to produce similar lines when he became his own boss. These were difficult and costly to produce, and the larger part of his substantial income was derived from the sale of coloured enamels, made up to his own special recipes, to other potteries for decorating china.

Goss also produced a small range of terracotta ware, using the local marl or clay. In 1867 he had a brief partnership with a Mr. Peake, and a few pieces exist marked *Goss and Peake*, mainly terracotta. Peake had financial difficulties as a result of his own activities, and Goss dissolved the partnership after one year.

Goss's other specialities included jewelled scent bottles and vases, which were produced from pierced and fretted parian, with inset cut-glass jewels in the Sévres style, but more successful than that firm in the setting and firing of

Adolphus Goss in retirement in the garden of his home, The Old Villa, Alsager, Cheshire.

the stones. This method was patented in 1872, but jewelled ware ceased to be made after 1885. The noted perfumier Eugene Rimmel, was one of the factory's customers, having perfumeries in Rome, Paris and London.

Other lines during this First Period of Goss china production included intricate flower baskets for table decorations, brooches, spill holders (one in the shape of Dr. Kenealy, the then Member of Parliament for Stoke, whom Goss loathed) and a bullock and sheep group - a special order from America.

The Second Period of Goss production is marked by the entry of his eldest son, Adolphus, into the management and the introduction of heraldic ware. This was to completely supersede the previous ware due to its popularity and ability to be mass produced (though not in the way things are today!) More importantly, Goss became a household name, and collecting Goss china a national hobby.

It was Adolphus who realised there was a growing market in providing for the day tripper, because of the introduction of bank holidays for workers by Queen Victoria in 1871, the expanding network of railways across Britain, and the increasing popularity of the seaside, approved of by the Queen herself.

It was his idea that visitors to seaside resorts and other places might like to take home a miniature china ornament as a souvenir. To give it local interest, he proposed that it should bear the town's coat of arms. The shape would be the reproduction of some vase, jar or urn of antiquarian interest, such as those found in the local museum. He and his father shared a love of heraldry and archaeology, and Adolphus hoped to use the porcelain models to create an interest amongst the middle and working classes in the subjects, whilst at the same time enticing the public to buy Goss china as an artistic memento of holiday visits.

He enthusiastically explained his idea to his father, expecting him to be delighted, but instead was immediately turned down and told that the scheme was not a viable proposition. Adolphus was naturally very disappointed, but being the strong minded person he was - his motto being to make up one's mind, and let no one alter it, he made up a few prototype glazed parian models, applied coats of arms in the form of transfers hand painted with enamels, and managed to get William to agree. Crested China, as it is now popularly known, started from there. It was not long before this heraldic ware entirely replaced the factory's previous output of figures and busts. This led to a five year building plan to treble the floor space in order to cope with the incredible demand.

Throughout this period of production, only one selected agent was appointed in each town. These agencies were only allowed to sell their own town's coat of arms or transfer printed views. After 1883 they could order any shape instead of being restricted to their own local shapes. For instance, the Gloucester agent could only sell Gloucester Jugs up until that date, and thereafter he would stock a wide variety of models, but they all bore the Gloucester crest. In those days, to obtain a Land's End crest entailed a journey there to purchase it; there was no other way!

TELEGRAMS:-
GOSS. STOKE-ON-TRENT.

WILLIAM H. GOSS,
Manufacturer of Ivory Porcelain Etc.,
FALCON POTTERY Stoke-on-Trent.

FULL PRICE ALLOWED FOR CASKS & PACKING MATERIALS, IF RETURNED. NO ALLOWANCE OTHERWISE.
NOT RESPONSIBLE FOR BREAKAGES. 5 % DISCOUNT UP TO TWO MONTHS FROM DATE OF INVOICE.
2½ % "   "   "   THREE "   "   "   "   "

30th August 1919

Miss Phillipps,

Fore Street,

Per N.S.Ry., Totnes. Devon.

P.T	1½ dozen	Asstd China Teas & Saucers Arms	12/ · 1	3	·
W.H.G.	11/12 ·	6ins China Plates ·	9/ ·	8	3
116	1/12 ·	Bournemouth Bottle ·	12/ ·	1	·
	3 1				
	1/3 ·	Rim Trays & Flemish Jars ·	5/ ·	1	8
	1 1				
	1/6 ·	Abergavenny & Glastonbury Vase ·	5 / ·		10
	1/12 ·	Famous Colchester Vase ·	5/ ·		5
	6 1				
	7/12 ·	Castletown & Stamp Box ·	6/ ·	3	6
	1 2				
	1/4 ·	Newbury & Cambridge Pitchers ·	8/ ·	2	·
	6 6				
	1 ·	Harrogate & Egyptian Jars ·	8/ ·	8	·
	1/2 ·	Manx Measures ·	8/ ·	4	·
	7/12 ·	Flemish Bottle &Tresco Braziers ·	9/ ·	5	3
	1/12 ·	Salisbury Kettle ·	10/ ·		10
	1/2 ·	Covered Jarra ·	11/ ·	5	6
	1/12 ·	Rose Bowl 3 ·	16/ ·	1	4
	1/12 ·	Lancaster Jug 1 ·	8/ ·		8
				3	6	3
		50% Advance		1	13	2
		Cask & Wood Wool			6	·
		£		5	5	5

5% DISCOUNT WILL
BE ALLOWED IF PAID BEFORE

OCT 30 1919

2½% ONE MONTH LATER,
NOTHING AFTERWARDS.

Invoice for Goss Heraldic Porcelain supplied to the Totnes Agent in 1919

It fell to Adolphus, with his business drive and enthusiasm, to be the firm's travelling salesman, spending more and more time away from home visiting suitable places to obtain permission to use the local arms, sketching new models for reproduction, securing and taking orders. He was so thorough and successful that he ceased to have anything more to do with the daily runnung of the firm. By 1900 he had organised 481 agencies inland. He considered he was the mainstay of the business and called himself Goss Boss, which irritated his father intensely. Letters that passed between father and son reveal a strained relationship and, as the author's research has shown, life in the Goss household was not easy with such a stern Victorian father as William.

In 1893 Adolphus introduced a new range of coloured miniature cottages. The first three were Ann Hathaway's, Shakespeare's Birthplace, and Burns' Cottage, Ayrshire. This new line proved immensely popular, and it was gradually extended to 42 buildings in various sizes. In the latter half of the firm's life, some cottages were glazed which tended to intensify the colouring. This was a good line for improving sales at a time that was particularly poor for British exports, and when the china trade was suffering a depression.

It is hardly surprising, therefore, that most of the other pot banks turned to producing crested china, though not one ever equalled the Goss quality in glaze, parian body, gilding or enamel colour. These were all the secret recipes of William Henry Goss, though they were leaked to the Irish firm Belleek in 1863 when eleven Goss workers were persuaded to leave in order to save the factory at Belleek in Co Fermanagh. Belleek china, using Goss recipes, was produced from 1863 onwards, and even today's pieces are similar to Goss. Far sighted firms such as Arcadian, Carlton, Shelley and Willow Art, found a viable trade in modelling animals, especially in amusing and comical poses; also buildings, the originals of which were to be found throughout Britain, and household objects, military and other items. In this way they catered for the lower end of the market. True Goss enthusiasts, however, would not accept these imitations.

J.J. Jarvis, a keen collector, began producing a series of booklets entitled *The Goss Record*, the purpose of which was to provide a catalogue of agents' names, addresses and opening hours. Agencies ranged from restaurants, bazaars, hotels, chemists, and station bookstalls to local libraries. The first edition was in 1900, and a supplement in 1902 includes 601 British agents, and the first foreign agent in Bermuda. By 1921, in the ninth edition, there were 1,378 British agencies, and 186 overseas in 24 countries.

The range of arms and models was extensive, all made with care and hand-painted to ensure perfection, with an exactness that could only be admired. The modern souvenir of today formed from Plaster of Paris is a sad reminder of how standards have fallen.

The death of the head of the firm in 1906, and Adolphus's exclusion from a share of the firm in his father's will, did not affect the boom years of 1900-1914. The third son, Victor, who took over the firm (second son Godfrey had also fallen from favour) was killed in a riding accident in 1913. Victor had been a good businessman, but not so Huntley, who was the last son and left in sole

William Henry Goss in the Summer-house at Ashfield Cottage. This photograph was taken by his son Adolphus, a keen photographer around 1880 when William was in his forties.

charge of the firm. In an attempt to survive the Great War, a range of warship crests and regimental badges was introduced, as were a couple of dozen copyright models. However, this was not enough to save the pottery from the decline in trade after the war, and Huntley Goss sold the firm, and the rights to the trademark, in 1929 to Cauldon Potteries, having paid every bill and all wages due.

The new owners continued producing heraldic ware for another four years, but began to specialise in good quality earthenware and pottery similar to that of their other factories which included Arcadian. All of this new ware was marked *Goss, Goss England,* or *Made in England.* A new company formed in 1931 by Harold Taylor Robinson, known as W H Goss Ltd, with himself as director, began trading, using the Goss mark on shapes made from moulds from other factories. He was declared bankrupt in 1932, having been personally responsible for the takeover of 32 companies, including firms which supplied his potteries with fuel and clay in order to produce more cheaply. He had had to weather the Great War, the 1921 Coal strike, and the loss of foreign trade with unsettled international markets; with Britain going off the gold standard in 1924, and the worldwide depression of the 30's. He said: 'When I saw the depression was developing to the extent it was, I left my country house and came to live practically next door to the works and I have been working 50 weeks out of 52 to try to circumvent the terrible effects of the depression. When you get down to the basic facts you realise that as the largest potter in Staffordshire, I have been the largest victim.'

The range produced during this Third Period of the factory was very colourful and distinctive. William Henry Goss would certainly not have approved, but it suited the changing tastes and moods of the roaring 20's. A popular line was the beige pottery tea sets called Cottage Pottery, decorated with pictures of cottages with hollyhocks and full beds of flowers.

Commemorative mugs and beakers were issued for the Silver Jubilee of King George V and Queen Mary in 1935, and for the Coronations of Edward VIII, and King George VI and Queen Elizabeth in 1937. The last commemoratives were for the 1938 Scottish Empire Exhibition at Glasgow, and were decorated with green trim instead of the usual gilding.

Production ended mid 1940 and all lines stopped, including the coloured Flower Girls in the style of the modern Doulton ladies. The Falcon works were used by a number of different companies after 1940, including a manufacturer of parachutes during the Second World War, and by a clothing manufacturer. The Goss ovens still stand, in a state of disrepair but deservedly the subject of a Preservation Order. Today, the entire site is owned by Portmeirion Potteries, Ltd.

For the complete history of the Goss family, the factory and their china see WILLIAM HENRY GOSS The story of the Staffordshire family of Potters who invented Heraldic Porcelain, by Lynda and Nicholas Pine (Milestone Publications). See the final pages in this book for further details.

Huntley and daughter Margaret Goss, 1920

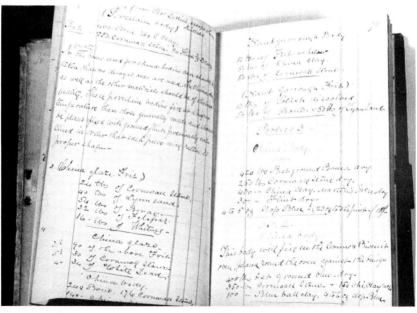

An original Goss recipe book detailing ingredients for parian

2 Factory Marks on W H Goss Porcelain

The wares of this factory are easy to recognise because virtually every piece was marked, usually on the base. W H Goss himself said that the black printed Goshawk with wings outstretched and the firm's name in capitals underneath, was in continuous use from 1862 onwards. This distinctive factory mark gave rise to the name of the Falcon Works, by which the pottery was known locally.

The earliest Goshawk was coloured red, gold, blue or puce, and appears without the firm's name printed beneath it. These marks appear on the earliest First Period pieces from 1858 to approximately 1862, and such pieces are rare.

The earliest products from the beginning of the firm in 1858 were impressed during manufacture whilst the clay was still damp. They were impressed **W H Goss** with serif type-face, that is, with cross-lines to the end of a stroke on a letter. This mark was used up until 1887 when the **W H GOSS** mark was used sans serif, i.e. plain lettering. This seems to have been applied to some shapes and not others right up until 1916 at least, usually with the Goshawk as well.

There are many examples of poorly placed impressed factory marks. Often just W H G is visible, or even perhaps the last two letters of GOSS. When inspecting an unmarked piece, it is advisable to carefully check the base and sides, and in the case of busts, the shoulders and back, for even a hint of the magic mark. Positive Goss identification will certainly add to the value of anything that at first sight appears unmarked.

Many of the First Period busts and figures were incised or printed in manuscript with details such as the following example, with minor variations occurring in the wording:-

> Published as the Act directs (See 54.Geo.III.C 56.)
> W. H. Goss.
> Stoke-on-Trent.
> 1 Dec 1873.
> Copyright

This identification became standard when used on the majority of the Parian busts, figures and groups produced during the mid-1870's through to 1911. It was either stamped into the still-wet porcelain or transfer printed on to the finished piece in black, for example:-

> Copyright as Act directs
> W. H. GOSS.
> Stoke-on-Trent.
> 1 November 1881.

Gold, red, blue or puce mark without words. Approx. 1858

Incised inscription on large bust in W.H. Goss's own hand

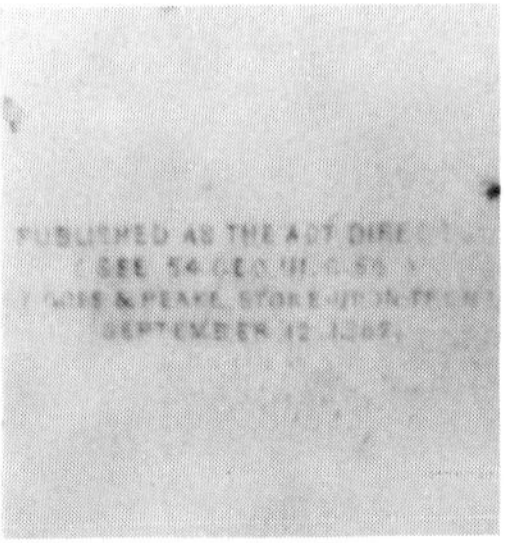

Black detailed printed mark on Figurine

Black printed mark, 1867

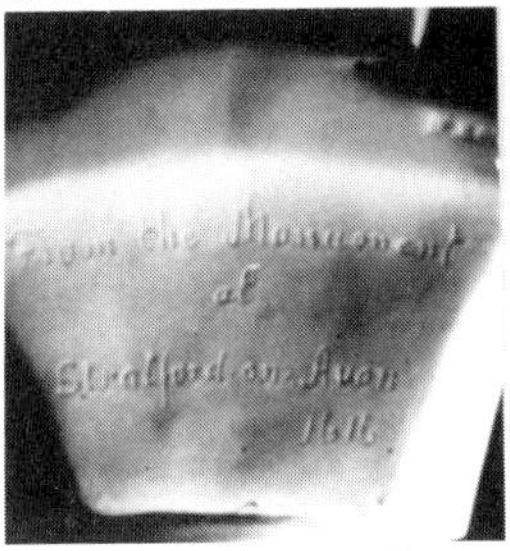

Incised inscription with impressed W H Goss

Black printed mark on terracotta

Serif impressed mark 1858–1887 approximately

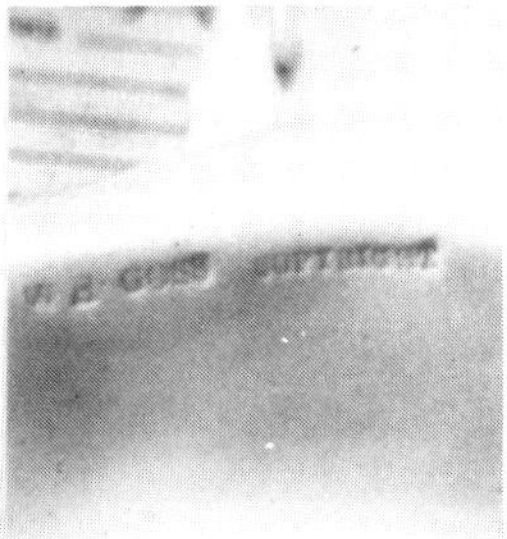

Impressed Serif Copyright Mark on a Bust, 1876

Sans-serif impressed mark 1887—1916 approximately

Incised mark on Dr. Kenealy Spill holder in W H Goss's own hand

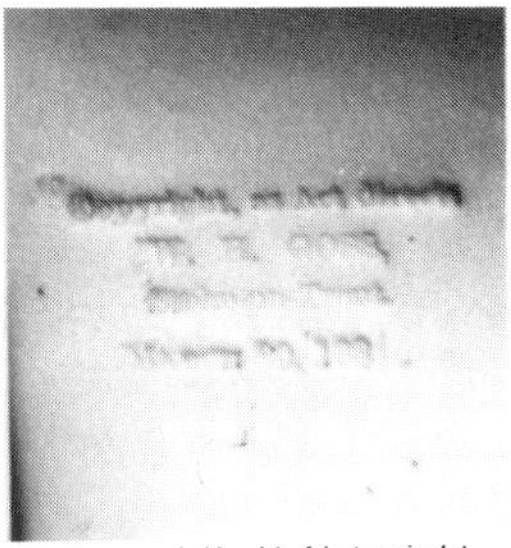

Impressed Serif Copyright Mark on a Bust, 1881

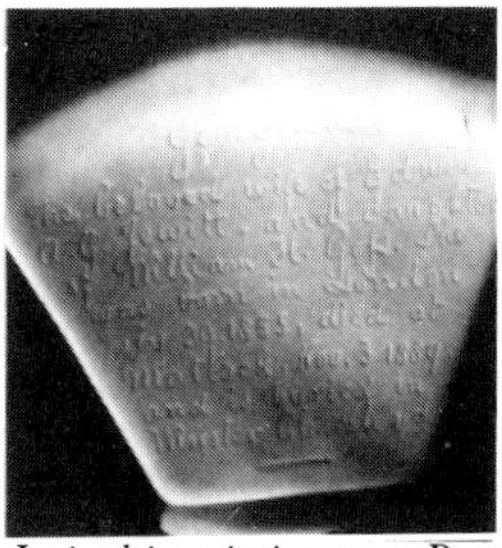

Incised inscription on a Bust in W H Goss's own hand

or, more fully:

Copyright
Pub. as Act Directs
(See 54. Geo III. C 56)
W. H. GOSS.
Stoke-on-Trent.
22 Jany 1893.

Identification details varied, and this style of marking, usually on the reverse, was in use from the early 1870s until 1911. The dates used in this way are the publication dates of the respective shapes, and not necessarily the date of manufacture. Often only one of a pair of figures, vases or ewers was marked.

Terracotta wares were marked with a black printed **W H GOSS or GOSS & PEAKE**, during a brief period of financial partnership with a Mr. Peake. See TERRACOTTA, Chapter 9D for full details.

Some First Period figures also carry a GOSS & PEAKE printed mark, usually the four or six line transfer printed mark.

The common black Goshawk was used up until 1934 on heraldic ware, and after 1935 the mark was distinctively blacker and thicker, and often applied over the glazed bases of the late colourful pottery, usually accompanied by the word ENGLAND under the firm's name. The printed titles on the base of beige pottery include Cottage Pottery, Royal Buff, and Hand Painted. These were Third Period and date between 1930 and 1939. Margaret (Peggy) Goss is said by her family to have introduced the Little Brown Jug as a new line. As her father, Huntley, sold the works in 1929, quite possibly some of the beige ware made afterwards could have been planned by Peggy and Huntley Goss.

Another late line was delicately coloured lustre which was applied to named models as well as to domestic ivory porcelain. No arms were applied to these pieces, and handles were thickly coated with gold as well as having gilded rims. It is generally believed these date from 1925 and were rubber stamped with an enlarged Goshawk some 16mm square.

The tiny coloured brush strokes on the bases of most armorial Goss are the factory signatures of the paintresses. W H Goss was particularly concerned to keep up his high standards, and in order to be able to detect any shoddy workmanship or incorrect colouring of the arms, each paintress had her own mark, which she painted on the base of each of her pieces, in whatever colour she happened to be using at the time. Offenders were given three warnings before being sacked, so in all probability this clever system kept them all on their toes! One only has to compare the products with those of other manufacturers to appreciate their skill. Occasionally a gilder's mark in gold can also be seen.

A blue Goshawk was used on an experimental range of models decorated with underglaze blue designs which are also marked SECONDS or REJECTS.

Many pieces are marked COPYRIGHT, and others have registration numbers on the base. For a detailed explanation of these see REGISTRATION NUMBERS and COPYRIGHT MARKS Chapter.

Incised mark on Dr. Kenealy Match and Spill Holder

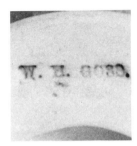

Serif impressed mark 1858–1887 approximately

Incised mark on The Boot Black, 1873

Written mark on Pepper Pot 1895–1925

The normal Goshawk 1862–1927

Black printed mark on a bust

Black printed mark on Bust

Black printed commemorative mark on Bust of Queen Victoria

Serif impressed mark 1887—1918 approximately Stamped mark with registration date

Scarborough Flags Plate special mark

Third Period Black Printed Mark

Goshawk and date on Churchill Toby Jug

Impressed mark G5 on a Goss doll

Model name, registration number and agents name

League model inscription. Note the artists mark

Goss England mark on a Flower Girl. Note also the Artists Mark.

Very late Goshawk mark. Post 1930

Post 1930 late mark

Large rubber stamp Goshawk 1925 and after

Royal Cauldon mark over-printed by a Goshawk Post 1925

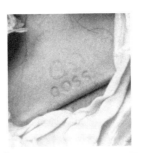

Impressed mark on a Goss doll 1916-1918 approximately

W.H. Goss England Cottage Pottery mark

W.H. Goss England Royal Buff mark

W.H. Goss England hand painted late mark

Some Goss pieces have been found marked **EMBLEMATIC T ENGLAND.**
One example seen is a beaker with the Harvard University Seal version
decoration [1], and another, a wall-pocket or posy-holder 173mm, with the
United States decoration E PLURIBUS UNAM.

Mark Used on Pieces for the
U.S. Market

Lower Portion of usual
Goshawk Mark on an
Oviform Salt Castor

Empire Exhibition Scotland
1938. Red Mark

Black Printed Mark on a
Bust of Lady Godiva

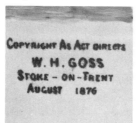

Black Printed Mark on a
Bust

Black Printed Mark on Busts
of Edward and Alexandra

League Model Inscription

Third Period Printed Mark

Mark on Cottage Pottery
Shakespearian Cottage Plate

3   Notes for the Collector

MINOR VARIATIONS IN SIZE

Where the dimensions of items are given, these have been obtained from actual specimens and refer to the height unless otherwise stated. Where an approximate measurement is quoted, no immediate specimen has been to hand, and the best available information source has been used.

Where no dimension is given, it has not been possible to gain access to information other than to confirm the existence of that model.

With regard to slight fluctuations in size in the same model, it must be borne in mind that variations in firing temperature can give rise to these and, in any case, shrinkage in firing can be as high as ten per cent. In early Goss items this figure is said to be higher, and certainly First Period wares have a tendency to firing cracks and flaws, but which the factory overcame around 1890. Examples of items particularly prone to having many minor differences in size are Loving Cups, Wall Pockets and Busts. These pieces, whilst lacking the excellence of Second Period wares, are rarer and equally desirable.

FORGERIES

Very few forgeries of Goss china have appeared. Those that have, usually take the form of a forged Goshawk on a piece that clearly did not originate from the Goss factory. These Goshawks are either crudely rubber stamped or drawn in Indian Ink. The giveaway must always be the quality of the piece the mark appears on. If it is not the fine parian body that is consistent with Goss, then look very closely at the mark. Compare a possible forgery with a correct normal mark, and also look at the quality of the porcelain.

In the end, however, recognition of forgeries rests with the experience and the knowledge of the collector, and there can be no substitute for handling Goss as often as possible in order to familiarize oneself with the ware.

Occasionally forged cottages appear. All Goss cottages produced are listed in the apppropriate chapter in this book. Any other ciottage which is purported to be Goss is most definitely not so, if it does not feature in the exhaustive list given. Shakespeare's Cottage is a particular exception, so many sizes having been produced by Goss and other crested manufacturers. A forged example has been found of the half-size solid base model, as well as the 110mm full length size. The latter cottage is well made and is only prevented from being condemned as a true forgery by carrying the inscription *Reproduction of Model of Shakespeare's House*. It carries the correct registration number and the usual Goshawk, so the words *Reproduction of.....* should be looked for in this particular case.

In 1990 a bronze/gold metallic bust of Queen Victoria came to light. The example seen had had the usual crown for the version in question filed down to a rim. The mark was the usual four line *Copyright as the Act directs, W. H. Goss,*

Stoke-on-Trent, and the year. This piece, whilst looking correct, is now believed to be a modern forgery.

THE BLACKPOOL COAT OF ARMS

Presumably at the request of the then Blackpool Agent, the Blackpool coat of arms was placed on a number of items which would not normally carry a coat of arms, the Abbot's Kitchen Glastonbury, Manx Cottage, Lincoln Imp, St. Columb Major Cross, Lucerne Lion, Goss Oven, and Cornish Stile, being but a few of the examples found.

Another practice of Mr. Naylor, the Blackpool Agent after 1913, was the sale of named models from which the descriptive matter had been omitted. This, together with an over generous use of gilding (e.g. on the ears of the Lincoln Imp) has tended to give some collectors the impression that Blackpool wares are second-rate and should be generally avoided. Almost all, however, that were sold through the Blackpool Agency, which changed hands at least four times between the years 1901 and 1921, were perfectly normal and correct.

With regard to value, items which should not be carrying arms, but are found to have the Blackpool coat of arms, tend to detract, thus reducing the value of the item by, say, one-third and two-thirds.

However, many items which would otherwise have been factory rejects (by virtue of firing flaws, distortion, etc.,) have been sold through the Blackpool agency and, therefore, carry the Blackpool arms. Such pieces would be worth around one-third of the normal perfect model, and every Blackpool crest item should accordingly be closely inspected in order to determine whether or not it was a factory second.

REGISTRATION NUMBERS

No piece of Goss is worth any more or less whether or not it carries a registration number. There is no reason why some pieces carry their number and some not. The production of Goss china was never an exact science, and the only reason for putting the registration number on a piece was to prevent other firms from using the design.

Two different aspects were registered. First, the shape or model, and secondly the decoration. Some pieces have one number which could refer to either, and some carry two numbers, indicating that both the model and decoration were designed and registered by the Goss factory.

Registration numbers were used from 1884 up until their discontinuance in 1914. The following tables give the dates of first registration of numbers between 1 and 630174. It should be noted that the dates given here indicate only the first registration of a design and not the exact year of manufacture. From the time patents began in 1883, registered designs could only run for four years, but were renewable, with a maximum life of 15 years.

Registration numbers were not used by the factory after July 1914, but it should also be remembered that a number indicates only when the registration took place, not when the piece was made, which might well be years afterwards.

Rd. No.   1   registered in Jan. 1884
Rd. No.   19754   registered in Jan. 1885
Rd. No.   40480   registered in Jan. 1886
Rd No.   64520   registered in Jan. 1887
Rd. No.   90483   registered in Jan. 1888
Rd. No. 116648   registered in Jan. 1889
Rd. No. 141273   registered in Jan. 1890
Rd. No. 163767   registered in Jan. 1891
Rd. No. 185713   registered in Jan. 1892
Rd. No. 205240   registered in Jan. 1893
Rd. No. 224720   registered in Jan. 1894
Rd. No. 246975   registered in Jan. 1895
Rd. No. 268392   registered in Jan. 1896
Rd. No. 291241   registered in Jan. 1897
Rd. No. 311658   registered in Jan. 1898
Rd. No. 331707   registered in Jan. 1899
Rd. No. 351202   registered in Jan. 1900
Rd. No. 368154   registered in Jan. 1901

First Registration No. for 1902   385088
First Registration No. for 1903   402913
First Registration No. for 1904   424017
First Registration No. for 1905   447548
First Registration No. for 1906   471486
First Registration No. for 1907   493487
First Registration No. for 1908   518415
First Registration No. for 1909   534963
First Registration No. for 1910   554801
First Registration No. for 1911   575787
First Registration No. for 1912   594175
First Registration No. for 1913   612382
First Registration No. for 1914   630174

COPYRIGHT MARKS

After the Great War the firm brought out a new range of models including numbered Egyptian and many other foreign shapes. Most of these had the word COPYRIGHT printed underneath in an attempt to stop other factories copying them. This does not add to, or detract from the value of the piece, but it does indicate that it was produced in the latter stages of the Second Period, or early part of the Thrid Period.

When the factory could not obtain a local authority's permission to use their coat of arms, or if a town did not possess arms, it became necessary to design them. These home-made arms were like Seal crests, within a consistent circular pattern, using some local symbol usually lifted from the town's arms, for the centre, such as a fish for Newquay to denote a fishing port. The registration number for these seals was 77966 and this was printed on the base of every piece bearing such arms. For further information, see *The Price Guide to Arms and Decorations on Goss China*, Section A, Geographical Place Names.

NON-PRODUCTION WARE

Fragments of pieces that did not go into production have been found in the factory spoil heap. Models seen have been listed below, and should perfect examples come to light, the author will be pleased to receive details. Some items are, of course, known with different colouring and glazing and will be found elsewhere in this Guide.

White Glazed:
Stratford Toby jug and basin
Churchill Toby jug
Bust of Lady Godiva
Ripon Hornblower and verse (Third Period)
Monmouth Mask, The Knight
Crucifix Pendants, varying floral designs
Cigarette Holders -
    numerous, with occasional examples in coloured lustres
Single Ear -
    on flat base with pierced hole for hanging. Not made as part of a head.
    70mm
Pixie on a toadstool

White Unglazed:
Shakespeare, standing, leaning on a lectern
    Very large size. Estimated height 330mm

Coloured:
Massachusetts Hall
Sandbach Crosses, brown
    As listed in *The 1978 Price Guide to Goss China* but not seen in one piece
St. Tudno's Church Font. Pale yellow
Thistle preserve pot and lid, with thistle knop
Tortoise (Third Period)
Brooches, black
Preseve Pot and lid. Multicoloured, Geometric Art Deco decoration.
Dolls Heads impressed Dorothy 10 or 12.

4   The Goss Records

Around 1900, it became obvious to the many collectors all over Great Britain that some sort of catalogue of agents' names and addresses was necessary to enable enthusiasts to plan their excursions. It could prove daunting to make a long, difficult trip to a far away town in search of a Goss agency which may or may not exist. Also the agent for any area could be a shopkeeper, hotel owner, pharmacist, librarian, or the owner of the local fancy stores or bazaar who often kept irregular hours.

J. J. Jarvis, an enterprising collector, approached William Henry Goss and put forward his idea of producing such a listing of agencies. William told him that he had been asked many times before, but he was a busy man, and thought it would be too time-consuming to continually keep updating such a publication with additions and changes of addresses. The thought of constant revision had deterred him. Eventually, mainly through Huntley Goss's help, Mr. Jarvis won William's confidence and gained the vital permission required to publish the first edition of *The Goss Record* towards the end of 1900, for a shilling a copy. Mr. Jarvis, who lived at Riverside, Enfield, Middlesex, did not have any financial interest in the Record's production, and the proceeds were donated entirely to a fund promoted by the Misses Evans of 58 Holly Road, Handsworth, Birmingham, for giving a Christmas tea and entertainment to some of the poor slum children in their area.

The first Record produced in 1900 was a hand-duplicated sheet not even stapled or bound. It listed the authorised agent in each town for which the factory produced arms, the address, the models and coats of arms stocked, together with details of opening hours. Jarvis was limited in the number of copies he could provide by duplication, and the few that he did produce sold out immediately. He was by now receiving letters from all over the country requesting still further copies, and he became determined to write a further edition with all the latest information about new models being made, to bind it properly, and to make this into a book. By having the Record printed and bound professionally, he could have a large quantity produced. Huntley Goss checked the rough draft and made any corrections and additions. In the interests of accuracy, Mr. Jarvis wrote to every known agent and asked them to reply confirming the particulars he had of them. Most complied with this request, but some were too lazy or too busy to reply, and so providing he thought their addresses were still correct, Jarvis kept them in his listing with their entries in italics. He was quite happy to send collectors details of any later changes on a free list that he was continually adding to, upon receipt of the stamps for the postage.

Certain statements had to be made in *The Goss Record* in order to satisfy the Goss factory arrangement. One was: 'I am not personally acquainted with Mr. Goss, or in any way financially interested in his business, but I take this opportunity of thanking him most sincerely for the trouble he has taken, and the

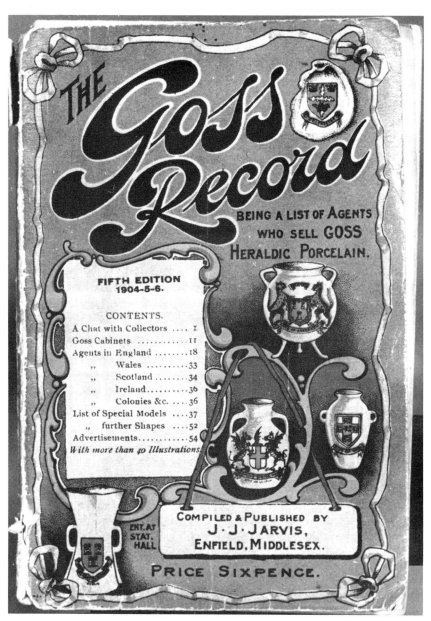

THE Goss Record

BEING A LIST OF AGENTS WHO SELL GOSS HERALDIC PORCELAIN.

FIFTH EDITION
1904-5-6.

COMPILED & PUBLISHED BY
J·J·JARVIS,
ENFIELD, MIDDLESEX.

ENT. AT STAT. HALL

PRICE SIXPENCE.

The Goss Record Fifth Edition 1904—5—6

assistance he has given me in compiling this book. J. J. Jarvis.' Another statement was: 'Mr. Goss will not supply any of his porcelain except through individual agents; arms of one town where an agency exists cannot be obtained off an agent in another town.' Also contained in *The Goss Record* was the warning: 'Collectors are warned against many inferior imitations of Goss porcelain, mostly of foreign manufacture, that are being sold.'

The agents themselves were very pleased with Jarvis as their trade increased. In April 1902, he published an 8-page supplement giving the latest corrections and amendments. In August of that year he produced the second of *The Goss Record*. By the time of the third edition, it was not just a list of agencies, but it also contained snippets and hints to collectors and details of the latest shapes being made, together with their historical background. With this edition there were also asterisks against certain agencies in the list signifying which particular shopkeepers would be prepared to open after hours to sell Goss to those collectors unfortunate enough to arrive after the close of business for that day. It also contained photographs of the latest Goss models, which were numbered. For example, the Salisbury Gill was No. 127. This was to facilitate the ordering of pieces from agents by post. Agents also advertised their own wares in *The Goss Record*, and other adverts included were for such ingenious inventions as the Doylesava, a circular glass pane for protecting lace doilies from cake stains, and the Dursley Pederson cycle, which looked remarkably uncomfortable and was supposed to be the featherweight of featherweights in cycling. The 4th edition was a supplement to the 3rd.

The 5th edition in 1905 had a shiny grey cover decorated with artistic sketches of various matching Goss models, which, incidentally, Jarvis collected. He related a tale in which he admitted he was responsible for Mr. Goss's office being bombarded with requests for an agency list in 1900 from all over Great Britain. This had led to Mr. Goss sending the requests to Jarvis' home in Enfield, together with permission for him to produce the first edition of *The Goss Record*.

By now his printing bills were in pounds, not shillings, and his postage bill was £50 a year alone - a terrific sum in those days when one considers that small Goss models were retailing for 9d each! *The Goss Record* could be obtained directly through him or through most Goss agencies. This fifth edition was 68 pages long and very much larger, thus reflecting the growing popularity of the porcelain and the increased output of the factory. Also announced was The League of Goss Collectors. Jarvis formed this in 1904 and was advertising for members in the 5th edition. All readers were eligible for membership.

A few years earlier he had formed a small exclusive club for his own friends, but now decided to make it national, as its usefulness might be extended if it had a wide following. Leaflets were enclosed advertising the aims of the League, and a form for joining. Cabinets were also advertised from this edition onwards.

The 6th edition of *The Goss Record* appeared in 1906. The copies produced before W. H. Goss's death on January 4th 1906 were encased in a red binding: those produced after his death had a purple binding and contained an obituary, extending the book to 96 pages. This was a very interesting booklet, full of information.

Three years elapsed before the 7th edition appeared in October 1909. Jarvis announced that a total of 70,000 of the various editions had been sold to date, and that the 8th would be printed in 1912. In fact, there was a short supplement to the 7th in 1911, and the 8th did not appear until 1913, not long before the outbreak of war. Jarvis had by that time handed over publication over to Evans Bros, the London publishers, who produced a 104 page book. It may be said that Goss collecting reached its peak that year and this edition was the best of them all.

The War edition was a supplement to the 8th and was produced in 1916 as a concise booklet due to the shortage of paper, and sold for only 3d. Earlier editions cost 6d, and the 9th and last edition in 1921 was one shilling. The War Edition announced the International League of Goss Collectors, and the Regimental badges, Naval crests, and war shapes available.

The 9th edition was 80 pages in length and in it Jarvis regretted that the Goss cabinets were no longer available due to difficulties in the furniture trade and the heavy demand for essential articles. Nine years after the last of *The Goss Record*, the Goss family sold the pottery. The editor became Sir Joseph John Jarvis, who kept his Goss collection until his death at Godalming in 1950.

A Lit of Every Edition with Present Value:-

		Value
The Goss Record		£ p
1900	1st edition. Duplicated leaflet with 4 subsequent pamphlets.	50.00
1901	1st edition. Printed booklet	60.00
1902-3	2nd edition (supplement to 1st)	60.00
1903	3rd edition	60.00
1903	4th edition (supplement to 3rd)	60.00
1904-6	5th edition	40.00
1906-7	6th edition Red binding (no obituary)	35.00
	Purple binding containing an obituary of W. H. Goss	30.00
1909-11	7th edition	35.00
1911	Supplement to 7th edition	30.00
1913-14	8th edition	25.00
1916-18	War Edition (supplement to 8th). Published by Evans Bros.	35.00
1921	9th edition. Published by Evans Bros.	25.00

5 Postcards

Goss postcards were published with the permission of W. H. Goss by S. A. Oates & Co. of Halifax who printed on them: None genuine without the name "Goss"

These cards were published in the latter half of the Edwardian era, postmarks ranging from 1905 to 1912.

They carry the word *Goss* in gold on a dark blue circular motif at the top left-hand corner, and the description of the particular model at the bottom, similarly in gold and on a blue background. The cards are basically photographs of selected models without coats of arms. It was then up to the local agent or stationer to order cards with their own particular town's coat of arms on them. These arms were then over-printed, a process which gives certain combinations of arms and models a peculiar flat/round appearance.

Originally, six cards were produced and sold, if required, in sets, in special envelopes. Later, two further cards were added to the range, and it is these two which are the rarities. The cards are numbered in gold in the top right-hand corner, and are as follows:

Card No.	Model	Value £ p
1	**Abbots's Cup, Fountains Abbey**	7.50
2	**Aberdeen Bronze Pot**	7.50
3	**Ancient Welsh Bronze Crochon**	7.50
4	**Roman Ewer from York**	7.50
5	**Loving Cup**	7.50
6	**Roman Vase from Chester**	7.50
7	**Bronze Ewer from Bath**	16.00
8	**Irish Mather**	16.00

Prices quoted are for cards in good condition.

Goss Postcard Album, with a postcard on the front cover,
and title *Album for Goss Post Cards;* green cloth cover, with 48
pages holding two cards per page;   Height 205mm Length 270mm   30.00

No. 1 Fountains Abbey Cup *No. 2 Aberdeen Bronze Pot* *No. 3 Ancient Welsh Crochon*

No. 4 York Roman Ewer *No. 5 Loving Cup* *No. 6 Chester Roman Vase*

No. 7 Bath Bronze Ewer *No. 8 Irish Mather*

£   p

Postcard advertising the Bournemouth Pilgrim Bottle,
illustrated in stone colour on a green background, with an
heraldic type cross in each corner and carrying the following
descriptive material in a panel below the picture:

Ancient Pilgrim Bottle

*One of the most perfect specimens of Early Christian Art ever
discovered in England. It is marked with the Sign of the Cross, and was
made about the year 600 A.D. Found at Southbourne, Bournemouth in
1907.*

*The Original may be seen and Goss Models obtained at
Bright's Stores, Ltd., Bournemouth*

20.00

Postcard in sepia: *"Welsh Girls at Snowdon"* in national
costume carrying baskets full of Goss china, including Welsh
Lady coloured cream jugs clearly in view, and with a *"Goss
Porcelain"* plaque attached to each basket.

20.00

Envelope in which the first six Goss Postcards were sold

6   Goss Cabinets

These were introduced by J. J. Jarvis, Editor of *The Goss Record* and were available from 1905 until 1919.

They were manufactured in six basic types by the firm which made bookcases for the Encylopaedia Britannica Company. The following details are taken from the Seventh Edition of *The Goss Record*;-

These cabinets have been specially designed to hold Collections of Heraldic Porcelain, although equally suitable for other varieties of China, Bric-a-brac, etc. Made by one of the leading wholesale Cabinet Makers in the country to the personal instructions of the compiler of the Goss Record, no expense has been spared to produce the most suitable Cabinets to display to advantage the varied shapes of Goss Porcelain obtainable, and the Arms emblazoned thereon.

Every cabinet is substantially made and well finished. The shelves are lined with green cloth and the doors fitted with lock and key. They may be had either in Chippendale or Fumed Oak as stated, whilst some are made in both, and each style is priced at the lowest possible figure consistent with the finest workmanship.

A fully illustrated list of Cabinets will be sent on application to the Goss Record Office.

The Cabinets will be sent from the makers direct on receipt of remittance, the carriage being paid by purchasers on delivery; 5s. will be charged for cases and packing unless these are returned carriage paid within 7 days.

The amount paid will be returned in full for any Cabinet not approved of and returned carriage paid upon receipt.

Cabinets may be obtained on the "Times" system of monthly installments, particulars of which may be had on application.

All Cabinets bear the "Goss Arms" on a specially designed porcelain shield, without which none are genuine.

There are seven types of Cabinets as under

Current Value £ p

Design A.   A small revolving cabinet in Chippendale to stand on a pedestal or table. 18-ins. square. Holding capacity, 50 average sized pieces inside and 25 outside. Step-shaped shelves from the bottom. Glass side and top.   **Price £2 2 0**   600.00

Design B.   Wall cabinet 3-ft. 3-ins. wide by 3-ft. 8-ins. high. Holding capacity, 85 pieces. Made in Fumed Oak. A very artistic and pleasing case.   **Price £2 18 6**   500.00

Design BB.   The same as B, but with an additional shelf. This will hold 100 pieces   **Price £3 3 0**   500.00

Design C.   A revolving case in Chippendale, somewhat similar to A, but 3-ft. 4-ins. high and 1-ft. 5-ins wide. This will hold 120 pieces, and where space is a consideration, is an excellent Cabinet.   **Price £3 7 6**   800.00

Design D.   4-ft. 6-ins. long by 3-ft. high. Made both in Chippendale and Fumed Oak. The centre door is hinged at the bottom enabling the entire contents to be displayed at once. By a unique mechanical contrivance this door is quite firm when opened. Holding capacity, 125 pieces   **Price £4 4 0**   600.00

Design E.   A handsome Cabinet on legs to stand on the ground, and sliding doors 3-ft. wide and 4-ft. high, will hold 160 pieces. Made in Chippendale or Fumed Oak.   **Price £5 5 0**   650.00

Design F.   5-ft. 2-ins. high by 4-ft. wide. Also made in both woods. A very fine Cabinet to hold nearly 200 pieces. The centre is recessed and enclosed by two doors below and one folding door above (as Cabinet D.) whilst the sides are glazed as well as the front.   **Price £7 7 0**   850.00

Unrecorded Design   Free standing two-tier Cabinet with plate glass elongated mirror between top and bottom sections, with the porcelain shield bearing the Goss Coat of Arms affixed inside the top case at the back of the top shelf. 5-ft. 3-ins. high by 3-ft. 6-ins. wide   **Original Price Unknown**   850.00

See *The Goss Record*. 8th Edition: Page 109 for illustration of Cabinet D in fumed oak.

The porcelain shield alone is worth £95.00 and this is included in the values given above.

Cabinets A and C were of the revolving variety, Cabinets B and D were for attaching to the wall, whilst E and F were free-standing.

Revolving cabinet Design A, no example of which is currently known to exist.

Arts and Crafts style wall-mounted cabinet Design B.

Revolving cabinet Design C, no example of which is currently known to exist.

Free-standing cabinet Design E.

Wall-mounted cabinet with drop-down centre door, Design D.

Large free-standing cabinet Design F.

This unique cabinet recently came to light. It was neither advertised nor recorded in The Goss Record. *Comparison with other cabinets reveals that it is definitely a Goss cabinet.*

Photograph Norman Pratten

7 The League and International League of Goss Collectors

The League of Goss Collectors was formed in 1904. The initial subscription was 2/6d which entitled the member to a certificate of membership, a copy of *The Goss Record* as and when published, and a special piece of porcelain bearing the Goss Arms surrounded by the wording: *The League of Goss Collectors.* Each model, except the first-issued, bore beneath it an inscription to the effect that it was issued to members and could not be bought. The inscriptions vary from model to model, for example some stating purchased instead of bought. The actual inscriptions will be found recorded under the individual pieces in SECTION 10E HISTORIC MODELS AND SPECIAL SHAPES.

Towards the end of the 1914-18 War, the League widened its scope to become the International League of Goss Collectors, and a new model was issued for each year until 1932. These models, together with re-issues of all but the first model, were inscribed *International League of Goss Collectors.* They bore the new arms, incorporating the Goss arms and motto *Se Inserit Astris;* a second shield for England, of the design borne by all the later Plantagenet kings, and a third shield of a design presumed to be indicative of the international aspect of the League. The arms are surrounded by green laurel wreathing tied with five crossed ribbons, and in tiny insets there appears the letters (FR) and the figures (16).

These are the League Models issued:

On joining the League	The Portland Vase.
For members of two years' standing	Ancient Costril or Pilgrims' Bottle.
For members of four years' standing	Staffordshire Tyg.
For members of six years' standing	King's Newton Anglo-Saxon Cinerary Urn.

1918	Cirencester Roman Ewer.	1925	Cyprus Mycenaean Vase.
1919	Contact Mine.	1926	Staffordshire Drinking Cup.
1920	Gnossus Vase.	1927	Colchester Roman Lamp.
1921	Greek Amphora Vase.	1928	Fimber Cinerary Urn.
1922	Italian Krater.	1929	Irish Cruisken.
1923	Egyptian Lotus Vase.	1930	Northwich Sepulchral Urn.
1924	Wilderspool Roman Tetinae or Feeding Bottle.	1931	Chester Roman Altar.
		1932	Cheshire Roman Urn.

HER MAJESTY'S FIRST LITTLE SHOES.

THE exquisite taste displayed by Mr. William Henry Goss, of Stoke-on-Trent, in his parian and porcelain wares, whether classic and ornamental, or adapted for ordinary domestic use, both in design and material, has been endorsed by prize medals at various of the world's great exhibitions. In one report we read:—"Few displays of porcelain are to be seen in the exhibition which excel those made by Mr. Goss. In the parian statuettes, vases, tazzi, &c., and other ceramic materials under notice, the perfection of art manufacture seems certainly to have been reached."

Mr. Goss is a Fellow of the Royal Geological and of several other learned societies, a chemical expert, an accomplished antiquarian, and the author of a number of valuable biographical, scientific, and literary works.

There is always something touching in looking at the shoe of a little child; for who can forecast the rough and often thorny paths the little pilgrim may have to tread !

Mr. Goss, accidently, in the following manner, got to hear of the Queen's first shoe, which he has now copied and reproduced in porcelain—imitating form, material and colour. The story we give, although it is a story, is quite true.

Her Majesty's father, the Duke of Kent, went to live at Sidmouth, in 1819, to get the benefit of the Devonshire climate. While there, a certain local shoemaker received the order for the first pair of shoes for the infant Princess Victoria. But instead of making two only he made three, while he was about it, facsimiles, and kept one as a memorial and curiosity. It has been preserved to this day, and is now in the possession of his daughter, who is the wife of Mr. Goss's porcelain agent at Sidmouth.

Hearing of this, Mr. Goss borrowed the shoe, and made an exact copy in porcelain. The dainty little shoe is four inches in length, has a brown leather sole, white satin upper, is laced and tied in front with a bow of light blue silk ribbon; and bound with the same round the edge, and down the back of the heel.

In 1820 the shoemaker received the Royal Warrant; and that, also, is preserved with the interesting little shoe.

This little porcelain model, so suggestive, will arouse the loyal thrill of love and blessing in thousands of British hearts, simple little Cinderella sort of thing as it is; while to Her Gracious Majesty herself, it must touch a minor chord that vibrates back to the far reach of memory.

A. J. S.

Queen Victoria's First Shoe leaflet

8 Advertising Ware and Leaflets

William Henry Goss disliked all forms of advertising, and considered that if a product was good enough it would sell itself. Therefore, the monthly *Pottery Gazette*, the trade magazine for pottery and glass manufacturers, did not carry advertisements for Goss until February 1906 - a month after his death!

It is not surprising that other potteries competed with the firm of Goss - W H Goss had left the field so wide open. Toward the end of his life he did accept that china dealers, solely engaged in legitimate trade, advertised in order to bring their wares prominently to the notice of their potential customers. Goss agents bought space in *The Goss Record* and probably elsewhere as well.

The advertising material below dates from 1905 with the exception of the shield-shaped Goss agents enamel sign which was earlier.

ADVERTISING WARE

		£	p
An unusual Oval Plaque distributed to Goss Agents after 1931 stating AGENT FOR W.H. GOSS ART-POTTERY in red between two Goshawks [3]*	Length 220mm	300.00	
The Shield from a Goss Cabinet. [2]	70mm	95.00	
The shield shape carrying the Goss family arms. Can also be found with town arms; BURFORD has been seen.		40.00	
A Goss Agent's Change Tray [2]*			
One was given to each Agent and bore the arms of his particular town. Inscribed around rim: *GOSS ORIGINAL HERALDIC PORCELAIN. CONNOISEURS COLLECT IT.*	Dia. 140mm	325.00	
Examples without arms may also be found		300.00	
Plaque shaped with Goshawk in relief at the top and some decoration *GENUINE GOSS COTTAGE POTTERY [3]*	100mm	250.00	
Plaque shaped to form Ann Hathaway's Cottage, coloured [3]		200.00	
Plaque featuring a Toby Jug in colour. [3]		200.00	
Goss Agent's enamel shop-front sign. Shield-shaped	Height 300mm	200.00	

"THE KEY-STONE OF THE KINGDOM.

" WE do not know whether Mr. Goss, to whose exquisite
and masterly works of Art we have more than once called
attention in our pages, intended in the preparation of the
well modelled portrait before us, to pay Lord Beaconsfield
the high compliment contained in the words we have placed
at the head of these few lines, or not—but this we do know,
that the form he has chosen carries out the idea in the most
emphatic and striking manner, and conveys to the mind an
impression that the compliment was as fully intended as it
was deserved. The design is, literally, a key-stone—the
centre stone of an arch—and from this, standing out in
alto-relievo, is a marvellously powerfully modelled, speaking,
and well-thought-out life-size head of the present Prime
Minister, Lord Beaconsfield, in all the freshness and vigour
of that mental capacity that so eminently distinguishes
him. Mr. Goss has won a high and deserved reputation for
the excellence and truthfulness of his portrait busts, and
this one is perhaps one of the happiest and best that even
he has produced. The head is not only a faithful portrait
of the *features* of the man, but is almost an inspired production, that presents a perfect reflex of the mind that animates
those features. The modelling is faultless. We ought to
add that, as a companion to this one, Mr. Goss has produced in a similar manner a very striking head of Lord
Derby, which deserves equal praise with that of Lord
Beaconsfield."

Leaflet sold with the Keystones of the Kingdom

Royal Buff Ashtray inscribed: *With Compliments. For all kinds of*
   Sanitary Ware and grates. W.E. Morris & Son Ltd.,
   Stoke-on-Trent Phone 4539.   Length 130mm Width 110mm   125.00

Taper Cream Jug 95mm carrying a transfer printed pictorial
   of a milkmaid milking a cow, surrounded by a ribbon
   containg the wording: *ST. ALDATE'S DAIRY OXFORD*
   F.J. WIGMORE, the whole being in green.   Height   95mm   100.00

LEAFLETS

Queen Victoria's Shoes	15.00
George & Mary Coronation 1911	15.00
Keystones of the Kingdom	60.00
The Loving Cup	15.00
Durham Sanctuary Knocker	20.00
The Potters' Oven	25.00
Glastonbury Bronze Bowl	20.00

Late Goss Agents Sign

Goss Agents Change Tray

Third Period Cottage Pottery
Advertising Stand

Royal Buff Advertising
Ashtray

The Shield from a Goss
Cabinet

THE POTTERS' OVEN.

A characteristic feature of the Potteries District, are the Potters' Ovens, shaped like immense inverted funnels.

After the potter has formed an article in clay, it has to be subjected to very great heat to change it into pottery. It is placed in a vessel made of a coarser clay, called a saggar, to protect it from fumes and smoke during firing. The saggars are filled and placed one on top of another making a column reaching from the floor to the top of the oven. When the oven is full the entrance is bricked up and the fires are lighted. The heat is raised very gradually, the process taking many hours, till the high temperature necessary is reached ; then it is allowed to cool slowly, requiring nearly the same length of time for cooling as for firing.

In consequence of the great heat developed, the oven is usually built away from other parts of the works to reduce the risk of fire. The building at the base gives shelter to the oven workers and provides storage for the saggars.

An interesting MODEL of the POTTERS' OVEN is
made in Goss Porcelain, and may be obtained from

RITCHIE & Co., Station China Stall, STOKE-ON-TRENT, Staffs.

Leaflet sold with the Goss Oven

THE LOVING CUP.

The late Lord Lyons, British Ambassador at Paris, used to relate the following history of the Loving Cup :

KING HENRY of Navarre, (who was also HENRY IV. of France), whilst hunting, became separated from his companions, and, feeling thirsty, called at a wayside inn for a cup of wine. The serving maid on handing it to him as he sat on horseback, neglected to present the handle. Some wine was spilt over, and his Majesty's white gauntlets were soiled. While riding home, he bethought him that a two-handled cup would prevent a recurrence of this, so his Majesty had a two-handled cup made at the Royal Potteries and sent it to the inn. On his next visit, he called again for wine, when, to his astonishment, the maid, (having received instructions from her mistress to be very careful of the King's cup), presented it to him, holding it herself by each of its handles. At once the happy idea struck the King of a cup with three handles, which was promptly acted upon, as his Majesty quaintly remarked, "Surely out of three handles I shall be able to get one." Hence the Loving Cup.

[P.T.O.]

The Loving Cup leaflet

9 The First Period 1858-1887

A   BUSTS
B   FIGURES
C   ORNAMENTAL AND DOMESTIC
D   TERRACOTTA

Period Symbols

Where a shape was known to have been made during more than one period, the number in brackets after its entry denotes the other period(s) during which it was manufactured.

The First period	[1]	**1858-1887**
The Second period	[2]	**1881-1934**
The Third period	[3]	**1930-1939**

A rare bust of The Prince of Wales, later King Edward VII, wearing the Masonic Collar of Grand Master of the Grand Lodge of England. 520mm.

A rare study of The Blind Highlander and Lass, with dog at feet. 280mm

A fine bust of Samuel Carter Hall, 376mm high on socle plinth.

AN INTRODUCTION TO PARIAN WARE

During his training and career as designer and artist with Copeland's of London and Stoke-on-Trent, William Henry Goss worked with the relatively new medium of parian. Whilst still in London, he made contact with the inventor of parian, John Mountford, and later wrote the history of that discovery. In his *Encyclopaedia of Ceramics,* W.P. Jervis revealed that 'It's origin has been disputed, both Minton and Copeland claiming to have invented it. Mr W H Goss, who, when all the experiments were being conducted, was a young boy, knew all the parties concerned and afterwards wrote the particulars of the discovery for a book published at The Hague in 1864, entitled *Verslag der Wereldtentoonstelling Te London in 1862,* which was an important work on the London Exhibition produced by order of the Goverment of Holland. Mr Goss states that it was during the year 1845 that experiments were made at the manufactury of Alderman Copeland to obtain a ceramic material that should resemble marble'.

S C Hall, Editor of the *Art Journal* (and guide and mentor of William Goss), suggested that reductions from stone sculptures of the modern masters be made in a material that could imitate the stone visually. These miniatures could be offered as prizes by the Art Union of London. Following this idea, a reduced model of Gibson's Narcissus was despatched to Copeland's works for the potters to work from, until there was success with John Mountford's invention. These experiments were conducted by several experienced artistic potters at Copeland, but the first parian was produced from Mountford's recipe, in the form of Narcissus, on Christmas Day, 1845.

This new medium was immediately known as porcelain statuary. Mountford's figure was sent to Mr Gibson himself for inspection, and he declared it to be the best material next to marble for the reproduction of sculpture. The new porcelain statuary was an instant success in the industry and it firmly established itself in the ceramic world. It was at about this time that Messrs. H. Minton & Co began similar experiments for imitation marble, and it was not long before they discovered their own version which they termed parian. It was noted that their parian was slightly tinted and approximated freshly chiselled marble as quarried on the Aegean island of Paros. Copeland's efforts were that of marble toned down with age. Each manufacturer obtained his own quality and hue using his own adaptations of the inventions, and William Goss, who conducted his own experiments in the outbuildings in the garden of Ashfield Cottage adjoining his factory, perfected his own recipes in the late 1850's.

Inside a book which once belonged to Llewellynn Jewitt was found a portion of a letter from his best friend Mr Goss, obviously saved for its contents, in which Goss stated his beliefs concerning parian. 'We believe the day will arrive when these cream-colour wares shall again be chosen in preference to the bluish tint. For we certainly think that if the materials were thoroughly magnetted, well lawned, and finely ground so as to leave a clean, pure tint, the prevalence of the cream or ivory colour of the Dorsetshire ball clay would form a much more pleasing ground for decoration in colours and gold than that of the stained ware'.

The term parian, for this new porcelain composition, was derived from Paros, an island in the Aegean Sea. The marble of Paros was known as parian marble. Only the wealthy could afford marble busts and statues. Now the middle classes would be able to obtain the porcelain equivalent.

W P Jervis concluded that parian was a non-plastic body composed of 3 parts china stone to 2 parts felspar. William Goss's ingredients, according to his notebook, were Norwegian and Swedish felspar, white glass (obtained from grinding up old bottles made of clear glass only), flints and kaolin or china clay. Goss obtained the latter from Messrs Varcoes Sales Co Ltd. High Cross Street, St Austell, Cornwall. Incidentally, the type of felspar used came from certain beds in Norway and Sweden, which were almost worked out by the end of the Goss factory's life in 1929, and there was no known similar alternative. It is the felspar which influences the colour, texture and feel of the final result, making each factory's products so different from their rivals. The felspar Goss favoured, resulted in the ivory translucency which was so distinctly his own.

Most pottery was thrown on a wheel and shaped by hand, but parian was mixed and ground into a liquid state and poured into moulds and left only until a sufficient coating had been absorbed into the walls of the moulds, then the excess poured out to be used again. In this way, simple hollow shapes were made in two halves, although for making the more complex figures, up to twenty moulds were used. Most of these were for the detailed floral headbands, or intricate fingers, etc.

Rare Eggshell Porcelain Tea Pot and Lid with Ivy decoration in relief, 130mm high. This type of porcelain was perfected by modeller Thomas Boden.

Bust of Llewellynn Jewitt, on socle plinth, 380mm high.

A Busts

The most important parian productions by Goss were portrait busts. Llewellynn Jewitt, in his *Ceramic Art of Great Britain*, described these portrait busts as ranking far above the average, and perfect reproductions of the living originals. 'It is not often that this can be said of portrait-busts, but it has been a particular study of Mr Goss, and in it he has succeeded admirably.' He later described Goss in *The Reliquary* as 'the leading portrait-bust producer of the age'. Vastly underrated by the majority of collectors who prefer the glazed heraldic ware so much easier to recognise, the busts nearly all date from the last century and mainly bear impressed titles.

The first parian bust to have been made was Mr Punch in 1861. William Goss was on friendly terms with two successive editors of *Punch* and made this study for the then editor Mark Lemmon.

Other early portrait busts for retail sale were those of Lord Palmerston whose second term of office was 1859 to 1865. The earliest models were marked *Copyright* and also signed by W H Goss in his own hand, on the shoulder. The majority of parian busts were made during a 30 year period after 1861, with subjects such as eminent musicians, members of the clergy, political and literary figures, royalty, and personal friends. A bust was eventually made of W H Goss himself in 1906, shortly before his death. Contrary to popular belief that he was so conceited that he made one of himself in large numbers, it was not his wish to be depicted in this way. It was only in his old age that enforced feebleness prevented him from standing up to his sons who organised the modelling of him as a good sales line.

Up until 1881 when he emigrated to America, the chief artist and modeller was W W Gallimore, except for the three years 1863-6 when he was induced to go to Ireland to work for the Belleek factory, taking the highly prized and secret Goss recipes with him, in particular the wafer thin eggshell method. After losing his right arm in a shooting accident, he returned to Stoke and worked with his left arm, and was said to have modelled even better than before!

After 1881 Joseph Astley became Goss's chief designer until his death in 1902. Astley had carried on where Gallimore left off with the creation of parian busts, with his boss often putting the finishing touches to his designs. William really valued his work and respected his talent. The two men worked well together for 21 years, with Astley religiously carrying out William's every instruction. It was as though William had two pairs of hands.

The portrait busts were favourably criticized by *The Reliquary* and *Art Journal*. The editors of these journals happened to be William's closest friends, Llewellynn Jewitt and Samuel Carter Hall, of whom he made busts!

The high quality of the busts, individually made from moulds from the one original, included detail about the eyes which most factories tended to ignore, giving the appearance of the subject being blind. Not so with the Goss versions, for the factory strove to obtain a true likeness. Reader of *The Reliquary* were recommended to purchase a Goss bust of Mr Gladstone because 'it conveys to the eye a far more truthful, and eminently pleasing likeness of the great statesman, than has ever been produced either by painting, engraving or sculpture.' Admirers of Charles Swain were also advised to purchase the Goss version of this well loved poet, because of its truthful and intellectual likeness.

The main series had either a square two-step plinth, or a socle base, the latter sometimes mounted on an octagonal plinth. The square base bust would carry the name of the subject impressed on to the lower step, or impressed into the back of the shoulder. Early busts had a circular (or socle) plinth, and tended to be of classical subjects. Plinths were affixed solidly with slip, or loosely with a steel or brass nut and bolt.

All Goss busts and figurines have an air hole at the back, usually in the rear of the neck on busts and smaller figures, and half way down the back on larger subjects.

Very little unglazed parian was issued after the turn of the century, with the exception of the busts of W H Goss, Shakespeare, King Edward VII, Queen Alexandra, The Prince of Wales (1911) and Scott. The ivory porcelain used for the production of heraldic ware was of the same recipe, but glazed.

All busts in Section A have square two step plinths unless otherwise stated and all dimensions refer to the height of the piece.

Queen Victoria, Mob Cap
Socle/Octagonal Plinth

Queen Victoria wearing Mob
Cap

Queen Victoria Wearing
Imperial Crown

The Prince of Wales

The Princess of Wales

King Edward VII

King Edward VII, Socle
Plinth

Queen Alexandra, Socle
Plinth

The Prince of Wales

Mary Queen of Scots

Ajax

Apollo, socle plinth

ROYALTY

		£ p

Queen Victoria in Mob-cap, socle/octagonal plinth   201mm   365.00
Impressed on plinth: *Victoria R.*   210mm   365.00
Impressed side or back: *Copyright as Act Directs W.H. Goss*   236mm   375.00
Stoke-on-Trent November 1886

Queen Victoria in Mob-cap, square plinth   101mm   110.00
Impressed on plinth: *Victoria R.*   Unglazed 129mm   145.00
Impressed on side or back: *Copyright as Act directs*   Glazed 129mm   125.00
W.H. Goss Stoke-on-Trent November 1886   150mm   185.00

Some busts of Queen Victoria have a single frill to the front of
the bonnet, others have a double frill. Value unchanged

Queen Victoria - wearing Imperial Crown,
the top of which is extremely fragile   Two step plinth 180mm   350.00
Impressed on plinth: *Victoria R.*   Socle/octagonal plinth 245mm   450.00
Impressed side or back: *Copyright as Act directs*
W.H. Goss Stoke-on-Trent January 1887

(NB. The 180mm version has been found in bronze colour, of heavy
earthenware with a large metallic content and is believed to be a
forgery.)

Note: Should any of the above busts bear reference on the back to
Queen Victoria's Diamond Jubilee, it will indicate that they
are commemorative items and of higher value, say £20.00 extra.
Inscribed on back: *1896-7 Memorial of 60th year*
of reign of Her Majesty Victoria R.I.

Mary, Queen of Scots socle plinth   131mm   225.00
Inscribed on back: *Mary Q. of Scots, Copyright.*
Pub. As Act Directs (See 54 Geo 111, C.56)
W.H. Goss Stoke-on-Trent 1st DecR 1894

Prince of Wales later King Edward VII wearing Masonic
collar; sculpted by W.W. Gallimore   520mm   2000.00
Inscribed: *Published by Bro. J.S. Crapper PM, PPAGDC,*
Staffs and Bro. C. Marsh PM, PPSGW Staffs 35 Design Office
April 16th 1875 Registered

Prince of Wales later King Edward VII, square plinth   167mm   275.00
Impressed on plinth: *H.R.H. The Prince of Wales*
Impressed side or back: *Copyright as Act directs W.H. Goss*
Stoke-on-Trent November 1882

Princess of Wales later Queen Alexandra, square plinth   176mm   275.00
Impressed on plinth: *H.R.H. The Princess of Wales*
Impressed side or back: *Copyright as Act directs W.H. Goss*
Stoke-on-Trent November 1882

Earl Beaconsfield Wearing
Coronet

Beaconsfield, Square base
440mm

Ludwig van Beethoven

Beaconsfield

Beaconsfield, Socle Plinth

The Beautiful Duchess
Coloured, White plinth

John Bunyan

Lord Byron

Lord Byron Socle/Octagonal
plinth

John Bright

Robert Burns, Socle plinth

Robert Burns, Socle/
Octagonal plinth

		£ p

King Edward VII square plinth   163mm   210.00
Impressed on plinth: *King Edward VII*
Impressed side or back: *Copyright as Act directs W.H. Goss*
Stoke-on-Trent, and sometimes the date *7 May 1901*

King Edward VII socle plinth   glazed 133mm   200.00
Inscribed on back: *Copyright. Pub. As Act Directs*   unglazed 133mm   200.00
(See 54 Geo 111, C.56) W.H. Goss Stoke-on-Trent 7 May 1901

Queen Alexandra socle plinth   132mm   215.00
Inscribed on back: *Copyright. Pub. As Act Directs*
(See 54 Geo 111, C.56) W.H. Goss Stoke-on-Trent 7 May 1901

Queen Alexandra square plinth   approx. 175mm   250.00
Impressed on plinth: *Queen Alexandra*
Impressed on side or back: *Copyright as Act directs*
W.H. Goss Stoke-on-Trent, and sometimes the date *7 May 1901*

Prince of Wales later King Edward VIII, bearing
details of Investiture, and mounted on column bearing arms   143mm   225.00
Inscribed on back: *Investiture of H.R.H. The Prince of Wales*
Carnarvon Castle 13 July 1911. Copyright. Pub. As Act Directs
(See 54 Geo 111, C.56) W.H. Goss Stoke-on-Trent 16 June 1911
As above but lacking Investiture details [2]   143mm   165.00

OTHER SUBJECTS

Adonis socle plinth   265mm   850.00
Impressed on back: *W.H. Goss*

Ajax socle plinth   330mm   950.00
Impressed on back: *W.H. Goss*

Apollo socle plinth-with some gilding   375mm   850.00
Impressed on back: *W.H. Goss*

Beaconsfield, Earl of square plinth   (a)   104mm   160.00
Impressed on plinth: *Beaconsfield*   (b) glazed   154mm   165.00
Impressed side or back: *Copyright as Act directs*   (c) unglazed 154mm   165.00
W.H. Goss Stoke-on-Trent August 1876   (d) bronzed 154mm   100.00
           (e)   440mm   950.00

Beaconsfield - wearing coronet, square plinth   181mm   400.00
Impressed on plinth: *Beaconsfield*
Impressed on side or back: *Copyright as Act directs W.H. Goss*
Stoke-on-Trent August 1876

Beaconsfield socle plinth, glazed   111mm   135.00

		£ p
Beautiful Duchess, The. (a) White, on 3-step plinth 242mm		1000.00
The Duchess of Devonshire (b) Coloured, on 3-step plinth 242mm		2000.00
(c) White, socle/octagonal plinth 242mm		1000.00

Impressed on the 3 steps of plinth (a) and (b): *The Beautiful
Duchess*
Impressed on back: *Copyright as Act directs W.H. Goss
Stoke-on-Trent December 1876* or *January 1877*

NOTE: This bust stands on a separate highly ornate plinth,
impressed on one foot: *W. H. Goss* (Also found unmarked)

(a) Unglazed, plain	135mm	200.00
(b) Glazed, four crests	135mm	100.00

Add the price of this plinth to that of the bust when present

Beethoven, Ludwig Van square plinth	glazed	116mm	165.00
Impressed on plinth: *Beethoven*	unglazed	116mm	165.00

Bright, John square plinth	glazed	165mm	165.00
Impressed on plinth: *Bright* and sometimes also on	unglazed	165mm	165.00

the rear of right shoulder
Impressed side or back: *Copyright as Act directs W.H. Goss
Stoke-on-Trent August 1876*

Bunyan, John square plinth	glazed	132mm	185.00
Impressed on plinth: *Bunyan*	unglazed	132mm	185.00
Impressed side or back: *Copyright as Act Directs*	coloured	132mm	375.00

W.H. Goss Stoke-on-Trent January 1884

Burns, Robert socle plinth	glazed	136mm	95.00
Impressed on back: *Robert Burns*	unglazed	136mm	95.00
		155mm	135.00

Burns, Robert socle/octagonal plinth	glazed	166mm	185.00
Impressed on plinth: *Robert Burns*	unglazed	166mm	185.00

See also 9D TERRACOTTA

Byron, Lord square plinth		179mm	225.00
Impressed on plinth: *Byron*			

Impressed side or back: *Copyright as Act directs W.H. Goss
Stoke-on-Trent March 30, 1881*

Byron socle/octagonal plinth	193mm	225.00
Impressed on plinth: *Byron*		

Byron socle plinth (Bust 162mm, plinth 50mm)	212mm	250.00

Cairns, Earl square plinth	172mm	350.00

Reputed to be, but unnamed

£   p

Children- A pair of busts, after the style of the 17th century
sculptor Francois Dugnesnoy, each with a cartouche affixed to the
front of the plinth. The cherub or cupid figures depicted on the
cartouches vary from model to model.

(a) Mirth (Laughing)		210mm	275.00
(b) Grief (Weeping and wearing shawl on head)		218mm	375.00

Christ square or socle plinth (Height 215mm, base 85mm)   300mm   850.00
Impressed on plinth: *W.H. Goss*
Impressed on back: *W.H. Goss*

Classical Bust of a Lady coloured, with butterfly upon shoulder.
Socle/octagonal plinth. Multi-coloured floral garland in
the hair. Early puce Goshawk. A similar bust was made by
Belleek, evidently after the Goss original   240mm   1200.00
Impressed on back: *W. H. Goss*

Classical Bust of a Maiden   180mm   450.00
Impressed on back: *W. H. Goss*

Clytie socle plinth, sunflower model   215mm   450.00
Impressed: *W. H. Goss*   270mm   650.00

Clytie socle plinth   275mm   650.00
Impressed on back: *W. H. Goss*

Clytie square base (not seen by the author)   approx. 160mm   450.00
Impressed on back: *W. H. Goss*

Cobden, Richard socle plinth   (a) Four Button Waistcoat   223mm   350.00
Impressed on base: *W.H. Goss*   (b) Two Button Waistcoat   223mm   350.00

Dawson, George socle plinth   215mm   400.00
See also 9D TERRACOTTA

Derby socle plinth   105mm   135.00
Impressed: *Copyright as Act Directs W. H. Goss*
Stoke-on-Trent Aug 1878

Derby square base   105mm   145.00
Impressed on base: *W.H. Goss*

Derby square plinth   115mm   130.00
Impressed on plinth: *Lord Derby*
Impressed side or back: *Copyright as Act*
Directs W. H. Goss Stoke-on-Trent August 1876

Child – Grief

Child – Mirth

Christ, square base

Clytie, sunflower model

Clytie, socle plinth

Classical Lady, coloured, butterfly on shoulder

Richard Cobden

Richard Cobden

Lord Derby

Lord Derby Socle Plinth

A Massive Bust of Dickens 650mm

Charles Dickens, 256mm

			£ p
Derby, Earl of square plinth	glazed	160mm	130.00
Impressed on plinth: *Derby*	unglazed	160mm	130.00

Impressed side or back: *Copyright as Act directs W.H. Goss*
Stoke-on-Trent August 1876

Dickens, Charles socle plinth		256mm	650.00

Impressed: *W.H. Goss*

Dickens, Charles socle plinth - Goss & Peake   650mm   5000.00
Incised in manuscript in W.W. Gallimore's own hand
on the back of the bust: *Published as the Act directs (see Geo. III,*
C.56) By Goss & Peake 12 October 1867 W.W. Gallimore ft

Giuseppe Garibaldi   174mm   450.00
Impressed on plinth: *Giuseppe Garibaldi*
Incised on rear in W.H. Goss's own hand:
Published as the Act directs under the Superintend J.A.P.
McBride

Gladstone, William Ewart square base   125mm   130.00
Impressed: *W. H. Goss*

Gladstone socle plinth   (a) With younger features 125mm   165.00
Impressed side or back: (b) With older features   130mm   165.00
Copyright as Act directs W.H. Goss
Stoke-on-Trent August 1876.

Gladstone square plinth   170mm   170.00
Impressed on plinth: *Gladstone*
Impressed side or back: *Copyright as Act directs W.H. Goss*
Stoke-on-Trent August 1876

Gladstone square base on socle plinth   445mm   950.00
Impressed on base: *Gladstone*
Impressed on back: *Copyright as Act directs W.H. Goss*
Stoke-on-Trent November 30, 1889

Godiva, Lady square plinth
(Goss Record, 9th Edition: Page 29)
Impressed on plinth: *Lady Godiva*
Inscribed on back: *Lady Godiva. Copyright, Pub.*
As Act Directs (See 54 Geo 111, C.56) W.H. Goss
Stoke-on-Trent 1st OctR 1902

(a) White	110mm	95.00
(b) Coloured	110mm	285.00

Giuseppe Garibaldi

William Henry Goss

General Gordon

William Ewert Gladstone

Gladstone, Socle Plinth

Gladstone, square base on socle plinth 445mm

Earl Granville

William Court Gully

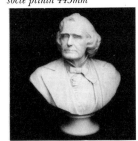

Samuel Carter Hall

George Frideric Handel

Lord Hartington, socle plinth

Lord Hartington

		£ p

Godiva, Lady socle/octagonal plinth   210mm   325.00
Incised on front of base: *Lady Godiva*
Impressed on back: *Copyright as the Act Directs*
W.H. Goss Stoke-on-Trent November 1891

Gordon, General square plinth   189mm   245.00
Impressed on plinth: *Gordon*
Impressed side or back: *Copyright as Act directs W.H. Goss*
Stoke-on-Trent January 1885

Goss, William Henry square plinth [2]   glazed 160mm   205.00
Impressed on plinth: *W.H. Goss*   unglazed 160mm   205.00
First sold in 1906 upon the death of W.H. Goss

Granville, Earl square plinth   glazed 176mm   175.00
Impressed on plinth: *Granville*   unglazed 176mm   175.00
Impressed side or back: *Copyright as Act directs W.H. Goss*
Stoke-on-Trent August 1877

Gully, William Court square plinth   165mm   275.00
(Speaker, House of Commons 1895-1905, and afterwards
first Viscount Selby)
Impressed on plinth: *W.C. Gully*
Impressed on back: *Copyright as The Act directs W.H. Goss*
Stoke-on-Trent August 1884
Inscribed: *Published by Wm. Workman, China Merchant, Whitehaven*

Hall, Samuel Carter socle plinth   376mm   2500.00

Handel, George Frideric square plinth   glazed 124mm   175.00
Impressed on plinth: *Handel*   unglazed 124mm   175.00

Hartington, Marquess of square plinth   glazed 174mm   195.00
Impressed on plinth: *Hartington*   unglazed 174mm   195.00
Impressed on side or back: *Copyright as Act directs*
W.H. Goss Stoke-on-Trent March 30, 1886

Hartington socle plinth   125mm   175.00
Impressed on rear: *W.H. Goss*

Hathaway, Ann on two books
(Goss Record. 9th Edition: Page 30) [2]   (a) White   75mm   85.00
                            (b) White   100mm   90.00
                            (c) Coloured   100mm   250.00

Inscribed on back: *Ann Hathaway. Copyright. Pub.*
As Act Directs (See 54 Geo. 111, C.56) W.H. Goss
Stoke-on-Trent 1st DecR 1894
See also THIRD PERIOD 11R for late examples of
busts of Ann Hathaway

Ann Hathaway, Coloured

Unknown Dignitary possibly Earl Cairns

Dr. Samuel Johnson socle/ octagonal plinth

Georgiana Jewitt

Llewellynn Jewitt

Sir Wilfrid Lawson

Henry W. Longfellow

Classical Maiden

John Milton

John Milton, Socle Base

Thomas Moore

Wolfgang Amadeus Mozart

		£ p

Irving, Washington square plinth 325mm 950.00
Impressed on plinth: *W. Irving*
Impressed on rear: *W.H. Goss*

Jewitt, Georgiana socle/octagonal plinth 198mm 1850.00
The inscription on the back of this bust reads: *'Georgiana. The*
beloved wife of Edwin A.G. Jewitt, and daughter of William H.
Goss. She was born in London July 30, 1855, died at Matlock,
Nov. 3, 1889 and is buried in Winster Churchyard'.
The grave may still be seen today in the delightful Derbyshire
   village of Winster.

Jewitt, Llewellynn socle plinth 380mm 2500.00
The inscription on the back of this bust reads: *This bust of*
Llewellynn Jewitt F.S.A. is made expressly for presentation
to his son Mr. Edwin Augustus George Jewitt on occasion
of his 21st birthday the 13th Oct. 1879 as a mark of the
the highest esteem for both by their devoted friend William Henry
Goss.
This bust was used as the frontispiece for *Ceramic Art in Great*
Britain, First Edition, 1878, by Llewellynn Jewitt

Johnson, Dr. Samuel socle/octagonal plinth 190mm 400.00
Impressed on plinth: *Dr. Samuel Johnson*
Impressed on back: *Copyright as the Act directs W.H. Goss*
Stoke-on-Trent

Johnson, Dr. Samuel socle/octagonal plinth 195mm 400.00
Unnamed Glazed Bust
Impressed on back: *W. H. Goss*

For **Lady Godiva** see **Godiva**

Lawson, Sir Wilfrid square plinth 170mm 350.00
Impressed on plinth: *Sir Wilfrid Lawson*
Impressed side or back: *Copyright as Act directs W.H. Goss*
Stoke-on-Trent August 1880
Inscribed on back: *Published by Marshall China Showrooms*
37-39-41 Scotch Street Carlisle

Longfellow, Henry W. square plinth 174mm 295.00
Impressed on plinth: *Longfellow*
Impressed side or back: *Copyright as Act directs W.H. Goss*
Stoke-on-Trent March 30th 1882

Mendelssohn, Felix square plinth glazed 125mm 250.00
Impressed on plinth: *Mendelssohn* unglazed 125mm 250.00

Sir Moses Montefiore with Hat

Sir Moses Montefiore without Hat

Napoleon

Sir Stafford Northcote

Ophelia, Socle plinth

Pallas Athena, socle plinth, armour and helmet gilded

Lord Palmerston, Socle Base 165mm

Lord Palmerston, Socle Base 223mm

Lord Palmerston on Socle Base and Fluted Column

Lady Godiva, White

Lady Godiva socle/octagonal plinth

Sir Isaac Pitman

				£	p

Milton, John square plinth — unglazed 125mm — 165.00
Impressed on plinth: *Milton* — glazed 165mm — 195.00
Impressed side or back: *Copyright as Act directs* — unglazed 165mm — 195.00
W.H. Goss Stoke-on-Trent January 1884

Milton, John socle plinth — 210mm — 185.00
Impressed on rear: *W.H. Goss*

Montefiore, sometimes **Montifiore, Sir Moses** with hat — 130mm — 195.00
Impressed on plinth: *Sir Moses Montefiore*
Impressed side or back: *Copyright as Act directs W.H. Goss*
Stoke-on-Trent August 1882

Montefiore, Sir Moses without hat, square plinth — 123mm — 165.00
Impressed on plinth: *Sir Moses Montefiore*
Impressed side or back: *Copyright as Act directs W.H. Goss*
Stoke-on-Trent August 30. 1882

The above Montefiore Models can usually be found
inscribed on the back:*Pub. by W. Ballard*
Royal Albion Stationery Bazaar, Ramsgate.

Moore, Thomas square plinth — 170mm — 225.00
Impressed on plinth: *Thomas Moore*
Impressed side or back: *Copyright as Act directs W.H. Goss*
Stoke-on-Trent March 30. 1881

Mozart, Wolfgang Amadeus square plinth — glazed 118mm — 175.00
Impressed on plinth: *Mozart* — unglazed 118mm — 175.00

Napoleon — (a) square tapered plinth, unglazed 142mm — 110.00
— (b) plinth only glazed — 142mm — 110.00
— (c) completely glazed — 142mm — 110.00

NOTE: This bust normally carried the arms of St. Helena, and
the above prices are for this model. Examples have been
found bearing the arms of Napoleon, which would increase
the above values by £30.00 [2]

Northcote, Sir Stafford square plinth — glazed 169mm — 185.00
Impressed on plinth: *Sir S. Northcote* — unglazed 169mm — 185.00
Impressed side or back: *Copyright as Act directs W.H. Goss*
Stoke-on-Trent November 3rd 1881

Ophelia socle plinth — 250mm — 750.00
Impressed on rear: *W.H. Goss*
See also 9B FIGURES

Pallas Athena socle plinth. The larger size has armour and — 248mm — 650
helmet gilded, with the face tinted in natural colours — 300mm — 750.00
Impressed on rear: *W.H. Goss*

Lord Salisbury

Lady Godiva, Coloured

Peeping Tom, Coloured

Sir Walter Scott Wearing Jacket and Cravat

Sir Walter Scott, socle/ octagonal plinth

Sir Walter Scott

Sir Walter Scott, Tartan Plaid

Shakespeare, Socle/Octagonal Plinth

The Davenant Shakespeare

Shakespeare from The Monument, Coloured

The Chandos Shakespeare

The Rysbrack Shakespeare

		£ p
Palmerston Lord socle plinth (unnamed)	165mm	185.00
Impressed on the back of the smaller bust: *W.H. Goss*	223mm	185.00

Copyright, and incised in manuscript on back of the larger:
Published by W.H. Goss Copyright.

| **Palmerston** socle plinth and fluted column (unnamed) | 240mm | 195.00 |
| Impressed on the back of the smaller bust: *W.H. Goss* | 333mm | 225.00 |

Copyright, and incised in manuscript on back of the larger:
Published by W.H. Goss Copyright.

Peeping Tom square plinth

(Goss Record. 9th Edition:	(a) White glazed	115mm	95.00
Pages 29 & 30)	(b) White unglazed	115mm	100.00
	(c) Coloured	115mm	165.00

Impressed on plinth: *Peeping Tom of Coventry*
Inscribed on back: *Peeping Tom of Coventry Copyright Pub.*
As Act Directs (See 54 Geo. 111, C.56) W.H. Goss
Stoke-on-Trent 22 Jany 1893

Pitman, Sir Isaac. This bust is an apparent anomaly. Sculpted	275mm	350.00

by T. Brock, R.A. in London in 1887, it has an unusual square
plinth, and carries the GOSS ENGLAND mark. In view of its
early date it is included in this section [3]
Impressed on plinth: *Sir Isaac Pitman*
Incised on back: *T. Brock RA, SC London 1887*

Salisbury, Marquess of square plinth	glazed 163mm	195.00
Impressed on plinth: *Salisbury*	unglazed 163mm	195.00

Impressed side or back: *Copyright as Act directs W.H. Goss*
Stoke-on-Trent December 29 1887

Scott, Sir Walter square plinth	glazed 176mm	175.00
Impressed on plinth: *Sir Walter Scott*	unglazed 176mm	195.00

Impressed side or back: *Copyright as Act directs W.H. Goss*
Stoke-on-Trent March 30. 1880

Scott, Sir Walter socle plinth, and wearing tartan plaid	135mm	50.00
Impressed on back or base: *W.H. Goss*		

Scott, Sir Walter socle plinth, and wearing jacket, waistcoat		
and cravat	138mm	95.00
Impressed on back: *Scott*		

Scott, Sir Walter socle/octagonal plinth, and wearing jacket,		
waistcoat and cravat	168mm	215.00
Impressed on back: *Scott*		

Shakespeare from the monument, socle plinth	unglazed 100mm	80.00
Impressed on back: *From the Monument at Stratford-on-Avon 1616*		

Sister Dora

Robert Southey

*Robert Southey,
Socle/Octagonal Plinth*

Charles Swain

Sir William Wallace

H.M. Stanley

William Wordsworth

The Veiled Bride

Venus de Milo

John Wesley

Virgin Mary

Black Bust of Wesley

Shakespeare from the monument, socle/octagonal plinth. $£$ p
Incised on back in manuscript: *From the Monument at*
Stratford-on-Avon. 1616.

(a) Unglazed	165mm	135.00
(b) Coloured	165mm	185.00

Shakespeare from tomb, mounted upon two books
(Goss Record. 9th Edition: Page 30) [2]
Inscribed on the back: *Copied from the Monument erected by*
Shakespeare's family in the Church at Stratford-on-Avon.

(a)	White	75mm	60.00
(b)	White	102mm	60.00
(c)	Coloured	102mm	85.00
(d)	White	158mm	85.00
(e)	Coloured	158mm	135.00
(f)	Black	158mm	100.00
(g)	White	200mm	135.00
(h)	Coloured	200mm	145.00

Shakespeare - The Chandos socle plinth   125mm   145.00
Incised in manuscript on back: *The Chandos Shakespeare*   135mm   145.00

Shakespeare - The Davenant square plinth   115mm   95.00
Impressed on plinth: *The Davenant Shakespeare*

Shakespeare - The Rysbrack   224mm   95.00
Impressed on bust, rear: *W. H. Goss*
This model is the unnamed Goss version of Shakespeare, but is the
likeness created by Rysbrack. It has been seen mounted on a square
pillar, and also on a fluted column impressed: *W. H. Goss*, but these
are believed to have been matched subsequently, and that the
original base is a socle plinth.

See also THIRD PERIOD 11R. for late examples of busts of
Shakespeare.

Sister Dora square plinth   174mm   225.00
Impressed on plinth: *Sister Dora*
Impressed on side or back: *Copyright as Act directs W.H. Goss*
Stoke-on-Trent November 1888

Southey, Robert square plinth   180mm   155.00
Impressed on plinth: *Southey*
Incised in manscript on back: From the Drawing by Hancock (1796)
Impressed on back: *W.H. Goss*

Southey, Robert socle/octagonal plinth.   205mm   185.00
Impressed on plinth: *Southey*
Incised in manuscript on back: *From a drawing by Hancock (1796)*
Impressed on back or side: Copyright as Act directs W.H. Goss
Stoke-on-Trent March 30, 1880

		£ p

Stanley, Sir Henry Morton socle/octagonal plinth   212mm   600.00
Impressed on plinth: *H. M. Stanley*
Impressed on back: *Copyright as Act Directs W. H. Goss*
Stoke-on-Trent March, 1878

Swain, Charles socle plinth   283mm   1250.00
Incised in manuscript on side or back: *Published as the Act*
directs by R.R. Bealey, Manchester July 1870
Impressed on back: *W.H. Goss*
See also 9D TERRACOTTA.

Veiled Bride, The after the original marble bust by   270mm   950.00
Raphael Monti, socle plinth
Impressed on rear: *W.H. Goss*

Venus de Milo socle plinth   273mm   950.00
Impressed on rear: *W.H. Goss*

Virgin Mary socle plinth   500.00
Impressed on rear: *W.H. Goss*

Wallace, Sir William socle plinth   134mm   325.00
Inscribed on back: *Sir William Wallace. Copyright.*
Pub. As Act Directs (See Geo. 111, C.56)
W.H. Goss Stoke-on-Trent 22 JanY 1903

Webb, Captain Matthew   230mm   650.00
Impressed on rear; *W.H. Goss*

Wesley, John square plinth   unglazed 168mm   195.00
Impressed on plinth: *Wesley*   glazed 168mm   195.00
Impressed side or back: *Copyright as Act directs W.H. Goss*
Stoke-on-Trent

NOTE Black Basalt busts of Wesley were also made, height
154mm - but these, whilst being perfect smaller replicas of
the above, carry no manufacturer's identification mark. The
author definitely believes them to be products of the Goss
factory. Half-price.

Wordsworth, William square plinth   164mm   145.00
Impressed on plinth: *Wordsworth*
Impressed side or back: *Copyright as Act directs W.H. Goss*
Stoke-on-Trent March 30, 1880

B Figures

William Henry Goss's extensive education and instruction in the arts influenced the products of his pottery from the start in 1858. The long reign of Queen Victoria had led to a very peaceful and stable era in fashions and art, and made the nation feel secure in the permanency of its beliefs and tastes, and this was reflected in Staffordshire china. The new parian medium was readily approved of by the Queen, and manufacturer's top ranges were aimed at the middle classes who were emulating the upper calsses in the collection of marble statues.

William Goss had a desire to create shapes of beauty, mostly relating to known subjects in order to teach the general public an appreciation of art, history and culture. He felt, as head of his firm, and of better education and intellect than most, that he had a responsibilty to educate others.

As a student he had studied art at Somerset House from the age of 16 to 19 years, and his love of art led him to model superb classical figures, in the popular fashion of that time, of partly clothed mythical figurines in a variety of poses, often taken from classical mythology. A lady holding an asp aloft was Cleopatra; a robed woman, deep in thought with a dagger partly concealed in her dress, was the Shakespearian character Tragedy. A young woman praying is thought to be the Virgin Mary. Not all figurines were plain; some were coloured or were trimmed with colours, particularly gold, rose and turquoise, these being William's favourite colours.

In 1862 he won the much desired award of a medal at the Great International Exhibition for his display of parian and figurines. Many laudatory articles and engravings of his exhibits appeared in journals such as *The Illustrated London News* and Cassells' *Illustrated Family Paper*. Cassells wrote on November 15th, 1862, when examining an exhibit belonging to Goss of Stoke, 'It is necessary to glance at our engraving to perceive with what exquisite taste this manufacturer has worked out the several designs he produced in fictile wares. Here, classic forms blend harmoniously with the more ordinary forms in use in our domestic life... With the parian statuettes, the perfection of art manufacture seems ceratinly to have been reached.'

The two largest and most important figurines are Leda and the Swan, and Wood Nymph (holding a kid), of which coloured examples are dated 1866. Figurines made and sold in pairs were usually only factory marked on one of the pair. Almost all these were First Period and production had ceased well before 1900. The only figures listed on sale in the editions of *The Goss Record* were St Cuthbert of Durham and the coloured statues of the Trusty Servant and William of Wykeham, the latter two of which could only be obtained from the Winchester Agency during the Second Period. The same exclusivity applied during the First Period when Goss's friend, the first Winchester agent, William Savage, stocked his products.

The Lincoln Imp was available during the First and Second Periods, in both brown and white, in a variety of sizes.

Many figurines have gilded edges to their robes, usually brushed, a process apparently unique to Goss of having the gilding brushed across every 2mm so as to give a bright gilded appearance over a matt line of gilding. The brush marks remain visible, the whole leaving a distinctive striped effect.

Often figures were highlighted with William Henry Goss's favourite colour, turquoise blue, and occasionally also red. The robes of some figures were, more rarely, decorated with spots or dots of turquoise blue enamel, covering the entire garment and are particularly attractive. Sometimes faces and hair would be lightly tinted in correct pastel shades, the beautiful figurines of Leda and the Swan, and Wood Nymph holding a kid being the best examples.

Prices should be increased by at least £100 for the presence of gilding, £200 for brushed gilding and/or blue highlighting, and £250 for blue enamel dots or coloured faces and/or hair.

Some figurines are also jewelled. This is a process, not of insetting gem stones, (although, confusingly this is also called jewelling as described in the introduction to 9.C. ORNAMENTAL AND DOMESTIC), but of richly decorating ware, in the case of the Goss factory figurines, with a dot, usually in turquoise blue enamel, and surrounding this with decorative gilding and sometimes other colours, predominantly red.

Jewelling is usually found on the shoulders and around the base of robes on Goss figurines.

This distinctive decoration, used by no other factory on parian statuettes, makes Goss figurines easy to recognise, especially when otherwise unmarked, as often only one of a pair were marked, and many pairs have been separated over the years.

All figures in this section bear the impressed W H Goss mark unless stated otherwise.

		£ p
Angel standing with hands clasped in front	318mm	350.00
Angel holding shell in left hand	318mm	350.00
Angel kneeling, holding large shell (stoup). Reputedly St. John's Church Font, Barmouth	148mm	375.00
Bather nude, in pensive mood, seated on rock, white (a) Decorated with blue dots and brushed gilding (b)	220mm 220mm	350.00 575.00
Bather seated on a draped rock, holding conch shell with fishnet draped over knees and purse on ground.	240mm	450.00
Bather nude, seated on stump with drape over left knee, wearing bonnet	280mm	450.00
Bather nude, standing beside pump	390mm	950.00
Blind Highlander and Lass with dog gazing up, on circular base	280mm	750.00

Bride of Abydos, The
Embossed on front of plinth: *The Bride of Abydos*   535mm   1500.00
Inscribed: *Published as the Act directs (See 54 Geo 111, C.56)*
By Goss & Peake Stoke upon Trent September 12, 1867

Bull, John
Impressed: *W H Goss Sons Ltd*   165mm Unpriced
(In bisque, and probably a forgery)

The Captive Cupid a winged putto, feet chained
with metal chains, holding bow, other arm to eye, weeping

(a) White unglazed	215mm	250.00
(b) Some colouring	215mm	350.00
(c) White unglazed, without wings	218mm	250.00

Cherub The naked child, sleeping on a coverlet edged in gold and
stippled with purple dots, draped on the lid of an oval casket; head
resting on a basket of multi-coloured flowers. The lid decorated
around the top with blue dots, and around the edge with blue dots
and orange diamond shapes. The casket decorated around the top
with a white ruche pattern in relief, interspersed with orange and
gold triangular shapes, and with blue dots around the bottom edge.
    Length 130mm   650.00

Angel Holding Shell

Angel kneeling holding large shell (St. John's Font)

Bather, Partly Draped, Seated on Rock

Bather, nude, seated on stump

Bather, nude standing beside pump

Blind Highlander and Lass, with dog at feet

Cherub standing, foot on book, holding slate

Cherub, standing, holding palette in left hand

Classical Group, young male and nude maiden

Winged Putto, The Captive Cupid

The Boot Black

The Crossing Sweeper

£ p

Cherubs - a pair
    (a) Cherub standing on circular base, right foot on book, left
        hand holding compasses, pencil and slate   235mm   300.00
    (b) Cherub standing on circular base holding palette in left
        hand   210mm   300.00

Child kneeling on cushion, at prayer
    (a) Coloured, the decoration is Third Period [3]   165mm   550.00
    (b) White, glazed or unglazed   165mm   400.00

Child Girl, seated on circular base, holding open book
and crying   150mm   350.00

Children, Happy and Unhappy, The. A pair of figures from
originals by M. Simonis of Brussels, shown at the Great
Exhibition of 1851
    (a) Happy Child, holding toy Punch   approx. 150mm   350.00
    (b) Unhappy Child, having broken drum   143mm   350.00

Children Standing Beside Pillar Boxes - a pair
    (a) Boot Black   210mm   400.00
    (b) Crossing Sweeper (also found glazed)   224mm   400.00
        Both impressed *LETTERS* and incised in manuscript
        on the back of the Pillar Boxes:
        Published as the Act directs by W.H. Goss Stoke-on-Trent
        1 Dec 1873 Copyright.

NOTE: This pair, originally published in 1873 as unglazed
figures were re-issued in the latter days of the firm, but in
colour. In the earlier models, the Post Box has a loose top always
missing, and more rarely a fixed top, while in the later models
it is always fixed.
    (a) Boot Black, coloured [3]   210mm   750.00
    (b) Crossing Sweeper, coloured [3]   224mm   750.00

See also Section 9D for TERRACOTTA version
of the Crossing Sweeper.

Children - a pair
    (a) Partly draped, standing with foot on stool   210mm   300.00
    (b) Seated on rock   210mm   300.00

Chimney Sweeps boys
    (a) Standing against street bollard, on base, brush under right
        arm; left hand to mouth, shouting his trade   195mm   600.00
    (b) Standing against street bollard, on base, holding hat in right
        hand; brushes under left arm   195mm   600.00
The above two figures are a pair, one usually unmarked, the other
inscribed on the base below the bollard at the rear: *W.H. Goss*

Classical Lady, partly draped, seated on triangular base

Child, Partly Draped standing with Foot on Stool

Child Seated on Rock

The Devil Looking Over Lincoln

Lady Godiva on horseback, white

Lady Godiva on Horseback, Coloured

Dr. Kenealy Spill and Match Holder

Dewdrops, Dr. Kenealy Spillholder

Child Kneeling on a Cushion

Ophelia

The Bride of Abydos

Little Red Riding Hood

£ p

Chimney Sweep boy, sack over shoulder
    (a) White unglazed   292mm   350.00
    (b) Coloured, decoration probably late [3]   292mm   950.00

Classical Figurine Comedy lady holding mask away from face
                              (a) White   328mm   350.00
                              (b) With some colour   328mm   550.00
                              (c) Earthenware   328mm   350.00

Classical Figurine Tragedy lady with dagger.
                              (a) White   320mm   350.00
                              (b) With some colour   320mm   550.00
                              (c) Earthenware   320mm   350.00

The above two figurines are a pair. The (b) versions
both have edges of garments decorated in brushed gold
scrollwork pattern with red dots in the scrollwork, the
pattern bordered each side with lines of turquoise, and
brushed gilding to outer edges of garments.
Comedy has a hair garland of gold edged ivy leaves with
turquoise berries, and a necklet of gold dots with
turquoise beads.
Tragedy has a hair bandeau of brushed gold and turquoise
beads, and is holding a dagger of brushed gold.

Classical Figurine holding pitcher aloft with right arm;   345mm   350.00
left arm extended downwards and holding a fold of her drapes

Classical Figurine holding pitcher aloft with left arm;   345mm   350.00
right arm resting across her body, with the hand supporting the
drapes at her breast

(The above two figurines are a matching pair)

Classical Figurine right hand on head, blue dots, brown hair   380mm   350.00

Classical Group of a young male figure looking down upon a
reclining nude maiden with dying swan at her feet, all on a rocky
base
Impressed: *W.H. Goss*   Length 395mm Height 280mm   900.00

Classical Lady partly draped, seated on large triangular shaped
base (similar to Eve at the Fountain by Edward Bailey)   270mm   850.00

The Unhappy Child

The Happy Child

Child, girl, on circular base, holding book

The Chimney Sweep

Chimney Sweep boy holding hat

Chimney Sweep boy shouting his trade

Classical Lady, seated on large base, looking to sinister

Classical Lady, seated on large base, pensive mood

Classical Lady, seated on large base, looking to dexter

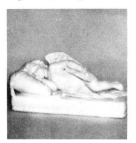

Cupid, asleep lying on a bed with bow and arrow

St. Cuthbert of Durham

Lady Holding a Child Playing Horn

£ p

Classical Ladies seated on large bases
  (a) Looking to dexter, with two money sacks, book and scroll
    at feet   350mm   400.00
  (b) Pensive mood, right hand under chin   350mm   400.00
  (c) Looking to sinister, holding scissors in right hand with
    hammer and chisel at feet   350mm   400.00

Cleopatra seated on draped tree stump holding aloft an asp.
On oval base   White (a) 240mm   650.00
         Decorated with blue dots and brushed gilding (b) 240mm   800.00

Cupid asleep lying on a bed with bow and arrow.   (a) 270mm x 140mm   400.00
Some colouring and gilded   (b) 280mm x 145mm   500.00
Impressed in manuscript: *Pub. as Act directs W.H. Goss
Stoke-on-Trent 15th May 1867*

Cuthbert of Durham, St.   134mm   400.00
(Goss Record. 9th Edition: Page 15) [2]
Inscribed on plinth, front: *St. Cuthbert* in Gothic script
and *Durham*

Devil Looking Over Lincoln, The   (a) White   147mm   90.00
Impressed in Gothic script around front and   (b) Brown   147mm   95.00
side faces of the plinth: *The Devil Looking Over Lincoln*

Fairy reclining in sleep, nude, natural colour, double wings, hands
clasped behind head, brown hair caught in a multi-coloured snood
of flowers, gilded star on forehead, lower limb drape with brushed
gilding to edges, turquoise blue waist cord with gilded tassels, three
porcelain back hooks for suspending the model. Found unmarked
but with all the hallmarks of Goss, as to familiar colours, gilding and
execution   Length 225mm   500.00

Figurine holding trumpet-shaped posy holder   300mm   350.00

Figurine Affection, standing with hand on breast   345mm   300.00

Figurine Meditation, standing in pensive mood with hand
under chin. Gown edged in gold   345mm   350.00

Figurine with hands partly outstretched   325mm   300.00

Figurine standing, looking to dexter at right hand and holding
lamp, whilst right hand holding gathered folds of garments to
chin   330mm   300.00

Figurine standing, playing lyre. Some colouring   340mm   350.00

Figurines a pair, each holding a baby   Each 375mm   350.00

*Classical Figurine, Comedy
Lady holding mask*

*Classical Figurine, Tragedy
Lady with dagger*

Figurine playing lyre

*Classical Figurine, holding
pitcher aloft*

**Classical Figurine, right hand
on head**

*Figurine looking to sinister,
right hand on stump*

*Figurine, hands partly
outstretched*

*Figurine, Seasons, holding
drape on head and cloak*

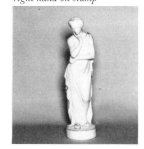

*Figurine, Meditation, with
hand under chin*

*Classical Figurine, right
hand on head, blue dots,*

*Figurine, Seasons, holding
sheaf of wheat aloft*

*Cleopatra Holding an Asp
Aloft*

		£	p
Figurines - a pair - **Seasons**			
(a) Holding sheaf of wheat aloft, blue dots, brushed gilding	340mm	450.00	
(b) Holding drape on head with left hand and edge of cloak with right hand. Blue dots, brushed gilding	340mm	450.00	

Figurine looking to dexter, with right hand on stump   320mm   350mm

Godiva, Lady, on horseback

(Goss Record. 9th Edition: Pages 29 & 30)
Impressed on plinth: *Lady Godiva* and *Copyright as Act directs. W.H. Goss Stoke-on-Trent 1st October 1902*
Inscribed on the base: *W. H. Goss Lady Godiva*, on the 112mm version. Also found with August 1876 or October 1880 on the 165mm size, and impresed *W. H. Goss* on the base in addition.
Sometimes found inscribed: *From the figure in Maidstone Museum, Maidstone*

(a)	White	112mm	275.00
(b)	White	133mm	300.00
(c)	White	165mm	350.00
(d)	White	182mm	550.00
(e)	Coloured	182mm	850.00

Goss, Evangeline the child sleeping on a cushion either forming the lid of a casket, white or coloured, or as a solid-based item
(Illustrated in Goss Record. 8th Edition: page 4. Bottom right.)

(a) White, on casket	Length 135mm Height	95mm	250.00
(b) Coloured, forming removable lid to casket	Length 145mm Height	95mm	350.00
(c) White, on cushion, blue trim, gilded	Length 135mm Height	55mm	275.00
(d) Natural coloured child on cushion, blue trim and gilded	Height	55mm	300.00
(e) As (d) but with crimson dots on cushion	Height	55mm	325.00

Dr. Kenealy caricature head modelled as a spillholder
Incised in manuscript on the base in W.H. Goss's own hand:
'Dew-drops' copyright Published as the Act directs (see 54 Geo 111, C.56) W.H. Goss Stoke-on-Trent 5th November 1875   130mm   200.00

Dr. Kenealy caricature figure standing and holding top-hat and umbrella, as spill-vase and match-holder
Incised in manuscript on the base: *'Dewdrops'* and on the back:
Pub. as Act directs by W.H. Goss See 54 Geo. 111 C.56, 5th November 1875 Copyright.   188mm   350.00

Dr. Kenealy depicted as a lion on circular plinth holding a shield *Sir Roger Tichborne and Magna Charta Defended*
Presumed to have been produced by W.H. Goss   350.00
Not seen by the author.

Evangeline Goss Lying on a Shaped Casket (b)

Evangeline Goss on a Cushion (b)

Evangeline Goss, white, blue trim, gilded (d)

Evangeline Goss, natural coloured child, crimson dots, blue trim, gilded (e)

Evangeline Goss, white, on casket (a)

Cherub on lid of oval casket, coloured

Mr Punch

Lincoln Imp

Lincoln Imp on Pedestal

Wood Nymph (holding a kid) coloured

Leda and the Swan, coloured

Shepherd Boy playing a flute

	£ p

Lady holding Child Playing Horn on oval base   275mm   650.00

Lady holding a kid, The Wood Nymph   (a) White   435mm   750.00
Inscribed: *Published as the Act directs*   (b) Coloured   435mm   1750.00
(See 54 Geo 111, C.56) by W. H. Goss Stoke upon Trent
November 18 1866

Leda and the Swan   (a) White   430mm   750.00
Inscribed: *Published as the Act directs*   (b) Coloured   430mm   1750.00
(See 54 Geo 111, C.56) by W.H. Goss Stoke upon Trent
November 18 1866

The above two figurines are a pair.

Lady with dove feeding from sea-shell   320mm   450.00

Lincoln Imp In high relief on beakers.
See L.11 DOMESTIC and UTILITY WARES

Lincoln Imp Miniature version on sconce of frilled candle-
holder. See L.14 DOMESTIC and UTILITY WARES

Lincoln Imp
(Goss Record. 9th Edition: Page 22)
Incised in manuscript on back: *The Imp of Lincoln*
From the carving in the Angel Choir at Lincoln Cathedral,
and intended as a wall hanging decoration.

(a)	White	44mm	100.00
(b)	White	80mm	45.00
(c)	Brown	80mm	40.00
(d)	White	110mm	40.00
(e)	Brown	110mm	45.00
(f)	White	120mm	60.00
(g)	Brown	120mm	55.00
(h)	White	145mm	55.00
(i)	Brown	145mm	60.00

These pieces often appear unmarked. Whilst some are from Goss
moulds they cannot all be properly considered as such and are
worth approximately £15.00
NOTE: Some of the above models are also found glazed, usually
with Blackpool Arms and are worth half the above prices.

Lincoln Imp seated on column
Impressed on base of column: *The Imp of Lincoln*

(a) White unglazed	114mm	85.00
(b) White glazed plinth, usually with matching arms	114mm	115.00
(c) Brown	114mm	175.00

Imperial Crown on square tasselled cushion, the tassels at each corner joined by gilded cord. The crown pierced and gilded.

Shakespeare standing leaning on lectern

Venus emerging from two shells

Virgin Mary

Trusty Servant implements, alternative version

The Trusty Servant

William of Wykeham

		£ p

Little Red Riding Hood   270mm   650.00
Impressed: *W. H. Goss*

Ophelia   535mm   1500.00
Embossed on front of plinth: *Ophelia*
Inscribed: *Published as the Act directs (see 54 Geo 111,*
C.56) By Goss & Peake Stoke upon Trent September 12, 1867
See also 9A BUSTS

Punch, Mr   295mm   1000.00
The three-quarter length figure resting on a base consisting of
four volumes of *Punch* and backed by two more.
Impressed: *Copyright as Act Directs*
Incised: *W. H. Goss*, and 1861 in Roman numerals

Shakespeare
Full length figure from monument in Westminster Abbey,   (a) 143mm   200.00
standing, leaning on a lectern.   (b) 175mm   275.00
    (a) also seen with the Third Period Goss England Mark

Shepherd Boy holding horn, wearing hat and sheepskin trousers,   280mm   750.00
sitting on a stone wall, flask by right elbow; bare footed; one
foot on the wall, the other on ground

Shepherd Boy wearing goatskin trousers, and playing a flute,   305mm   500.00
on naturalistic base.
Impressed: *W. H. Goss*

Trusty Servant, The [2]   202mm   2000.00
Inscribed on base: *A piece of antiquity painted on the wall*
adjoining to the kitchen of Winchester College.
Inscribed in manuscript on front of column:

> *A Trusty Servant's Portrait would you see,*
> *This Emblematic Figure well survey;*
> *The Porker's Snout - not Nice in diet shews;*
> *The Padlock Shut - no Secrets He'll disclose;*
> *Patient in the Afs - his Master's wrath will bear;*
> *Swiftness in Errand the Staggs Feet declare;*
> *Loaded his Left Hand - apt to labour Saith;*
> *The Vest - his Neatnefs; Open hand-his Faith;*
> *Girt with his Sword, his Shield upon his Arm,*
> *Himself and Master He'll protect from harm.*

Variations of the implements held by the Trusty Servant can
be found - see illustrations page 92

Figurine; Lady playing lyre. 340mm Note the decorated hem and jewelling to sleeve.

		£	p
William of Wykeham [2]	202mm	2000.00	

Inscribed on front: *William of Wykeham founder of Winchester College 1393.*

The above two are a Winchester pair in full colours.
William of Wykeham carries a removable crozier with a wire stem
without which the figure is incomplete. This crozier bears the
Rd. No. 208046 which dates the first year of manufacture to 1893
See also the story of the Winchester Goss Agencies on page 251

Venus emerging from between two large shells, supported by dolphins. Unglazed or part glazed	175mm	450.00
Woman Praying standing, possibly the Virgin Mary	275mm	300.00

Left: Bather, nude, in pensive mood, seated on rock 220mm
Right: Classical figurine, right hand on head, jewelled hem 380mm

Cockatoo sitting on perch on rocky base 270mm

C   Ornamental and Domestic

Apart from the range of busts and figures, the factory, under the management of the founder, produced many other wares. These included a variety of artistically tasteful wares: scent bottles with pierced sides (the scent was contained in the outer hollow rim of the round pierced bottles), large wall plaques, flagons and flasks, and wall vases with faces in relief.

The most costly wares were the jewelled vases and scent bottles, which were made up until 1885. The jewels were, in most cases, paste which had their colours enhanced by being placed into hollows coloured with the Goss enamels. These processes were patented in 1875, and were a successful improvement on the methods used by the Sèvres factory whose enamel jewels frequently rubbed off. Real jewels and pearls were used on certain precious pieces, but the author is unaware of any still in existence.

Pieces in this chapter usually bear impressed marks, sometimes with the addition of a Goshawk. In order to avoid confusion or duplication, nothing which could be expected to be found in another chapter has been listed in this section, but those pieces also produced during the First Period have been marked thus [1] in other chapters.

THE BULLOCK AND SHEEP GROUP

Albert Loring Murdock, a native of Boston, Massachusetts, discovered around 1860 that liver, then only given to animals, was the life saving treatment for pernicious anaemia. Murdock perfected a potion which was called Murdock's Liquid Food to treat this disease. He expanded his business, eventually supplying almost every drug store in the USA and many in Europe and the Orient. Every two years he went to Europe to maintain his agencies. He wanted a model of a cow, sheep and a pig in white to be manufactured as an advertisement for his medicines. He was told that William Henry Goss's china was the finest, so he contacted the factory and asked Goss to design some suitable models.

The chosen group of a bullock and two sheep on an oval plinth, was produced with the printed advertising slogan on the side of the beast MURDOCK'S LIQUID FOOD IS CONDENSED BEEF, MUTTON & FRUITS. It is surprising that William undertook the order, considering his dislike of advertising. Murdock and Goss, both eccentrics, became good friends and were regularly in contact with one another.

Murdock was a very generous and charitable man, who built and ran a free 175 bed hospital for the poor women and children of Boston. He also sent free cases of his liquid food to the Civil War wounded. Yet a member of his family can recall him as stingy! He was married with two sons and his unfulfilled ambition was to have a daughter, so he much admired Goss for having four beautiful girls. He particularly liked the youngest, Florence, and asked William if he could adopt her, pay her school fees and bring her up as his own. This offer was, no doubt, firmly rejected.

Murdock remained in contact with Florrie, as she was called, by sending her letters and postcards from his travels all over the world, and when, by chance, he returned to Stoke in 1905, he found a beautiful, mature, composed young woman in her thirties and was amazed to find her still single. She had had many suitors and offers of marriage, but had declined them all. Murdock had lost his wife and he proposed to Florrie, who eventually accepted. They married on St. Valentine's Day in 1906, one month after her father's death. Albert Murdock was older than her father! In his wedding photograph he had white hair and long grey whiskers. Life with him looked to be a life of luxury. Their honeymoon was a six month world tour including Paris, New York, California and Japan. But Murdock's real ambition was realised when they had a daughter in 1907.

Murdock died aged 82 years old, when his daughter was still only 5. His headstone holds pride of place in a South Hingham, Massachusetts cemetery, and his home, Maple Hall, still stands nearby.

Examples of the bullock and sheep group often come to light in the USA, but a purported group with a pig has yet to be seen.

Monmouth Mask, The Knight

The magnificent Alhambra Vase 516mm

The Alhambra Vase

Noah's Ark

Bird, Wren, on Edge of Nest

Bird on Tree Stump

Bird, Falcon, on Rock, Inkwell

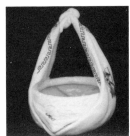

Bird's Nest in a Napkin

Cockatoo, sitting on perch on rocky base

Bullock and Sheep Group, Reverse

Bullock and Sheep Group

Dolphin, Inkwell

Guillemot Egg, open and closed

Bear and ragged staff coloured chain and harness

C. Ornamental and Domestic

£ p

The Alhambra Vase - after the Alhambra Palace at Granada, Spain.
William Henry Goss was fascinated with Moorish design and made a copy of this fabulous multi-coloured winged vase in earthenware especially for the 1861 Crystal Palace Exhibition. The vase adorned the mantlepiece of his cottage in Barthomley, Cheshire and has remained in the family until recently. 516mm 10,000.00
An Illustration showing the decoration of the vase in more detail may be found on page 99

The Ark (Noah's) - an excellent model of The Ark, with every plank detailed, and a decorated rubbing straight; the superstructure interior decorated in turquoise blue, with a pitched roof, and open at the stern end.
Impressed: sans-serif mark and brown Goshawk, but without W. H. Goss printed beneath it   Length 150mm Height 80mm 2500.00

Basket, Fruit Glazed, with acanthus-leaf pattern and strap
handle   (a) Length 215mm Height 145mm 325.00
                                    (b) Length 195mm Height 130mm 325.00

Basket, Fruit Glazed, fluted with turquoise strap
handle   Length 120mm 125.00

Basket, Dutch style blue coral handle, multi crested
                            Length 215mm Width 130mm 300.00
                            Length 215mm Width 140mm 300.00
(Illustrated. Goss Record. 8th Edition: Page 4. Upper Shelf.)

Basket, Posy Glazed. Fluted sides with twisted handle (Illustrated Goss Record. 8th Edition. Page 4, at bottom)
                            Length 140mm Height 105mm 250.00

See also Basket 11S THIRD PERIOD for late examples

Bear and Ragged Staff
(Goss Record, 9th Edition: Page 31)
Impressed on top of plinth: *Warwick*
Inscribed in the base: *Copyright. Pub. As Act Directs*
(See 54 Geo. 111, C.56) W.H. Goss Stoke-on-Trent 7 May 1898

(a) White unglazed   90mm 150.00
(b) White glazed with shield and arms
    (Add £50.00 for Warwick Arms)   90mm 175.00
(c) White unglazed with gilded harness and chain   90mm 175.00
(d) White unglazed, coloured harness and chain, plain base 90mm 265.00

Early Jug, Acanthus Leaf Pattern

Bowl, fluted, inscribed Homeopathic Medicine

Cream Jug, Sea-Urchin design White Glazed

Small Basket with Flutes and Strap

Basket with Coral Handle

Basket with Acanthus Leaves and Strap

Eggshell Cup with twig handle and feet

Eggshell Cream Jug

Posy Basket, fluted, twisted handle

Early Tea Pot with Raised Floral Decoration

Eggshell Cup and saucer with raised floral decoration

Imperial Crown on tasselled cushion, gilded

		£ p
(e) White unglazed with brown harness, yellow chain and green and yellow striped base	90mm	300.00
(f) Beige with brown harness and green and yellow striped base. Glazed or unglazed	90mm	350.00
(g) Brown unglazed	90mm	250.00
(h) Brown and coloured unglazed	90mm	350.00

Bird a wren standing on the edge of a nest, coloured light blue inside ..... 70mm 250.00

Bird on Tree Stump as posy vase ..... approx. 100mm 175.00

Bird, Falcon, on a rock as inkwell ..... 125mm 250.00

Bird's Egg Apart from the named Guillemot's Egg with a pointed end, for which see 10E HISTORIC MODELS, there is also a similar-sized sea-bird egg with a rounded base. Both varieties were produced in beige, blue and green speckled colourings.

(a) Closed, coloured	95mm	65.00
(b) Closed, white	95mm	85.00
(c) Open, to hang as posy vase	83mm	65.00

Bird's Nest in Napkin

(a) White glazed with and without arms	185mm	250.00
(b) Forget-Me-Nots covering piece	185mm	350.00

Bowl and Lid circular. The body formed from pink rose petals trimmed with green leaves. The lid has a rosebud knop ..... Dia. 73mm 55.00

Bowl (heavy), slightly fluted edge; ..... Dia. 90mm Height 52mm 60.00
decorated with two primrose sprays (Rd. No. 25947)

Bowl fluted, inscribed *HOMOEOPATHIC MEDICINE* with measurement scale on the inside and pattern around outside of body. All decorations in sepia ..... 70mm 100.00

For **Brooches** see FLORAL DECORATIONS page 109

Bullock and Two Sheep on oval plinth ..... 148mm 1000.00
Inscribed with the following advertising slogan on one side of the Bullock: *Murdock's Liquid Food is Condensed Beef, Mutton & Fruits.*
Impressed on the base: *Copyright as Act directs.*
W.H. Goss Stoke-on-Trent 1st September 1882
See also the story of this group on page 97

Cockatoo sitting on perch on rocky base ..... 270mm 400.00

Elephant with Howdah on oval base

Elephant and Howdah, no base

A Special Plaque. Bulls fighting

Fox and its Prey

Game Pie Pin Oval Box and Lid

Lion and Mouse group on ornamental base with bamboo

Early Sheep

Squirrel beside tree-trunk

Swan

Hand as Ring tree, natural colour, blue cuff

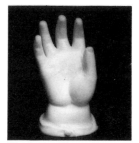
Hand Ring Tree, white glazed

Hand Holding Bag Vase

			£	p

Comport with three 50mm short legs.
Floral decoration of nasturtiums, with star pattern
centrally, in bas-relief inside bowl.   Dia. 224mm Height 170mm   100.00

Cream Jug and Sugar Basin sea-urchin design.
                    Jug Height 60mm   Bowl Dia.   100mm
                    (a) White glazed   Each   55.00
                    (b) Some turquoise colouring   Each   55.00

Cream Jug and Sugar Basin with vertical blue dots in relief
                                    Basin Dia.   100mm   30.00
                                    Jug Height   60mm   30.00

Cream Jug. Glazed, having acanthus leaf pattern in low relief.
Many variations of pastel coloured decoration predominently
pink, blue and green, both to handle and body can be found as
well as plain white, in addition to inscriptions in Gothic script.
'A PRESENT FROM....' or 'FROM....'   75mm   75.00

Cream Jug. Unglazed, with two cherubs in high relief, grape and
vine decoration in low relief   90mm   65.00

for Cream Jug
see also **Leaf Pattern**, this section

Crown, Imperial, on square tasselled cushion, the
tassels at each corner joined by gilded cord. The crown
pierced and gilded.
           Height 45mm Width 60mm Length   60mm   350.00

Dog Bowl. Illuminated lettering in relief around rim:
Quick at Work, Quick at Meals   Dia. 210mm   100.00

Dolphin on seaweed base with flat scallop shell dish supported
on raised tail   90mm   220.00

Dolphin - Tail uppermost on small round hollow plinth,
presumably for use as posy holder or inkwell   98mm   200.00
One example seen has an early puce Goshawk mark without
lettering and the registration mark for 1874. Found either
white or tinted pink glazed, after Belleek. The other has only
the serif impresed mark.

Eggshell Porcelain Tea Service
Cups, saucers, plates and jugs, bearing only the
impressed W.H. GOSS mark. Cups and saucers are very
fine wafer-thin glazed parian ware with apple blossom, violets
or vine and grape decoration in bas-relief. Belleek later used
the same design.

Leaf Pattern Cream Jug

Leaf Pattern sugar basin

Sark Milk Churn, Early

Pierced Bowl

Pierced Comport

Pierced Dish 242mm

Pin Cushion, Acanthus Leaf Pattern

Pin Cushion

Pierced Dish, beige, coloured floral decoration

Keystone of the Kingdom, Lord Beaconsfield

Monmouth Mask, The Knight

Monmouth Mask, The Miller

			£ p
Cup with twig handle and three feet		60mm	150.00
Cup and saucer Taper		65mm	65.00
		80mm	100.00
Cream Jug blue handle		65mm	100.00
Milk Jug		70mm	100.00
Sucrier on three legs, with pierced cover		92mm	250.00
Plate. Crested, glazed, violets in relief	Dia.	148mm	75.00
Plate. Round, unglazed	Approx. Dia.	200mm	150.00
Bread or Cake Plate. Oval, unglazed	Max. width	215mm	175.00
Tea Pot and Lid. three feet (Also found gilded)		130mm	350.00

One unique set has been decorated with butterflies in relief
and apple blossom in relief and has forged Chamberlain
Worcester marks concealing the impressed W.H. GOSS -

Tea Pot		130mm	1000.00
Sucrier and cover on three legs		92mm	350.00
Milk Jug on three legs		76mm	350.00
Cup and saucer	Dia.	138mm	300.00

Cup and Saucer, bagware with gilded trim.
No other decoration in relief. Glazed   55mm   75.00

Elephant with Howdah on oval base
(a) White glazed   153mm   650.00
(b) Some colouring, pink or green blanket   153mm   1250.00
(c) Earthenware   160mm   650.00

Elephant with Howdah. No base, coloured, unmarked   140mm   1250.00

For **Ewer,** early, see **Vases**

Coloured Box and lid with floral decoration (4)

Turquoise/white Bowl and lid with floral decoration (3)

Patterned Bowl and lid with fixed floral spray (5)

Coloured Puff Box with floral decoration (2)

Puff Box and lid with floral decoration (1)

Bowl and patterned lid with large floral spray (3)

Puff Box and lid with floral decoration (1)

Box and lid with floral decoration (6)

Floral decoration in Bowl (8)

Early Lozenge Vase, Oval Mouth floral decoration

Lozenge Vase, Oval Mouth with floral decoration

Pendant Cross, Ivy decoration, brown (13)

FLORAL DECORATIONS

Brooches were a successful line for the factory and these were sometimes affixed to the sides of First Period lozenge and other vases (for which add £50.00). They were also affixed to the tops of powder bowls and puff boxes, which were often highly decorative with fern and similar patterns in relief and usually multi-coloured in pastel shades, blue, green, pink and yellow predominating.

Floral decorations were used in the Third Period and are often finished in lustre.

Certainly anything with a lustre finish would only have been produced during that period.

Specific items are listed below but generally a floral decoration affixed to a piece would add some £50-£75.

BOWLS AND BOXES
                                                          £   p

1   Puff box and lid, white, with a large spray of coloured flowers
       affixed to lid.   Dia. 82mm Height   47mm   60.00
       Several variations including:
          Zinnia, periwinkle and carnation   110.00
          Three primroses   110.00
2   Puff Box and lid coloured, with a single rose as knop; petals
       mostly white, with the innermost ones tinted yellow
                          Dia 80mm Height   50mm   60.00
3   Circular box and lid with fern and similar pattern in relief and
       criss-cross brooch as a knop.   Dia. 70mm Height   70mm
       Also brooch knop without criss-cross centre on this version
       (a) White   200.00
       (b) Coloured
              (i) green and white bowl and lid   300.00
              (ii) turquoise and white bowl and lid   300.00
4   Box and lid, floral knop; leaf green and orange leaf patterns in
       relief   Dia. 70mm Height   93mm   250.00
5   Circular taper box and lid with pattern in relief and floral spray
       as a knop.   Dia. 100mm Height   75mm   150.00
6   Circular box and lid, white, patterned in relief and with floral
       spray as a knop.
       (a)   Dia. 102mm Height   70mm   75.00
       (b)   Dia. 110mm Height   55mm   95.00
7   Circular box and lid, fern pattern in relief in green,
       coloured brooch as knop, orange and green in relief on the
       box   Dia. 100mm Height   98mm   350.00

CROWN STAFFORDSHIRE TYPE FLORAL SPRAYS, BOWLS OR BASES

8   (a) Three yellow roses in bud on long stems, with small
          flowers at the base   Dia. 43mm Height   75mm   85.00
       (b) Mother of pearl lustre, assorted flowers [3]   45mm   50.00
       (c) Floral decoration inset, into lip-salve pot base   40mm   50.00
9   Four yellow/pink tulips and leaves on circular base; four
       tiny leaves on the green moss-like base.
                          Dia. 53mm Height   77mm   95.00

Pendant Cross, Lily of the Valley, white (15)

Pendant Cross, mixed floral, white (16)

Pendant Cross, mixed floral, black unglazed (14)

Lily of the Valley (53)

Daisies and Anemones, coloured (55)

Red Grapes with Green Vine Leaves, Oval, Coloured (37)

Three Rosebuds, oval, coloured (51)

Petunias and Leaves, tied with ribbon (28)

Forget-me-not spray, oval, coloured (43)

Roses, oval bouquet tied with ribbon, coloured (34)

Daisy and forget-me-nots, oval, coloured (46)

Rose and lily of the valley buds, oval spray, coloured (47)

Pink Rose (52)

Carnation, two tone, coloured (33)

Daisy with buds and leaves, circular, coloured (38)

Speedwell, petunia and daisy, coloured (45)

Violets with scarlet, yellow primroses, circular (42)

Double Daisy, circular, coloured (32b)

Poppy, speedwell and petunia, triangular, coloured (44)

Rose, forget-me-nots and speckled buds, circular (48)

Anemone with yellow primroses, circular (31)

Roses, two with three in bud and forget-me-nots (54)

Roses, forget-me-nots on criss-cross background, coloured (39)

Petunia, rose and forget-me-nots, oval, coloured (30)

111

Daisy and forget-me-nots, white (21)

Petunia, rose and forget-me-nots, white (19)

Rose with speckled buds, round, white (23)

Oval spray of violets, white (20)

Rose, Snowdrops and forget-me-not spray, oval (24)

Rose with speckled buds, circular, coloured (49)

Forget-me-not circle, coloured (29)

Daisy, Zinnia and rose, coloured (35)

Violet with buds and foliage, oval, coloured (36)

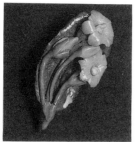

Spray of yellow Primroses, oval (41)

Wild anemone spray, oval, coloured (40)

Forget-me-not spray, oval, coloured (43)

£   p

10   Four daisies with long stems and green leaves on circular
      base (two yellow, one pink, one purple). One tiny
      flower between each stem, all on green moss-like base.
                                        Dia. 55mm Height   98mm   95.00

FLORAL JEWELLERY - PENDANTS, ETC.

11   Pendant, in form of a Cross with Clematis decoration in gold.
      Unglazed, (Red Goshawk).   80mm   150.00
12   Pendant, white glazed, with roses and speckled buds.   56mm   150.00
13   Pendant, in form of a Cross with ivy decoration, unglazed
      brown (Red Goshawk).   80mm   200.00
14   Pendant, in form of a Cross with roses, forget-me-nots,
      peonies in relief. Unglazed black.   90mm   150.00
15   Pendant, in form of a Cross with lily of the valley in relief.
      White glazed.   80mm   150.00
16   Pendant, in form of a Cross with roses, daisy, lily of the valley
      and forget-me-nots in relief. (a) White unglazed.   80mm   150.00
                              (b) Fully coloured   80mm   150.00
17   Stick Pin, blue forget-me-nots, pink buds, green leaves. 80mm   75.00
18   Earrings, to match above stick pin. Priced as a pair. 20mm   100.00

BROOCHES

Some thirty-five different designs were made, some white unglazed and others
coloured and glazed. As well as being produced during the First Period, some of these
designs were re-introduced during the 1920's in the Second Period.
After manufacture, the brooches were casually stored and little care was taken to see
that they remained perfect. Exceptionally, light damage would not affect the values
quoted here as all brooches are chipped to some extent.
All dimensions of brooches are diameter or length, whichever is the greatest.

Brooches, white unglazed   £   p

19   Petunia, rose and forget-me-nots, oval   47mm   75.00
20   Spray of three violets, oval   58mm   85.00
21   Daisy and forget-me-nots, oval   47mm   75.00
22   Rose and speckled buds, oval   50mm   75.00
23   Rose and speckled buds, circular   45mm   75.00
24   Rose snowdrops and forget-me-not spray, oval   50mm   85.00
25   Forget-me-not spray, oval   50mm   65.00
26   Forget-me-nots in border of leaves, circular   50mm   75.00

Brooches, white glazed

27   Scarab   40mm   75.00

Stick pin and earrings to match, forget-me-nots (17/18)

Scarab, Brooch, white glazed (27)

Crown Staffordshire type floral spray, two tulips on a base

Late Floral Brooch inset into Lip-salve Pot Base, Lustre (8)

Late Floral Spray planted in bowl (8)

Crown Staffordshire type floral spray, four daisies (10)

Delicate Limpet Shell on Coral Tripod

Brown Mushroom, green grass to stem base

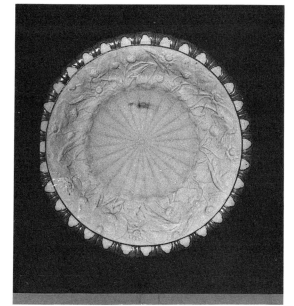

Plate, Water Lillies pattern in relief, Dia. 200mm

£   p

Brooches, coloured glazed

28	Petunias and leaves, tied with ribbon, oval		66mm	75.00
29	Forget-me-not circular		42mm	65.00
30	Petunia, rose and forget-me-nots, oval		47mm	75.00
31	Anemone with yellow primroses, circular		40mm	85.00
32	Daisy, circular, coloured purple, green centre	(a) single	30mm	75.00
		(b) double	37mm	75.00
33	Carnation, two-tone, circular		45mm	75.00
34	Bouquet of roses, tied with ribbon, oval	60 and	70mm	85.00
35	Daisy, zinnia and rose, circle		60mm	85.00
36	Violet with buds and foliage, oval		58mm	65.00
37	Bunch of red grapes and vine leaves with trailing creepers, oval		46mm	75.00
38	Daisy with buds and leaves, circular		40mm	65.00
39	Roses and forget-me-nots on criss-cross background, circular.		50mm	125.00
40	Wild anemone spray, oval		60mm	100.00
41	Spray of yellow primroses, oval		55mm	95.00
42	Violets with scarlet and yellow primroses, circular		45mm	145.00
43	Forget-me-not spray, oval	45 and	55mm	125.00
44	Poppy, speedwell and petunia, triangular		40mm	65.00
45	Speedwell, petunia and daisy, triangular		40mm	85.00
46	Daisy and forget-me-nots, oval		50mm	70.00
47	Rose (pink or yellow) and lily of the valley buds, oval		50mm	75.00
48	Rose (pink or yellow) forget-me-not and speckled buds, circular		50mm	70.00
49	Rose and speckled buds, circular		40mm	80.00
50	Large initial F on lily of the valley, roses and forget-me-nots on criss-cross background		80mm	160.00
51	Three rosebuds on leaf base, tied with ribbon, oval		70mm	85.00
52	Rose, pink		40mm	145.00
53	Lily of the valley, pink, oval		50mm	145.00
54	Roses, two, with three in bud and forget-me-nots		65mm	95.00
55	Daisies and anemones		60mm	75.00

Brooches, Terracotta

56	Terracotta base with floral brooch of forget-me-nots and roses	55mm	100.00

Fox and Its Prey a rooster, on oval plinth.   Height 90mm Length 200mm

(a) parian		200.00
(b) earthenware		145.00

For **Fruit Basket.**
see Basket

Game Pie oval pin box with pheasant and ferns decoration on lid and ivy around base.   Length   95mm   85.00

Hand Glazed. A ring tree.	(a) White	93mm	50.00
	(b) White, blue button	93mm	55.00
	(c) Natural colour, blue cuff	93mm	85.00

*St. Cross Hospice, Winchester
Plate Dia. 345mm*

*Plate Dia. 345mm with
Proverb*

*Winchester Plate
Dia. 345mm*

*Oval Plate: Think, Thank
and Thrive*

*Oval Platter: Give Us This
Day Our Daily Bread*

*Oval Platter: Where Reason
Rules The Appetite Obeys*

*Early Plate with Glazed
Recessed Centre*

*Unglazed Plate with Vine
Pattern in relief*

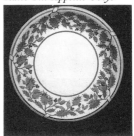

*Christmas Pudding Plate
coloured Holly Dia. 348mm*

Pierced Plate Dia. 225mm

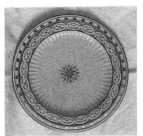

*Pierced plate, coloured with
medallions in relief,
225mm dia.*

*Plate Dia. 218mm A Merry
Christmas in Ribbon*

116

£   p

Hand Glazed, holding bag vase.
Some fine gliding and turquoise cord and button.   122mm   95.00

Japan Ewer [2]
Unglazed with ring of blue dots below neck, the
body decorated with two buff coloured transfers of a
radiating Grecian figure on a chariot drawn by three
horses rearing before an arc of eight stars; possibly
Apollo the Sun God riding his chariot.   200mm   150.00

For **Jewelled Ware** see **Vases, Jewelled**

Keystones of the Kingdom, The being almost life-size
heads of
    (a) **Lord Derby**   400.00
    (b) **Lord Beaconsfield**   400.00
Impressed on back: *Copyright as Act Directs W.H. Goss*
Stoke-on-Trent August 1880
These Heads are mounted on keystone shaped slabs.
Dimensions. Height 300mm; Width 175mm reducing to 144mm
See also 9D TERRACOTTA.
An advertising leaflet was issued with those models and is
valued at £60.00

Leaf pattern folded leaves with	(a) Cream Jug	Length	80mm	150.00
butterfly handles sometimes	(b) Cream Jug	Length	100mm	175.00
enamelled	(c) Sugar Basin	Length	100mm	175.00

Lion, and mouse group on ornamental base, with bamboo
poles at rear. Originally, lion trapped in netting which is usually
found disintegrated   Length 150mm Height 180mm   400.00

Lithophane A wafer-thin porcelain circle depicting an
art nouveau style girl with a star in her hair.   Dia.   89mm   2500.00
Signed and dated *J.A. 1888* (Joseph Astley, chief
modeller at the time).

Milk Can unglazed, early, with coloured spray of flowers
in bas-relief on both sides. Similar to the First Period
Sark Milk Churn. Marked No. 885X   64mm   250.00

Monmouth Masks [2]
(Goss Record. 9th Edition: Page 23)
Inscribed: *Model of Mask from Geoffrey of Monmouth's Study*
at Monmouth.
Although there are actually three masks in Geoffrey of
Monmouth's study: the Miller, the Knight, and the Angel, only
the former two have so far been found reproduced by Goss:

				£ p

The Miller   (a)   White glazed   81mm   225.00

The Miller	(a)	White glazed	81mm	225.00
	(b)	White unglazed	81mm	225.00
	(c)	Brown	81mm	300.00
	(d)	White	95mm	275.00
	(e)	Brown	95mm	375.00
	(f)	White glazed	120mm	300.00
	(g)	White unglazed	120mm	300.00
	(h)	Brown	120mm	375.00
The Knight	(a)	White glazed	80mm	225.00
	(b)	White unglazed	80mm	225.00
	(c)	Brown unglazed	80mm	300.00
	(d)	White unglazed	96mm	275.00
	(e)	Brown unglazed	96mm	375.00
	(f)	White glazed	115mm	300.00
	(g)	Brown unglazed	115mm	395.00

Mushroom Brown unglazed, with green grass around base
of stem [2]   60mm   250.00

Noah's Ark (see Ark)

Pierced Bowl
A latticed window bowl with turned over rim.
(Illustrated Goss Record. 8th Edition: Page 4,
Middle Shelf)   Dia. 140mm   250.00

Pierced Dish in imitation basket-work, oval, glazed with
a coat of arms in base of dish, usually of Boston.   Length 242mm   125.00
Alternatively, with beige ground and coloured floral
decoration around border   Length 242mm   150.00

Pinbox and lid, see Cherub, and Goss, Evangeline

Pin-cushion holder with three sprays of coloured thistles   Dia. 57mm   45.00

Pin-cushion A round, glazed porcelain base with shell pattern,
to be filled with sawdust and top covered in velvet. Inscribed
in Gothic lettering 'A PRESENT FROM...'   (a) Dia. 70mm   50.00
     Plain white (b) Dia. 70mm   40.00

Pin-cushion A round unglazed porcelain bowl with two bands
of turquoise and A PRESENT FROM THE CRYSTAL
PALACE in orange capitals around top, and moulded leaf
pattern to lower half.   95mm   60.00

£ p

Plaque. Fighting Bulls (Illustrated, Goss Record. 8th Edition:
Page 4, Top Shelf) was made specially for the Exhibition at
Stoke-on-Trent in 1913 on the occasion of Their Majesties,
King George V and Queen Mary's visit to the Potteries.
The only one specimen is known and the piece is believed to be
unique. It depicts two bulls fighting, in bas-relief and is
unglazed. The border is perfectly plain. [2]   335mm x 275mm   2000.00

Plates Circular. The following various early
unglazed plates, measuring about 345mm in diameter were
produced. Some were left completely white while others had the
wording, coat of arms or other decoration in colour. The most
common is the Winchester plate, which often bears the
inscription: *Designed and Published by W. SAVAGE* on the back,
often without the W.H. Goss impressed mark.

Manners Makyth Man
Embossed around rim, with Arms of Bishop William of
Wykeham centrally and his See at the bottom.
(a) White	345mm	185.00
(b) Coloured	345mm	250.00

Domus Eleemosynaria Nobilis Paupertatis (sic)
Embossed around rim with **Arms of St. Cross Hospital
Winchester,** centrally
Translation: ALMS HOUSE OF THE NOBLE POOR
(a) White unglazed	345mm	185.00
(b) White or cream glazed	345mm	150.00
(c) Coloured	345mm	250.00

Eat Thy Bread with Thankfulness
embossed around rim
(a) White	345mm	185.00
(b) Coloured	345mm	250.00

A Little Cheese if you Please
embossed around rim - White   345mm   150.00

Think Thank and Thrive
embossed around rim [2]
(Illustrated. Goss Record. 8th Edition: Page 4)
(See also Platters)
(a) White	345mm	185.00
(b) Coloured	345mm	250.00

A Merry Christmas
inscribed in a ribbon on a circular plate, with magenta border,
and in the centre a coloured bouquet of holly, ivy and mistletoe
Dia. 218mm   650.00

£   p

Christmas Pudding Plate
with holly decoration around rim

(a) White	Dia. 348mm	145.00
(b) Coloured	Dia. 348mm	300.00

Plate, Toft style with glazed recessed centre and heavy
relief decoration around wide unglazed rim   Dia. 200mm   50.00

Plate Celandine pattern, in relief   Dia. 227mm   75.00

Plate Nasturtium pattern, in relief   Dia. 227mm   75.00

Plate Water Lillies pattern, in relief   Dia. 200mm   75.00

Plate circular, wavy edge with vine and grape decoration
in low relief, found both marked and unmarked

(a) Gilded around edges of leaves.	Dia. 210mm	90.00
(b) Ungilded.	Dia. 210mm	70.00

Plate pierced, with piercings left in place, with pink band as
decoration. The body is of cream earthenware, and a matching
comport was made of three twisted cornucopia, with fruit and
foliage at the base of the legs, which open up to a triangular pierced
base to support the plate.
This plate may also be found with an early transfer of
a child in the centre for which add £50.00   Plate Dia. 225mm   75.00
                                                    Comport Dia. 170mm   100.00

Plate square pierced with ring of oval medallions around
rim, coloured - Creamware   Dia. 225mm   150.00

Plate, pierced with linked chain decoration in relief
Bournemouth coat of arms in centre. This is from the same
mould as that used for the comport featured in the 1862
International Exhibition. (See page 14)   Dia. 234mm   70.00

Platters Oval Bread 310mm x 250mm which appear (a)
unglazed, with coloured lettering and (b) glazed with plain or
coloured lettering, and with arms or other motif central.
   (a) *Where Reason Rules, The Appetite Obeys* embossed around rim.   125.00
   (b) *Give Us This Day Our Daily Bread* embossed around rim.   125.00
White or cream glazed.

Platters almost Oval 328mm x 245mm carrying the *Think,*
Thank and Thrive wording embossed around the border are
found with two differing types of lettering

(a) White unglazed	150.00
(b) White, coloured lettering, glazed or unglazed	200.00

	£	p

Sark Milk Churn parian with small handle and gilded acanthus decorations in relief and bearing in gilded lettering *Souvenir de Sercq* in gilt script. It has no lid　　　　　　　64mm　　250.00

Scent Bottle circular and pierced, with an openwork twisted stopper. Richly gilded with a wide turquoise band around the circular scent tube, which can be found with plain edge, or decorated with turquoise blue dots. This item is jewelled with tiny gilt stones set around a central ruby. Originally supplied in a fitted leather case lined with purple velvet, for which add £200.00　　　　　　　120mm　　1000.00

Scent Bottle with decoration in relief of crown over cipher in orange colour. Floral cartouche, oval, on reverse. Unglazed. Can be found unmarked and uncoloured　　　　130mm　　200.00

Sheep lying down, identical to those featured in the Bullock and Sheep group. (See also 10I Animals and Birds) This same sheep re-appeared some half a century later, this time glazed and on an oval plinth as one of the series of animals produced in the 1920s. [2]　　　　　Glazed or unglazed 115mm　　150.00

SHELLS:

Limpet [2]
An extremely fine glazed limpet shell mounted on a coloured coral tripod base, another example of eggshell porcelain. (Illustrated. Goss Record. 8th Edition: Page 4. Bottom Shelf front)　　　　　　　　　　　　　　66mm　　150.00

Nautilus
(a) large glazed and crested version [2] (See 10K.5 Miscellaneous)　　　　　　　　　　155mm　　150.00
(b) As (a) in Earthenware　　　　　　　　155mm　　100.00
(c) a finer smaller, glazed, uncrested version tinted in pink　95mm　　325.00
　　(Illustrated. Goss Record. 8th Edition: Page 4. Middle
　　Shelf). [2] This is an example of Goss eggshell porcelain.

Whelk
(a) a single glazed whelk shell supported on a coral and rock base　144mm　　100.00
(b) a group of three glazed whelk shells mounted on a stone base
　　and having coloured coral between the shells　137mm　　250.00
(c) one large whelk shell supported by three smaller ones, standing
　　on four coral legs (Glazed)　　　　　185mm　　250.00
(d) eight whelk shells on rocky base surrounding the nautilus
　　shell, the latter supported on coral　　200mm　　600.00

Winchester Flagon patterned in relief, blue trim, gilded handle

Lithophane

Wall Plaque, with bust of Shakespeare in bas-relief

Winchester Flagon

Jewelled scent bottle in original fitted leather case

Vase, oval, flat faced, wreath surround, rectangular base

First Period Scent Bottle with Crown over Cipher

Rare Vase 293mm, flying cherubs in relief

Rare jewelled vase

Vase, round, flat faced, wreath surround, rectangular base, round mouth

Rare Jewelled Vase, octagonal, raised Ivy Leaf pattern

Jewelled Vase with oviform body and pedestal foot

£   p

Squirrel standing beside a hollow tree-trunk, glazed and
unglazed. Trunk glazed inside for use as a posy vase   117mm   150.00

for Sugar Basin
see also **Leaf Pattern**, this section

Sugar Bowl and Pierced Lid on three tiny feet.
Periwinkles in relief; lid with periwinkle knop surrounded
with lattice work in relief.
Impressed: *W. H. Goss*   93mm   250.00

Swan				
	(a)		60mm	95.00
	(b)		73mm	95.00
	(c)		94mm	100.00
	(d)	Glazed	130mm	145.00
	(e)	Unglazed	130mm	145.00
	(f)	Glazed	135mm	145.00

Can be either a cream jug or posy holder. Occasionally found
with arms or decorations to rear. Same value.

Trinket Box and Lid see Cherub, and Goss, Evangeline

Vase, Bulbous With cup top and strap handle
Turquoise trim to cup top and handle. Two purple transfers of
Oxford High Street, believed to be an early experimental piece
unglazed [1]   135mm   150.00

Vase Round, flat faced, turquoise or plain leaves on border,
oval base and mouth   120mm   75.00

Vase Round, flat faced, wreath surround in blue or plain;
rectangular base and round mouth   107mm   75.00

Vase Oval, flat faced, wreath surround, rectangular base and
oval mouth

(a)	115mm	75.00
(b)	120mm	90.00
(c)	170mm	90.00

Vase decorated with flying cherubs in relief and two gargoyles
on shoulder. Exhibited at International Exhibition 1862.   293mm   900.00
See illustration page 14

*Vase, whorl pattern in relief
No. 890X*

*Ewer, rounded handle
No. 889X*

*Ewer, flat handle
No.889X*

Rare Early Vase

*Rare Early Vase
No. 895X*

*Vase, dove in circle and leaves,
white*

*Vase, green and beige
decoration No. 891X*

*Vase, coloured flowers in
relief, taper stem No. 881X*

*Pompeian Vase, with coloured
Grecian Scenes*

*Vase, round, flat faced, oval
base and mouth*

Three Whelk Shells on Base

*Three Whelk Shells on coral
base*

Vases, Jewelled

These are probably the finest and most beautiful pieces ever
produced by the Goss factory. William H. Goss carried out
hundreds of experiments in order to perfect the parian body,
which the author considers to be among the finest ever
produced. Into this he set stones; some semi-precious, others
glass, in the most attractive and decorative way. He patented
this process which was the object of widespread acclaim, for
nobody had yet been able to successfully produce high quality
work of this nature, although many, even Sèvres, had tried.
Only a few examples of jewelled ware are known to exist; all
known are illustrated in this Chapter, and one again in colour on
the jacket of *Goss China Arms, Decorations and their Values*
(1982 Edition) Milestone Publications

(a) **Vase** with oviform body, and pedestal foot, having 597 jewels
     coloured green, red, yellow and magenta set amongst rich
     and ornate gilding. Goshawk mark   155mm   3500.00

(b) **Vase** octagonal with two shaped handles. Raised ivy leaf
     pattern, richly gilded with 740 magenta and green jewels inset   240mm   3500.00

(c) **Vase** with fluted body and two pierced fluted handles.
     Beautifully decorated on beige ground set with red, yellow
     and green stones. Glazed interior   170mm   2000.00

(d) **Scent Bottle** See page 121

Vases A number of early parian vases 70-385mm in height
were produced, each unique. Illustrations of these may be
found in the engraving of W.H. Goss's exhibit for the
International Exhibition of 1862 (illustrated on page 14, and in
Goss for Collectors, The Literature, John Magee. Milestone
Publications, but now out of print)
All unglazed except one, numbered 888

Some specific known examples are given here:

(a) **Vase** Having multi-coloured sprays of flowers in relief on both
     sides of body, and two gilded bands around narrow taper stem.
     Inscribed on base:*881X*   96mm   1500.00

(b) **Ewer** glazed, vertical blue lines, raised pattern on vertical
     white stripes (numbered 888)   67mm   1250.00

(c) **Vase** Whorl pattern in relief with lines of alternate blue dots
     and gilding   70mm   1250.00
     Inscribed on base: *890X*

Oval plaque 'Can't you talk'

Oval Plaque Oakley Coles

Oval Plaque J.S. Crapper

Oval Plaque Robert Garner

Oval Plaque Rev. Lovelace Stamer

Oval Plaque The Prince of Wales

Two House Martins on nest shaped wall pocket

Humming Bird Wall Vase

Florence Goss Wall Vase

Wall Name Plate decorated with scrolls, jewelled and surrounded by turquoise. The name Georgiana in flowers and foliage. Glazed. 190mm x 83mm

		£ p
(d) **Vase** Having vertical green leaves around base, and beige and green decoration to body. Inscribed on base: *891X*	122mm	1500.00
(e) **Ewer** Having vertical blue lines and raised ivy leaf pattern with two horizontal bands of blue dots enclosed by gilded bands. One shaped handle to side, rounded or flat Inscribed on base: *889X*	70mm	1250.00
(f) **Vase** Having vertical flutes with rich multi-coloured floral pattern around bulbous centre Inscribed on base: *895X*	100mm	1250.00
(g) **Vase** Fluted pattern in relief with three horizontal bands of blue dots enclosed by gilded lines. Ivy pattern in relief at neck	70mm	1250.00
(h) **Vase** of Pompeian slender form and having Grecian scenes in light pastel shades	385mm	1500.00
(i) **Vase** Unglazed, no colouring or gilding, having a dove in a circle within crossed sprays of leaves.	130mm	500.00

Wall plaque large upright oval, with bust of Shakespeare in bas-relief centrally Height 435mm Width 390mm Impressed: *W.H. Goss*		450.00

Wall Plaques, Oval, upright. A number of these were produced with busts in bas-relief centrally. The plaques were normally edged in richly gilded acanthus leaves with red berries, and surmounted by a porcelain ribbon bow trimmed in turquoise blue. The title for each will be found lightly impressed under the subject.

(a) **Oakley Coles**	200mm	550.00
(b) **J.S. Crapper**	200mm	550.00
(c) **Robert Garner**	200mm	550.00
(d) **William Ewart Gladstone**	190mm	550.00
(e) **The Prince of Wales** (later King Edward VII)	200mm	600.00
(f) **Eugene Rimmel**	200mm	550.00
(g) **The Rev Sir Lovelace Stamer,** Bart	200mm	550.00
For an example found uncoloured	200mm	350.00
(h) **Wall Plaque, Oval, horizontal etc.** **Child with Large Dog** Length 180mm		550.00
with title on front: *can't you talk*		

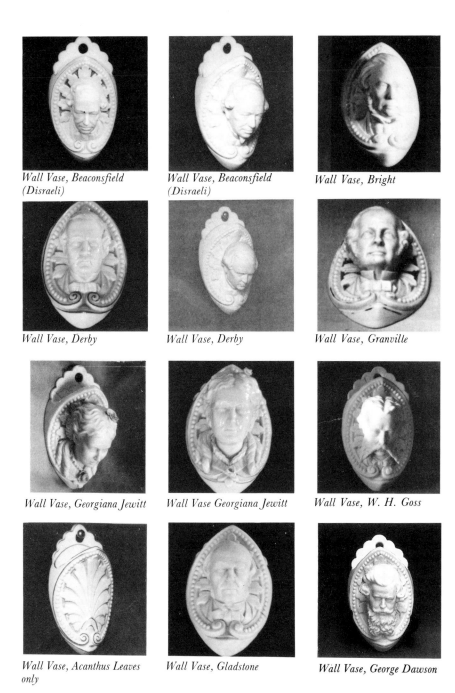

Wall Vase, Beaconsfield
(Disraeli)

Wall Vase, Beaconsfield
(Disraeli)

Wall Vase, Bright

Wall Vase, Derby

Wall Vase, Derby

Wall Vase, Granville

Wall Vase, Georgiana Jewitt

Wall Vase Georgiana Jewitt

Wall Vase, W. H. Goss

Wall Vase, Acanthus Leaves
only

Wall Vase, Gladstone

Wall Vase, George Dawson

£   p

The above wall plaques were commissioned and published by J.S. Crapper, a colleague of W.H. Goss, and the following is impressed on the reverse, in addition to W.H. Goss:

Plaques (a) (b) and (h)

> *COPYRIGHT*
> *as the Act directs*
> *(See 54 Geo iii, c56)*
> *J S Crapper*
> *Hanley*
> *1st May 1876*

Plaques (e) and (f)

> *COPYRIGHT*
> *as the Act directs*
> *(See 54 Geo iii, c56)*
> *William H Goss*
> *Stoke-on-Trent*
> *May 1st 1876*

Plaques (c) (d) and (g)

> *Copyright as the Act directs*
> *W.H. Goss*
> *Stoke on Trent*
> *January 1877*

Wall Vases

(a) **Child's Head** with radiating hair and feathers. The face is that of Florence, William Henry Goss's youngest daughter. Impressed on back: *Copyright as Act directs W.H. Goss Stoke-on-Trent January 1882* Usually glazed, but occasionally unglazed.

		£
	125mm	250.00
	150mm	275.00
	190mm	300.00

(b) Heads of the following in high relief on front of a glazed or unglazed oval wall-pocket, with plain, blue, or green background and acanthus leaf surround, with the name of the subject usually found impressed on the front at the base of the oval mount:-

Beaconsfield (Disraeli)
John Bright
George Dawson
Earl of Derby
William Henry Goss
Earl Granville
Georgiana Jewitt

		£
White, glazed or unglazed	180mm	225.00
Part-coloured, glazed	180mm	350.00

One of a series of seven oval Wall Plaques, 200mm high depicting the Bust of the Perfumier Eugene Rimmel in bas-relief. The name is lightly impressed under the subject on the front.

    The acanthus leaves are richly gilded with red berries and the ribbon trimmed with turquoise. The figure is raised from a cream ground.

		£	p

(c) As (b) but without head, i.e. a wall-vase decorated with turquoise blue acanthus leaves. — 180mm — 350.00

(d) **A Humming Bird** taking nectar from a passion flower, and with a nest above containing three eggs in the surrounding foliage. Glazed
Impressed on back: *Copyright as Act directs W.H. Goss Stoke-on-Trent January 1888* — 257mm — 275.00

(e) **Two House Martins** on nest-shaped wall pocket, decorated with fern leaves on front, and a snail shell at the bottom.
Impressed on back: *W.H. Goss* — Overall Height 235mm
Overall width 180mm — 350.00

Winchester Flagons These are a pair, unglazed, carrying coloured likenesses in bas-relief of:

(a) **The Trusty Servant** fully coloured version can be found decorated with brushed gilding — 160mm — 200.00

(b) **William of Wykeham** white and coloured. The coloured version is marked, and the white is unmarked, but the same mould. — 160mm — 200.00

Many of these appear unmarked and may possibly have been made by the Goss factory. One pair, marked, is reputed to exist but has not been seen by the author. Similar flagons were made by Copeland and other factories for William Savage, the first Winchester Agent. Unmarked varieties would be worth £70.00-£120.00 depending on size and desirability.

Winchester Flagon (Unmarked) patterned in relief, turquoise blue rim and base, gilding to rim and handle — 150mm — 250.00

Wall Name Plate
Personalised ornamental name plate made for William Henry Goss's eldest daughter. Decorated with gilded scrolls, jewelled, and surrounded by turquoise. The name Georgiana in flowers and foliage. Glazed. — Length 190mm Height — 83mm — 2000.00

Two House Martins on nest shaped wall pocket decorated with fern leaves on front and a snail shell at the bottom.

£ p

D Terracotta

In 1856 a valuable deposit of red clay was found in the Stoke area giving birth to the red clay tile industry. One manufacturer involved in this trade was a Mr Peake who entered into a brief partnership with W H Goss in 1867. It was short lived due to Peake's own financial difficulties and lasted for less than a year.

The partnership concentrated on the production of terracotta ornamental and utility ware, marked GOSS & PEAKE in fine black lettering. Terracotta manufactured after the partnership dissolved was marked W H GOSS. Few of the utility items such as tobacco jars with lids are to be found perfect today as they were made to be used. Decorations on these heavy wares included transfers of Egyptian and Greek influence in black, red, yellow and green, and amusing cartoons in black silhouette.

Wares marked GOSS & PEAKE are more desirable, being scarcer in number, and £20.00 should be added for this mark.

Terracotta was produced between 1867 and 1876 and Goss appeared to be one of the few factories to mark their wares. Probably for this reason much unmarked terracotta is hopefully, but incorrectly attributed to Goss.

Terracotta Jardinière and Base Plate

Terracotta Spill Holder, Cartoons

Terracotta Cambridge Jug with hinged Pewter lid

Terracotta Vase, Cartoons and Patterned

Terracotta Spill Holder, Patterned

Terracotta Vase, Patterned

Terracotta Keystone, Lord Beaconsfield

Terracotta Keystone of the Kingdom, Lord Derby

Terracotta Bust of Burns

Terracotta comport, Patterned

Terracotta Jug, with thumb rest

Terracotta Tobacco Jar, Patterned

Terracotta Tobacco Jar, Patterned

Terracotta Tobacco Jar Cartoons

Terracotta Tobacco Jar Cartoons

Black Enamelled Terracotta Vase

Terracotta Bag-Vase, Barbados Transfer

Terracotta Vase and Stopper, Cartoons

			£	p

Busts   (a) **Robert Burns** socle/octagonal base   170mm   375.00
          (b) **George Dawson** socle base, dated 1871   280mm   500.00
          (c) **Charles Swain** socle base   280mm   500.00
See also FIRST PERIOD 9A BUSTS for white parian varieties

Cambridge Jug sometimes with hinged pewter lid
                              Overall height   117mm   100.00

Candle Holder   85.00

Coffee Pot   125mm   100.00

Comport   Dia. 245mm   115mm   100.00

Crossing Sweeper in varied brown shades; the Child standing
beside a Pillar Box with impressed word LETTERS and a loose
lid; incised in manuscript on the back of the Pillar Box:
Published as the Act directs by W. H. Goss, Stoke-on-Trent 1 Dec 1873
Copyright, and impressed below: *WETLEY BRICK AND*
POTTERY CO. LIMITED. W.K.   224mm   200.00

See also FIRST PERIOD 9B FIGURES for white parian variety

Jardinière normally found with an unmarked base plate, but
correct   190mm   100.00

Jug sometimes with hinged pewter lid   Approx.   130mm   100.00
with hinged thumb lever; sometimes with   180mm   110.00
thumb rest affixed to top of handle   190mm   110.00

Spill Holder   130mm   85.00

Tea Pot   Length   150mm   100.00

Tobacco Jar with damper and lid.   105mm   70.00
These are relatively common   110mm   70.00

A Black-enamelled Terracotta Vase having Classical Figures
stencilled around the body.   180mm   300.00

Vase, Bag with pictorial view of *The Cassino, Barbados Aquatic*
Club, and *Arms of Barbados* on the reverse.   50mm   75.00

Vase slender waisted, patterned   120mm   100.00
                                     140mm   100.00
                                     210mm   100.00

		£	p
Vase bulbous bottom glazed interior	140mm	100.00	
Vase and stopper usually missing, and base plate	250mm	100.00	

The Keystones of the Kingdom
being almost life-size heads mounted on keystone shaped
slabs of -
  (a) Lord Derby
  (b) Lord Beaconsfield
Impressed on back: *Copyright as Act directs W.H. Goss*
Stoke-on-Trent August 1876
One example also has additionally impressed on the back
WETLEY BRICK AND POTTERY CO. LIMITED. W.K.
thus posing the question as to whether they were all
made by this firm.
Height 321mm; Width 195mm reducing to 150mm   Each   400.00
See also FIRST PERIOD 9C ORNAMENTAL for an unglazed
white parian variety. An advertising leaflet was issued with
these models and is valued at £60.00

A rare terracotta bust of Robert Burns on socle/octagonal plinth. Height 170mm

10 The Second Period 1881-1934

E   HISTORIC MODELS AND SPECIAL SHAPES
F   COTTAGES AND COLOURED BUILDINGS
G   CROSSES
H   FONTS
I   ANIMALS AND BIRDS
J   MINIATURES
K   ORNAMENTAL
L   DOMESTIC AND UTILITY WARES
M   METALWARE
N   DOLLS

Period Symbols

Where a shape was known to have been made during more than one period, the number in brackets after its entry denotes the other period(s) during which it was manufactured.

The First Period	[1]	**1858-1887**
The Second Period	[2]	**1881-1934**
The Third Period	[3]	**1930-1939**

Photograph sent by Adolphus Goss to Agencies to assist them in ordering

Six of the earliest models to be produced, all are First Period. Top Row: Avebury Celtic Urn, Swindon Vase, Itford Lewes Urn Bottom Row: Norwich Urn, Bath Urn, Abingdon Roman Vase

E   Historic Models and Special Shapes

The majority of models in this section were manufactured during the Second Period between 1888 and 1929. However, certain shapes, especially the larger versions, were test-marketed during the First Period up to seven years earlier, and more popular lines continued for four years into the Third Period after the sale of the pottery in 1929. Numbers in square brackets throughout the listing indicate other periods where particular models were known to have been in production. It is possible to tell by the thicker feel and slightly gritty texture plus the more yellow hue of the porcelain, if a piece was made pre-1888. Thereafter, the quality of china, enamel and gilt improved drastically and became consistent. Second Period named models are very much whiter in appearance and the quality is excellent. The original factory photograph on page 141 shows an example of armorial ware made from 1929 to 1934. The named models are the most widely known of all the factory's products and they dominated production for the larger part of its existence. This chapter will probably be the most important to collectors because it contains the six hundred plus models which are most avidly collected. Cottages, Fonts, Animals and Crosses are also models, but due to their importance will be found under their own sub-headings.

Two sets of values are given where applicable, one for any arms and the other for matching arms. For example, an Exeter Vase with the Arms of Exeter will be worth very much more than one with, say, City of Edinburgh arms. No general percentage can be added for matching arms as examples vary so much in rarity. Many collectors prefer to have the correct arms on a model and where possible these are stated. Where there are no arms for a particular model, such as the Ashley Rails Urn, the nearest town or the local agency in this case Christchurch or New Milton (Manor of New Milton) is considered correct. If a model relates to a specific person rather than a place, such as Dorothy Vernon's Porridge Pot, then the arms of that person is to be preferred. Ethnic shapes such as the Welsh Leek, Welsh Picyn, Welsh Milk Can etc relate to the Principality as a whole and not just to one town. Any Welsh arms can be considered matching although the true correct arms are the Arms of Wales. Foreign models such as the Norwegian Dragon and Horse shaped Beer Bowls and Bucket are matching with the arms of Norway and also with those of any Norwegian town. Matching arms also include the arms of any school, hospital, or nobleman relevant to the respective town of the model concerned. Nearby towns and correct county arms will attract premiums ranging from ten per cent to fifty per cent to be added to the price given with any arms. For the values of the various arms and decorations to be found on any piece of Goss see the Price Guide's companion volume - *The Price Guide to Arms and Decorations on Goss China* by Nicholas Pine (Milestone Publications).

Some models are listed with only one price. This is where the item is known only with or without matching arms as the case may be. For instance, the Alderney Fish Basket appears only with the matching arms of Alderney so no price is given for a variety with any other arms.

The inscription on each model is given in italics in every case. There is no inscription if none is stated.

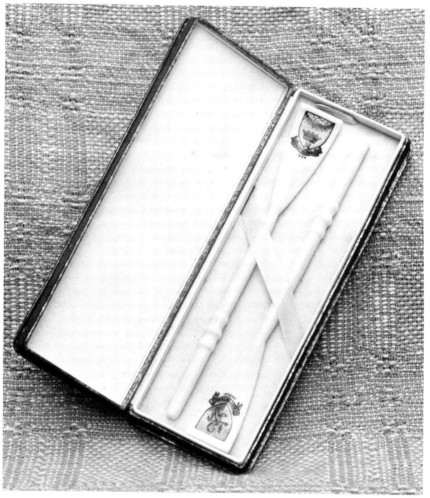

A pair of Hawkins Famous Henley Sculls in original Presentation Box. These only appear with correct matching Arms

A selection of Second Period Goss Models and Shapes sold during the Third Period between 1929 and 1934 displayed on an Agent's ordering card

Aberdeen Bronze Pot

Abergavenny Ancient Jar

Abingdon Roman Vase

Acanthus Rose Bowl

Alderney Fish Basket

Alderney Milk Can and Lid

Alnwick Celtic Sepulchral Urn

Amersham Leaden Measure

Ancient Costril or Pilgrims Bottle (League model)

Antwerp Oolen Pot

Appleby Elizabethan Bushel Measure

Arundel Roman Ewer

Models which bear no arms are included in the first column and are marked thus †.
All dimensions refer to the height unless otherwise stated.
Where no price is given, no piece exists in that particular category

Model		With any Arms £ p	With Matching Arms £ p

for ABBOT BEERE'S JACK
see Glastonbury (Abbot Beere's) Jack

for ABBOT'S CUP, FOUNTAINS ABBEY
see Fountains Abbey, Abbot's Cup

ABERDEEN BRONZE POT — 63mm — 9.00 — 26.00
(Goss Record. 8th Edition. Page 4) — 89mm — 23.00 — 30.00
Inscribed: *Model of Bronze Pot found in Upperkirkgate* — 133mm — 34.50 — 45.00
Aberdeen May 31st, 1886. Containing 12267 silver pennies.
(Can be found with inscription omitting reference to the pennies).
See also POSTCARDS Chapter 5.
Variation with unusually short legs attached to the large
size pot — 110mm — 75.00
Matching Arms: *ABERDEEN*

ABERGAVENNY ANCIENT JAR — 54mm — 7.00 — 22.50
(Goss Record. 8th Edition. Page 29)
Inscribed: *Model of Ancient Jar found at*
Abergavenny. Rd. No. 633432.
Matching Arms: *ABERGAVENNY*

ABINGDON ROMAN VASE — 95mm — 28.00 — 40.00
(Goss Record. 8th Edition: Page 16)
Inscribed: *Model of Roman Vase dug up at The Abbey,*
Abingdon.
Matching Arms: *ABINGDON*

ACANTHUS ROSE BOWL — with wire cage 130mm — 95.00
(Goss Record. 8th Edition: Page 45) — without wire cage 130mm — 75.00
Inscribed: *The Acanthus Rose Bowl.*
Rd. No. 633431
This model was originally sold with a
wire cage which is often missing nowadays.
It has no correct arms.

Ashbourne Bushel

Ashley Rails Roman Urn

Avebury Celtic Urn

(Cup of) Ballafletcher

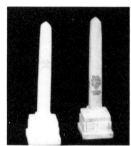
Barnet Stone
White and Brown

Bartlow Ewer

Bath Ancient Roman Cup

Bath Bronze Roman Ewer

Bath Roman Ewer

Bath Roman Jug

Bath Urn

Beachy Head Lighthouse

Model		With any Arms £ p	With Matching Arms £ p
ALDERNEY FISH BASKET	40mm		65.00
(Goss Record. 8th Edition. Page 17)	58mm		75.00
Inscribed: *Model of Alderney Fish Basket*			
Matching Arms: *ALDERNEY*			
ALDERNEY MILK CAN and lid	70mm		56.50
Inscribed: *Alderney Milk Can*	108mm		56.50
This model has a lid without which it is incomplete.	140mm		65.00
Value approximately £10.00			
Matching Arms: *ALDERNEY*			
ALNWICK CELTIC SEPULCHRAL URN	68mm[1]	19.00	35.00
(Goss Record. 8th Edition. Page 30)			
Inscribed: *Model of Celtic Urn dug up at Alnwick.*			
Matching Arms: *ALNWICK*			
AMERSHAM LEADEN MEASURE	48mm	17.00	43.00
(Goss Record. 8th Edition. Page 17)			
Inscribed: *Model of Leaden Measure circa 1682, found in the Old Lock up in the Town Hall, Amersham. Rd. No. 626749.*			
Matching Arms: *AMERSHAM*			

for AMPHORA VASE
see Greek Amphora Vase or
    ORNAMENTAL 10K chapter

ANCIENT COSTRIL or **PILGRIMS BOTTLE**	(a) 56mm		56.50
(Goss Record 9th Edition. Pages 22, 28, 40 and	(b) 56mm		82.50

Plate B)
Inscribed: *Model of Ancient Costril or Pilgrims' Bottle.*
Rd. No. 526384. This model is only issued to Members of the League and cannot be bought
This model was first introduced bearing **The League of Goss Collectors** motif (a), and re-introduced later bearing the **International League of Goss Collectors** motif (b).

for ANCIENT STONE VESSEL, DOVER CASTLE
see Dover Mortar

for ANCIENT TYG (One Handle)
see Staffordshire One Handled Tyg

for ANCIENT TYG (Two Handles)
see Staffordshire Two Handled Tyg

Model			With any Arms £ p	With Matching Arms £ p

for ANGLO-SAXON CINERARY URN
see King's Newton Anglo-Saxon Cinerary Urn

ANTWERP OOLEN POT	(a) 1 coat of arms	70mm	7.50	29.00
(Goss Record. 8th Edition. Page 42)	(b) 3 coats of arms	70mm	14.50	35.00

Inscribed: *Model of Oolen Pot 16th century.*
Found inside a Caisson at Antwerp. Now in Liebaert
Museum at Ostend. Rd. No. 495668.
Matching Arms: *ANTWERPEN*

APPLEBY ELIZABETHAN BUSHEL MEASURE

(Goss Record. 8th Edition: Page 36)	Dia. 59mm	15.50	35.00

Inscribed: *Model of Elizabethan Bushel Measure now*
in Appleby Moot Hall.
Matching Arms: *APPLEBY*

ARUNDEL ROMAN EWER	55mm	14.50	25.00
(Goss Record. 8th Edition: Page 34)	102mm	26.00	41.50

Inscribed: *Model of Roman Ewer, found at*
Avisford Hill, Arundel.
Matching Arms: *ARUNDEL*

ASHBOURNE BUSHEL	Dia. 51mm	12.50	30.00

(Goss Record. 8th Edition: Page 18)
Inscribed: *Model of Ashbourne Bushel. Rd. No. 450628.*
Matching Arms: *ASHBOURNE*

ASHLEY RAILS ROMAN URN	108mm	56.50	75.00

Inscribed: *Model of Roman Urn found at Ashley Rails,*
New Forest. Copyright.
Matching Arms: *MANOR OF NEW MILTON* OR
CHRISTCHURCH

for ASHMOLEAN VASE, GNOSSUS
see Gnossus Ashmolean Vase

for ATWICK VASE
see Hornsea Roman Vase

AVEBURY CELTIC URN	105mm[1]	23.00	40.00

(Goss Record. 8th Edition: Page 36)
Inscribed: *Model of Celtic Urn, dug up near Avebury.*
Matching Arms: *CALNE, MARLBOROUGH* OR *DEVIZES*

for AYSGILL URN
see Hawes Ancient British Urn

Model			With any Arms £ p	With Matching Arms £ p
(CUP OF) BALLAFLETCHER		95mm	27.50	65.00

(Goss Record. 8th Edition: Page 24)
Inscribed: *Model of the Lhannan Shee (Peaceful Spirit) Cup of
Ballafletcher in the possession of J.C. Bacon Esq Seafield,
Isle of Man. Rd. No. 448432.*
Matching Arms: *DOUGLAS, ISLE OF MAN*
With *ANY ISLE OF MAN ARMS*   35.00

for BARGATE, SOUTHAMPTON
see Southampton, Bargate

BARNET STONE	(a) White†	172mm	110.00	
(Goss Record. 8th Edition: Page 24)	(b) Brown†	172mm	125.00	

Inscribed on base: *Barnet Stone Rd. No. 489664.*
Inscribed on front: *Here was fought the famous Battle
between Edward the 4th and the Earl of Warwick April
the 14th ANNO 1471 in which the Earl was Defeated
and Slain.*
Inscribed on reverse: *From St. Albans VIII
miles 3/4.* Left side: *To Hatfield VII miles 3/4.*
Right side: *This was erected 1740.*

for BARROW'S MONUMENT
see Sir John Barrow's Monument, Ulverston.

BARTLOW EWER	104mm[1]	35.00	56.50

(Goss Record. 8th Edition: Page 22)
Inscribed: *Model of Roman Bronze Ewer. Found in 1835 at
Bartlow Hills. Near Saffron Walden.*
Matching Arms: *SAFFRON WALDEN*

BATH ANCIENT ROMAN CUP	102mm	95.00	145.00

(Goss Record. 8th Edition: Page 31)
Inscribed: *Model of Ancient Roman Cup found at Bath.
Rd. No. 543009.*
Matching Arms: *BATH*

BATH BRONZE ROMAN EWER	120mm[1]	30.00	45.00

(Goss Record. 8th. Edition: Page 31)
Inscribed: *From Bronze original found in Roman Bath
at Bath.*
(An example has also been seen erroneously inscribed
as a Bartlow Ewer
See also POSTCARDS Chapter 5
Matching Arms: *BATH*

Beccles Ringers Jug

Bettws-y-Coed Ancient Bronze Kettle

Bideford Ancient Mortar

Blackgang Cannon

Blackgang Tower, St. Catherine's Hill

Blackpool Tower

Bognor Lobster Trap

Bolton Abbey Wine Cooler

Boston Ancient Ewer

Boulogne Milk Can and Lid

Boulogne Sedan Chair

Boulogne Wooden Shoe

Model			With any Arms £ p	With Matching Arms £ p
BATH ROMAN EWER		63mm	5.50	22.50
(Goss Record. 8th Edition: Page 31)		130mm	21.00	35.00

Inscribed: *Model of Roman Ewer in Dorset Museum Found in Bath.*
Matching Arms: *BATH*

BATH ROMAN JUG		150mm[1]	35.00	56.50
(Goss Record. 8th Edition: Page 31)				

Inscribed: *Model of Roman jug found at the Roman Bath at Bath.*
Matching Arms: *BATH*

BATH URN		75mm[1]	30.00	45.00
(Goss Record. 8th Edition: Page 31)				

Inscribed: *The Bath Urn from original in Museum.*
Matching Arms: *BATH*

for **BATTLE OF LARGS MEMORIAL TOWER**
see Largs Memorial Tower

BEACHY HEAD LIGHTHOUSE	(a) Brown band	125mm	47.50	65.00
(Goss Record. 8th Edition: Page 34)	(b) Black band	125mm	47.50	65.00

Inscribed: *Model of Beachy Head Lighthouse.*
Rd. No. 622475.
The black band version also found with a brown rim around
the top, below the lantern
Matching Arms: *EASTBOURNE* (with or without addition of
BEACHY HEAD)

This exact model also appears as the extremely rare
DUNGENESS LIGHTHOUSE only one example of
which has been found

BECCLES RINGERS JUG		87mm	250.00	475.00

Inscribed on base: *The Ringers Jug in Beccles Parish Church.*
The original was made by Samuel Stringfellow, Potter.
Inscribed on the side with the ringers verse: *When I*
am fill'd with Liquor strong, Each Man drink once & then
ding dong. Drink not to much to Cloud your Knobs. Least
you forget to make the Bobbs, a gift of JOHN PATTMAN Beccles
Impressed: *(1827).*
Very rare; only seen bearing matching arms until 1990,
when a model was found bearing the Hastings crest and the usual
(1827) impressed, but with no inscriptions on the base or side.
Matching Arms: *ANCIENT SEAL OF BECCLES*

Bournemouth Ancient Bronze Mace Head

Bournemouth Ancient Egyptian Lamp

Bournemouth Pilgrim Bottle

Bournemouth Pine Cone

Bournemouth Bronze Urn

Brading Stocks

Brading Roman Ewer

Braunton Lighthouse

(The nose of) Brasenose

Bridlington Elizabethan Quart Measure

Bristol Puzzle Cider Cup

British Six Inch Shell

Model		With any Arms £ p	With Matching Arms £ p

BETTWS-Y-COED ANCIENT BRONZE KETTLE　　73mm　14.50　28.00
(Goss Record. 8th Edition: Page 38)　　　　　　114mm　26.00　35.00
Inscribed: *Model of Ancient Bronze Kettle dug up near*
Bettws-y-Coed 1877. Rd. No. 543011.
Matching Arms: *BETTWS-Y-COED*

BIDEFORD ANCIENT MORTAR　　　　　　　42mm　12.50　33.50
(Goss Record. 8th Edition: Page 20)
Inscribed: *Model of Ancient Mortar dredged out of the*
Torridge at Bideford. Rd. No. 622407.
Matching Arms: *BIDEFORD*

for BLACK AND BROWN CUP
see Newcastle (Staffordshire) Cup

BLACKGANG CANNON　　　　　Length 95mm　14.00　25.00
(Goss Record. 8th Edition: Page 26)
Inscribed: *Model of Ancient Cannon found on the beach at*
Blackgang Chine, I.W. Rd. No. 554472.
Matching Arms: *BLACKGANG*

BLACKGANG TOWER, ST. CATHERINE'S HILL　112mm　30.00　45.00
(Goss Record. 8th Edition: Page 26)
Inscribed: *Model of Tower on St. Catherine's Hill, Blackgang,*
I.W. Built in 1323 by W. De Godyton for a chantry priest to
sing mass for the souls of mariners and in the tower a light was
placed to warn ships off this dangerous coast. Rd. No. 630366.
Matching Arms: *BLACKGANG*

BLACKPOOL TOWER
(Goss Record. 9th Edition: Page 21 & Plate J)　　118mm　34.50　56.50
Inscribed: *Model of Blackpool Tower.*
Matching Arms: *BLACKPOOL*

BOGNOR LOBSTER TRAP　　　　　　　51mm　　　　　75.00
Identical to the Lobster Trap but specifically named.
Inscribed: *Model of Bognor Lobster Trap*
Matching Arms: *BOGNOR*

BOLTON ABBEY WINE COOLER　　Dia. 68mm　23.00　30.00
(Goss Record. 8th Edition. Page 38)
Inscribed: *Model of Wine Cooler at Bolton Abbey.*
Rd. No. 633428.
Matching Arms: *BOLTON ABBEY*

Model		With any Arms £ p	With Matching Arms £ p
BOSTON ANCIENT EWER	70mm	13.50	26.00

(Goss Record. 8th Edition: Page 28)
Inscribed: *Model of Ancient Ewer now in Boston Museum.*
Rd. No. 594871
Matching Arms: *BOSTON*

BOULOGNE MILK CAN and lid	74mm	25.00	45.00

(Goss Record. 8th Edition: Page 42)
Inscribed: *Model of Boulogne Milk Can. Rd. No. 521974.*
The model is incomplete without its lid, value £10.00
Matching Arms: *BOULOGNE-SUR-MER*

BOULOGNE SEDAN CHAIR	(a) 69mm	40.00	65.00
	(b) 69mm	250.00†	

(Goss Record. 8th Edition. Page 42)
Inscribed: *Model of Sedan Chair used by the Countess*
of Boulogne. XVII Century. Rd. No. 539423.
In the 8th Edition of the Goss Record (Page 1) a
version specially decorated in Turquoise Blue is
advertised (b).
This model has very fragile handles. With one of
these broken it would be worth only one-quarter of
its perfect price.
Matching Arms: *BOULOGNE-SUR-MER*

BOULOGNE WOODEN SHOE	Length 118mm	28.00	77.50

(Goss Record. 8th Edition: Page 42)
Inscribed: *Model of wooden shoes worn by the*
fisherwomen of Boulogne sur Mer and Le Portal.
Rd. No. 539421.
Matching Arms: *BOULOGNE-SUR-MER*

BOURNEMOUTH ANCIENT BRONZE			
MACE HEAD	80mm	23.00	37.50

(Goss Record. 8th Edition: Page 22)
Inscribed: *Model of Ancient Bronze Mace Head circa A.D. 300.*
Found in Kings Park, Bournemouth. Rd. No. 613962.
Matching Arms: *BOURNEMOUTH*

BOURNEMOUTH ANCIENT EGYPTIAN			
LAMP	Length 105mm	23.00	35.00

(Goss Record. 8th Edition: Page 23)
Inscribed: *Model of Ancient Egyptian Lamp Circa B.C.*
100 to A.D. 100. Found at Southbourne, Bournemouth.
Rd. No. 638371.
Matching Arms: *BOURNEMOUTH*
With Egyptian Arms add £10.00

Model			With any Arms £ p	With Matching Arms £ p
BOURNEMOUTH PILGRIM BOTTLE		90mm	13.00	30.00

(Goss Record. 8th Edition: Page 23)
Inscribed: *Model of Pilgrim Bottle (circa 600 A.D.) Found at Southbourne, Bournemouth 1907. Rd. No. 562740.*
Matching Arms: *BOURNEMOUTH*

BOURNEMOUTH PINE CONE		90mm	12.50	21.50

(Goss Record. 8th Edition: Page 23)
Inscribed: *Pine Cone. Rd. No. 559524.*
Matching Arms: *BOURNEMOUTH*

BOURNEMOUTH BRONZE URN		52mm	13.00	23.00

(Goss Record. 8th Edition: Page 23)
Inscribed: *Model of Ancient Bronze Urn in the Museum of the Royal Bath Hotel, Bournemouth. Rd. No. 489583.*
Matching Arms: *BOURNEMOUTH*

BRADING STOCKS		Length 87mm	155.00	285.00

Inscribed: *Model of The Stocks, Brading, I.O.W. Copyright.*
The stocks are unglazed Brown on a white glazed base.
Matching Arms: *THE KING'S TOWN OF BRADING, SEAL OF BRADING* OR *ANCIENT ARMS OF BRADING*

BRADING ROMAN EWER	(a)	70mm	9.00	23.00
(Goss Record. 8th Edition: Page 26)	(b)	125mm[1]	17.00	26.00
	(c)	125mm[2]	17.00	26.00

Inscription [1]: *Model of ewer found on site of Roman Villa*
Inscription [2]: *Model of Ewer Found on Site of Roman Villa Brading I. of W.*
Also known as the Isle of Wight Roman Ewer by J.J. Jarvis in The Goss Record. As it is not so named on the piece itself the author prefers to call it the Brading Ewer.
Either *THE KING'S TOWN OF BRADING, SEAL OF BRADING* OR *ANCIENT ARMS OF BRADING* OR *ISLE OF WIGHT* may be considered as Matching Arms.

for BRAMPTON WARE MUG
see Chesterfield Brampton Ware Mug

BRAUNTON LIGHTHOUSE		133mm	600.00	750.00

Inscribed: *Model of Braunton Lighthouse near Westward Ho. Copyright.*
The third rarest lighthouse, it has a grey roof.
Matching Arms: *WESTWARD HO.*

British Tank

Brixworth Ancient Cup

Broadway Tower

Burton Beer Barrel

Bury St. Edmunds German Bomb

Bury St. Edmunds Kettle and Lid

Caerhun Roman Burial Urn 833

Caerleon Glass Lachrymatory or Tear Bottle

Caerleon Lamp

Cambridge Pitcher

Cambridge Roman Jug

Canary Porron

154

Model		With any Arms £ p	With Matching Arms £ p

(THE NOSE OF) BRASENOSE   104mm   27.50   37.50
(Goss Record. 8th Edition: Page 31)
Inscribed: *The Nose of Brazenose, Oxford.*
Brasenose is frequently spelt Brazenose.
The Matching Arms are *BRAZENOSE* OR *ARMS OF THE CITY OF OXFORD.*

(THE NOSE OF) BRASENOSE   98mm   65.00
Flat back with a pointed nose.
Inscribed: *H.N.W. Goss 20/11/19*
Impressed: *W H Goss*
Unique example; probably a prototype for the Second
Period, except that it is too late.
The model was listed in *The Goss Record* 8th Edition, and this 1919
example was made for William Huntley's son, Huntley Noel
William Goss, who attended Brasenose College

for (OLD) BRAZIER AT TRESCO
see Tresco Old Brazier

BRIDLINGTON ELIZABETHAN QUART
    MEASURE   50mm   11.00   26.00
(Goss Record. 8th Edition: Page 38)
Inscribed: *Model of Bridlington Quart Measure now in "The
Old Bayle Gate", Bridlington. Rd. No. 509868* and with E.R.
1601 embossed on the side.
Also found with *Rd. No. 500865*
Matching Arms: BRIDLINGTON

BRISTOL PUZZLE CIDER CUP   51mm   26.00   43.50
(Goss Record. 8th Edition: Page 22)
Inscribed: *Model of Puzzle Cider Cup made at the Bristol Pottery
1791. Now in Bristol Museum. Rd. No. 562739.*
Matching Arms: *CITY OF BRISTOL*

for BRITISH CONTACT MINE OR BRITISH SEA MINE
see Contact Mine

BRITISH (SIX INCH) SHELL   110mm   25.00
(Goss Record. World War Edition. Pages 5 [illustrated]
and 7). This model is COPYRIGHT but is not usually
so marked.
Inscribed: *Model of British 6 in Inciendiary Shell.*
(Note misspelling of incendiary)
The value of any military crest is to be added to the price,
say £20.00-£60.00 depending upon rarity and suitability.
Correct Arms: *ANY ARTILLERY REGIMENT*

Model			With any Arms £ p	With Matching Arms £ p

BRITISH TANK — Length 110mm (two moulds) — 56.50
(Goss Record. 9th Edition: Plate L)
Inscribed: *Model of British Tank - "England Expects that every Tank will do its Damn'dest." Copyright.*
Matching Arms: *(a) LINCOLN* — 75.00
(b) TANK CORPS — 80.00

BRIXWORTH ANCIENT CUP — 55mm — 11.00 — 14.50
(Goss Record. 8th Edition: Page 30)
Inscribed: *Model of Ancient Cup found at Brixworth, Northamptonshire. Rd. No. 423199.*
Matching Arms: *NORTHAMPTON (SHIRE)*

BROADWAY TOWER — (a) White — 75mm — 110.00 — 190.00
(Goss Record. 8th Edition: Page 36) — (b) Grey† — 75mm — 195.00
(c) Brown† — 75mm — 250.00
Inscribed: *Model of Broadway Tower. Rd. No. 634630.*
Matching Arms: *BROADWAY*

BURTON BEER BARREL — 60mm — 9.50 — 22.50
(Goss Record. 8th Edition: Page 32) — 73mm — 19.00 — 28.00
Inscribed: *Model of Burton Beer Barrel.*
Matching Arms: *BURTON UPON TRENT*

BURY ST. EDMUNDS GERMAN BOMB — 75mm — 28.00 — 43.50
(Goss Record. 9th Edition: Page 28)
Inscribed: *Model of German Bomb dropped on Bury St. Edmunds from a Zeppelin 30 April 1915. Copyright.*
This model has an extremely delicate handle, without which it is of little value.
Matching Arms: *BURY ST. EDMUNDS*

BURY ST. EDMUNDS KETTLE and lid — 76mm — 21.50 — 40.00
(Goss Record. 8th Edition: Page 34) — 121mm[1] — 35.00 — 56.50
Inscribed: *Model of Roman Libation Vessel found at Suffolk. Now in Bury Museum.*
This model is not complete without its lid, worth £10.00 of the price shown.
Matching Arms: *BURY ST. EDMUNDS*

for BURY ST. EDMUNDS LIBATION VESSEL
see Bury St. Edmunds Kettle

for CAERHUN BRONZE CROCHON
see Welsh Crochon

Model		With any Arms £ p	With Matching Arms £ p

CAERHUN ROMAN BURIAL URN　　　　　　54mm　21.50　40.00
Inscribed: *Model of Roman Burial Urn found at Caerhun*
(Conovium) in 1878 containing calcinated female bones.
Copyright.
This model is the rarest of the smaller urns and is
numbered 833
Matching Arms: *CONWAY*

CAERLEON GLASS LACHRYMATORY
　　(or Tear Bottle)　　　　　　　　86mm　　8.50
(Goss Record. 8th Edition: Page 29)
Inscribed: *Model of Glass Lachrymatory or Tear Bottle found in*
stone coffin. Discovered in the excavations for the railway, near
Caerleon, July 1847. Now in Caerleon Museum.
Rd. No. 559520.
Matching Arms: *(a) CAERLEON*　　　　　　　　　　30.00
　　　　　　　　(b) NEWPORT　　　　　　　　　　26.00

CAERLEON LAMP
(Goss Record. 8th Edition: Page 29)
Inscribed: *Model of Ancient Lamp in Museum at Caerleon*
(City of Legions, King Arthur's Capital).
Matching Arms: *(a) CAERLEON*　Length 88mm　10.00　26.00
　　　　　　　　(b) NEWPORT　　　　　　　　　　19.50

CAMBRIDGE PITCHER　　　　　　　　63mm　　5.50　22.50
(Goss Record. 8th Edition: Page 17)　　108mm　14.50　23.00
Inscribed: *The Cambridge Pitcher from the original in*
Archaeological Museum.
Matching Arms: *CAMBRIDGE*

CAMBRIDGE ROMAN JUG　　　　　　70mm　17.50　26.00
This model is not found named in the usual way,　76mm　17.50　26.00
but it is a well known shape produced by many　82mm　17.50　26.00
factories during Victorian and Edwardian times.　88mm　17.50　26.00
It is also one of the few Goss models not to be named　94mm　22.00　30.00
and the reader is referred to the illustration　120mm　30.00　37.50
for identification. See also 9D TERRACOTTA　130mm　32.50　37.50
Matching Arms: *CAMBRIDGE*　　　　　　140mm　40.00　50.00
　　　　　　　　　　　　　　　　　155mm　50.00　60.00

for CANADIAN MAPLE LEAF
see (The) Maple Leaf of Canada

Canterbury Jug

Canterbury Leather Bottle

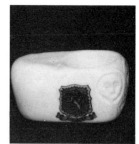

Capel Madoc Stoup

Cardinal Beaufort's
Candlestick

Cardinal Beaufort's Salt
Cellar

Carlisle Old Salt Pot

Carmarthen Coracle

Carnarvon Ewer

Castletown Cinerary Urn

(The) Cenotaph, Whitehall

Cheddar Cheese

Cherbourg Milk Can and Lid

Model		With any Arms £ p	With Matching Arms £ p

for CANARY ANCIENT COVERED JARRA
see Las Palmas Ancient Covered Jarra

for CANARY ANCIENT EARTHEN JAR
see Las Palmas Ancient Earthen Jar

for CANARY ANCIENT JARRA
see Las Palmas Ancient Jarra

CANARY PORRON	68mm	24.50	40.00

(Goss Record. 8th Edition: Page 42)
Inscribed: *Model of Canary Porron. Rd. No. 449120.*
This model is identical to the Gibraltar Alcaraza, but rarer,
so the inscriptions on all models found should be carefully
checked.
Matching Arms: *LAS PALMAS, GRAND CANARY*

for CANNON BALL
see Rye Cannon Ball

CANTERBURY JUG	113mm[1]	17.50	28.00

(Goss Record. 8th Edition: Page 26)
Inscribed: *The Canterbury Jug.*
Matching Arms: *CANTERBURY*

CANTERBURY LEATHER BOTTLE	46mm	5.50	14.00

(Goss Record. 8th Edition: Page 26)
Inscribed: *Model of the Pilgrim 'Leather Bottell' in
Canterbury Museum. Rd. No. 392067.*
Matching Arms: *CANTERBURY*

CAPEL MADOC STOUP	Length 80mm	28.00	65.00

(Goss Record. 9th Edition: Page 34)
Inscribed: *Model of Stoup from Capel Madoc near
Rhayader removed to Dderw, circa 1855. Rd. No. 643962.*
Matching Arms: *RHAYADER*

CARDINAL BEAUFORT'S CANDLESTICK	152mm[1]	110.00	225.00

(Goss Record. 8th Edition: Page 23)
Inscribed: *Model of Cardinal Beaufort's Candlestick.
(1404-1447).*
Matching Arms: *CARDINAL BEAUFORT* OR
    WINCHESTER

Model		With any Arms £ p	With Matching Arms £ p
CARDINAL BEAUFORT'S SALT CELLAR	70mm[1]	65.00	125.00

(Goss Record. 8th Edition: Page 23)
Inscribed: *Model of Cardinal Beaufort's Salt Cellar.*
(1404-1447).
Matching Arms: *CARDINAL BEAUFORT* OR
   WINCHESTER

CARLISLE OLD SALT POT	46mm	5.50	17.00

(Goss Record. 8th Edition: Page 18)
Inscribed: *Model of Old Salt Pot in Carlisle Museum.*
Rd. No. 403422.
Matching Arms: *CARLISLE*

CARMARTHEN CORACLE	Length 133mm[1]	40.00	100.00

(Goss Record. 8th Edition: Page 38)
Inscribed on the seat or base: *Model of Carmarthen Coracle.*
Pub. by E. Colby Evans Guildhall Sq. Carmarthen.
The arms can be found either inside or on base of this model.
Matching Arms: *CARMARTHEN*

CARNARVON EWER	63mm	7.50	22.50
	89mm[1]	14.50	30.00

(Goss Record. 8th Edition: Page 39)
Inscribed: *From original found at Carnarvon. (Roman*
Segontium), now in Carnarvon Castle.
Matching Arms: *CARNARVON*

CASTLETOWN CINERARY URN	40mm	11.00	26.00

(Goss Record. 8th Edition: Page 24)
Inscribed: *Model of Cinerary Urn found at Gretch Veg I. of*
Man Jany. 1899. Now in Museum Castle Rushen Castletown
I. of Man. Rd. No. 599333.
Matching Arms: *CASTLETOWN, ISLE OF MAN*

CENOTAPH, WHITEHALL	(a) White glazed	145mm	30.00	40.00
	(b) White unglazed†	145mm	47.50	

Inscribed: *The Cenotaph Whitehall.*
See also THIRD PERIOD 11.O for later varieties.
Matching Arms: *CITY OF LONDON*

for CHARLOTTE'S (QUEEN) FAVOURITE
   WINDSOR KETTLE
see Windsor Kettle

Model			With any Arms £ p	With Matching Arms £ p
CHEDDAR CHEESE	(a) Yellow	62mm	33.50†	47.50
(Goss Record. 8th Edition: Page 31)	(b) White glazed [3]	62mm	22.50	47.50

Inscribed: *Model of a Cheddar Cheese.*
Rd. No. 521975.
Also so named on side in Gothic script.
Matching Arms: *CHEDDAR*

CHERBOURG MILK CAN and lid	65mm	22.50	65.00

(Goss Record. 8th Edition: Page 42)
Inscribed: *Model of Cherbourg Milk Can. Rd. No. 605734*
This model is not complete without its lid which is
worth £12.00 of the price shown.
Matching Arms: *CHERBOURG*

CHESHIRE ROMAN URN	90mm	400.00

Inscribed: *Model of Roman Urn found at Condate*
(Kinderton) Cheshire 1820. Copyright 1932. This model is only
issued to Members of the League and cannot be bought.
International League Model for 1932
Correct Arms: *INTERNATIONAL LEAGUE OF GOSS*
    COLLECTORS

CHESHIRE SALT BLOCK	80mm	28.50	40.00

(Goss Record. 9th Edition: Page 11 and Plate K)
Inscribed: *Model of Cheshire Salt Block. Copyright.*
Matching Arms: *CHESHIRE*

CHESTER ROMAN ALTAR	117mm	150.00	800.00

Inscribed: *Model of Roman Altar found buried off Pepper*
Alley Chester 1861. This model is only issued to Members
of the League and cannot be bought. Copyright 1931.
International League Model for 1931
Correct Arms: *INTERNATIONAL LEAGUE OF GOSS*
    COLLECTORS

CHESTER ROMAN VASE	59mm	5.50	14.50
(Goss Record. 8th Edition: Page 17)	89mm[1]	16.00	28.00

Inscribed: *Model of Roman Vase found at Chester*
from the original in Museum.
see also Chapter 5 POSTCARDS
Matching Arms: *CHESTER*

Cheshire Roman Urn
League Model, 1932

Cheshire Salt Block

Chester Roman Altar
League Model, 1931

Chester Roman Vase

Chesterfield "Brampton
Ware" Mug

Chichester Roman Ewer

Chichester Roman Urn

Chicken Rock Lighthouse

Chile Stirrup

Chile Hat

Chile Mate Cup

Chile Spur

Model		With any Arms £ p	With Matching Arms £ p
CHESTERFIELD BRAMPTON WARE MUG	93mm	40.00	65.00
(Goss Record. 9th Edition Page 13) Inscribed: *Model of "Brampton Ware" Mug found on a beam during repairs to roof of Chesterfield Church, the original being left by workman in 1750. Copyright.* Matching Arms: *CHESTERFIELD*			

for CHESTERFIELD MUG
see Chesterfield Brampton Ware Mug

CHICHESTER ROMAN EWER	63mm	5.50	15.50
(Goss Record. 8th Edition: Page 34) Inscribed: *Model of Roman Ewer in Chichester Museum. Rd. No. 403420.* Matching Arms: *CHICHESTER*			
CHICHESTER ROMAN URN	81mm[1]	17.50	30.00
(Goss Record. 8th Edition: Page 34) Inscribed: *Model of Roman Urn found at Chichester now in the Museum.* Matching Arms: *CHICHESTER*			
CHICKEN ROCK LIGHTHOUSE	127mm	34.50	47.50
(Goss Record. 8th Edition: Page 26) Inscribed: *Model of Chicken Rock Lighthouse, Isle of Man. Rd. No. 602906.* Matching Arms: *ISLE OF MAN*			
CHILE HAT	Dia. 86mm	215.00	300.00
(Goss Record. 9th Edition: Page 37 and Plate O) Matching Arms: *CHILE*			
CHILE MATE CUP	60mm	100.00	175.00
(Goss Record. 9th Edition: Page 37 and Plate O) Matching Arms: *CHILE*			
CHILE SPUR	Length 150mm	200.00	300.00
(Goss Record: 9th Edition: Page 37 and Plate N) Matching Arms: *CHILE*			

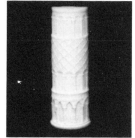

Christchurch Ancient Bowl

Christchurch Priory Church Norman Tower

Christchurch Romano-British Urn

Cirencester Roman Ewer League Model, 1918

Cirencester Roman Ewer

Cirencester Roman Urn, 784

Cirencester Roman Vase

Cliftonville Roman Jug

Cliftonville Roman Vase

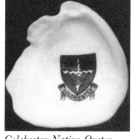

Colchester Gigantic Roman Wine Vase

Colchester Native Oyster Shell

Colchester Roman Lamp League Model, 1927

Model		With any Arms £ p	With Matching Arms £ p
CHILE STIRRUP 50mm		100.00	175.00

CHILE STIRRUP   50mm   100.00   175.00
(Goss Record. 9th Edition: Page 37 and Plate N)
Matching Arms: *CHILE*

N.B. The Chilean pieces do not carry the usual named model
inscriptions, but when bearing the arms of Chile titled
RECUERDO DE CHILE, they are inscribed above the arms
respectively, as follows:-
> CHURAYA (Hat)
> MATE (Cup)
> ESPUELA (Spur)
> ESTRIBO (Stirrup)

for CHIPPING NORTON FOURSHIRE STONE
see Fourshire Stone

CHRISTCHURCH ANCIENT BOWL   Dia. 60mm   7.50   22.00
(Goss Record. 8th Edition: Page 23 and the
advertisement on page 65)
Inscribed: *Model of Ancient Bowl found near Christchurch,
Hants. Rd. No. 639534.*
Matching Arms: *CHRISTCHURCH*

CHRISTCHURCH PRIORY CHURCH NORMAN TOWER
(Goss Record. 8th Edition:
Page 23), and the advertisement   (a) White glazed†   123mm   56.50
on page 65)   (b) White unglazed† 123mm   65.00
                                   (c) Grey†   123mm   82.50
                                   (d) Brown†   123mm   155.00
Inscribed: *Model of Norman Tower, Priory Church
Christchurch, circa 1100, built by Ralph Flambard Bishop
of Durham 1099-1128. Rd. No. 567379.*

CHRISTCHURCH ROMANO-BRITISH URN   52mm   7.50   25.00
(Goss Record. 8th Edition: Page 23, and the advertisement
on page 65)
Inscribed: *Model of Romano-British Urn, found near
Christchurch, Hants. Rd. No. 639533.*
Matching Arms: *CHRISTCHURCH*

for CHRIST'S HOSPITAL WINE FLAGON
see London Christ's Hospital English Wine Flagon

Model			With any Arms £ p	With Matching Arms £ p
CIRENCESTER ROMAN EWER	(a) 78mm			82.50
(Goss Record. 9th Edition: Pages 22, 41 and Plate C)	(b) 78mm			117.50

CIRENCESTER ROMAN EWER (a) 78mm   82.50
(Goss Record. 9th Edition: Pages 22, 41 and Plate C) (b) 78mm   117.50
Inscribed: *Model of Roman Ewer found at Cirencester.*
Issued to Members only & cannot be purchased. Copyright.
This model was first introduced bearing THE LEAGUE OF
GOSS COLLECTORS motif (a), and re-introduced in 1918
bearing the INTERNATIONAL LEAGUE OF GOSS
COLLECTORS motif (b).

CIRENCESTER ROMAN EWER   (a) 1 Arms   115mm [1]   32.50   46.50
(Goss Record. 8th Edition: Page 22)   (b) 2 Arms   115mm [1]   40.00   60.00
Inscribed: *Model of Roman Ewer found at*   (c) 3 Arms   115mm [1]   47.50   65.00
Cirencester now in the museum.
Matching Arms: *CIRENCESTER*

CIRENCESTER ROMAN URN   165mm   87.00   130.00
This model is marked COPYRIGHT and numbered 784
(see Roman Vase 783 for comparison)
This model often appears in coloured lustre glaze and
uncrested
Matching Arms: *CIRENCESTER*

CIRENCESTER ROMAN VASE   80mm   7.50   24.50
(Goss Record. 8th Edition: Page 22 and   124mm   17.50   28.00
advertisement Page 66)
Inscribed: *Model of Roman Vase found at Cirencester,*
now in the museum.
Matching Arms: *CIRENCESTER*

CLIFTONVILLE ROMAN JUG   180mm   175.00   220.00
Inscribed: *Model of Roman Jug found during excavations*
in Avenue Gardens, Cliftonville 1924.
Matching Arms: *MARGATE*

CLIFTONVILLE ROMAN VASE   70mm   195.00   265.00
Inscribed: *Model of Roman Vase found during excavations*   107mm   195.00   265.00
in Avenue Gardens, Cliftonville 1924.
Matching Arms: *MARGATE*

Model	With any Arms £ p	With Matching Arms £ p

Colchester enthusiasts should refer to The Goss Record 8th Edition: Page 63 for a full page advertisement.

COLCHESTER GIGANTIC ROMAN WINE VASE   157mm   56.50   95.00
(Goss Record. 8th Edition: Page 21)
Inscribed: *Model of Gigantic Roman Wine Vase in Colchester Castle. Found in Castle Yard.*
Matching Arms: *COLCHESTER*

COLCHESTER NATIVE OYSTER SHELL   Width 68mm   12.50   21.50
(Goss Record. 8th Edition: Page 22)
Always appears unnamed.
Matching Arms: *COLCHESTER*

COLCHESTER ROMAN LAMP   Length 100mm   185.00
Inscribed: *Model of Roman Lamp found at Colchester.*   Height   75mm
Copyright 1927. This model is only issued to Members of the League and cannot be bought.
International League Model for 1927
Correct Arms: *INTERNATIONAL LEAGUE OF GOSS COLLECTORS*

COLCHESTER VASE (Cloaca)   45mm   7.50   21.50
(Goss Record. 8th Edition: Page 22)
Inscribed: *Model of Roman Vase found in the "Cloaca". Now in Colchester Castle.*
Cloaca refers to the place where the original vase was found. It is included with the model's name to distinguish the piece from the Colchester Vase (Famous).
Correct Arms: *COLCHESTER*

COLCHESTER ROMAN VASE (Famous)   44mm   5.50   15.50
(Goss Record. 8th Edition: Page 22)   90mm   15.50   26.00
Inscribed: *The Famous Colchester Vase in the museum.*   127mm   23.50   30.00
Famous refers to that part of the full name listed in *The Goss Record* viz. Famous Roman Colchester Vase... etc. and is quoted to distinguish this model from the Colchester Cloaca Vase.
Matching Arms: *COLCHESTER*

CONTACT MINE   Length 73mm   205.00
(Goss Record. 9th Edition: Pages 22,41 and Plate C)
Inscribed: *Model of Contact Mine. Copyright. Issued to Members only and cannot be purchased.*
International League Model for 1919.
Correct Arms: *INTERNATIONAL LEAGUE OF GOSS COLLECTORS* (in Gothic script)

Colchester Vase (Cloaca)

Colchester Roman Vase (famous)

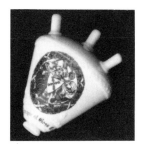

Contact Mine League Model, 1919

Corfe Castle Cup

Cornish Bussa

Cornish Pasty

Cornish Stile

Cuckfield Ancient Bellarmine

Cumbrae, The Monument Tomont End

Cyprus Mycenaean Vase League Model, 1925

Dartmouth Sack Bottle

Denbigh Brick

Model			With any Arms £ p	With Matching Arms £ p
CORFE CASTLE CUP		62mm[1]	15.50	25.00

(Goss Record. 8th Edition: Page 20)
Inscribed: *Model of Ancient Cup dug up near Castle Corfe.*
Matching Arms: *CORFE CASTLE*

CORNISH BUSSA		55mm	8.50	19.50

(Goss Record. 8th Edition: Page 18)
Inscribed: *Model of Cornish Bussa. Rd. No. 594377.*
Matching Arms: *CORNWALL*

CORNISH PASTY
Inscribed: *Cornish Pasty. There are so many Saints in Cornwall
that the Devil was afraid to cross the Tamar for fear of being
put into a Cornish Pasty. (Ancient Legend).*

Matching Arms: *CORNWALL*		Length		
	(a) White glazed	82mm	47.50	75.00
	(b) Yellow	82mm	70.00	110.00
	(c) White glazed	87mm	47.50	75.00
	(d) White glazed	110mm	60.00	82.50
	(e) Yellow	110mm	82.50	117.50

CORNISH STILE	(a) White unglazed†	Length	70.00	
	(b) White glazed†	72mm	52.50	
	(c) Brown†		95.00	

Inscribed: *Model of a Cornish stile. Rd. No. 567378*
Variety (b) can be found with the Blackpool arms,
which would reduce its value by half.

for CORONATION CHAIR IN WESTMINSTER ABBEY
see Westminster Abbey Coronation Chair

for CORONATION CHAIR, PERTH
See Perth Coronation Chair

for COSTREL
see Luton Bottle

for CRICKET STONE, HAMBLEDON
see Hambledon Cricket Stone

for CRONK AUST CINERARY URN
see Ramsey Cronk Aust Cinerary Urn

Devizes Celtic Drinking Cup

Devon Cider Barrel

Devon Cooking Pot

Devon Oak Pitcher

Dinant Wooden Shoe

Doncaster Ewer

Doncaster Urn

Doncaster Vase

Dorchester Jug

Dorchester Roman Cup

Dorothy Vernon's Porridge Pot

Dover Mortar (or Stone Vessel)

Model			With any Arms £ p	With Matching Arms £ p

CUCKFIELD ANCIENT BELLARMINE   75mm   12.50   25.00
(Goss Record. 9th Edition: Page 29)
Inscribed: *Model of Ancient Bellarmine found in a pond at*
Horsgate, Cuckfield. Rd. No. 647236.
This model is identical to the Rochester Bellarmine
The effigy of a bearded man is embossed on the neck of this
model, also known as a Greybeard
Matching Arms: *CUCKFIELD*

CUMBRAE, THE MONUMENT, TOMONT END
(Goss Record. 8th Edition: Page 40)   Brown† 175mm   375.00
Impressed on front: *The Monument Townontend*
Cumbrae.
There are several mis-spellings of Tomont End on the
Goss model

CYPRUS MYCENAEAN VASE   Dia. 90mm   145.00
Inscribed: *Model of Mycenaean Vase from Cyprus in*
British Museum. Copyright 1925. This model is only issued
to Members of the League and cannot be bought.
International League Model for 1925
Correct Arms: *INTERNATIONAL LEAGUE OF GOSS*
    COLLECTORS

for DART SACK BOTTLE
see Dartmouth Sack Bottle

DARTMOUTH SACK BOTTLE   63mm   7.50   15.50
(Goss Record. 8th Edition: Page 20)   92mm[1]   14.50   22.50
Inscribed: *Model of Sack Bottle dredged from the Dart*
from the original in Exeter Museum.
This model depicts an embossed medallion with -
Thos. Holdsworth, Dartmouth, 1735 in relief.
He was the Governor of Dartmouth Castle at the time.
Matching Arms: *DARTMOUTH*
When matching arms are shown without a shield, as a
pictorial presentation: Add £10.00

DENBIGH BRICK   (a) White glazed   82mm[1]   75.00   87.50
(Goss Record. 8th Edition: Page 39) (b) White unglazed†   82mm   87.50
                                     (c) Brown or red†   82mm   265.00
Inscribed: *Model of a Brick found at*
Denbigh Castle representing the Legend of
St. Hubert. Date about 1620.
Matching Arms: *DENBIGH*

Model		With any Arms £ p	With Matching Arms £ p
DEVIZES CELTIC DRINKING CUP	63mm	10.00	25.00
(Goss Record. 8th Edition: Page 36)	82mm	14.50	28.00
Inscribed: *Model of Celtic Drinking Cup found at Devizes.*			
Matching Arms: *DEVIZES*			
DEVON CIDER BARREL	60mm	15.00	30.00
Inscribed: *Model of Devon Cider Barrel. Copyright.*			
This model is identical to the small version of the Burton Beer Barrel but rarer.			
Matching Arms: *DEVON* OR *ANY DEVONSHIRE ARMS*			
DEVON COOKING POT	46mm	15.00	30.00
Inscribed: *Model of Devon Cooking Pot. Copyright.*			
This model is identical to the Manx Peel Pot but scarcer...so that every apparent Peel Pot requires close examination.			
Matching Arms: *DEVON* OR *ANY DEVONSHIRE ARMS*			

NOTE: The two models are only found with arms of places in Devonshire, or rarely, Cornwall. The only truly correct arms are those of Devon itself.

Model		With any Arms £ p	With Matching Arms £ p
DEVON OAK PITCHER	59mm	5.50	17.50
(Goss Record. 8th Edition: Page 20)	114mm[1]	17.00	33.00
Inscribed: *Model of Oak Pitcher peculiar to Devon.*			
Matching Arms: *DEVON* OR *ANY DEVONSHIRE ARMS*			
DINANT WOODEN SHOE	Length 74mm	25.00	47.50
(Goss Record. 8th Edition: Page 42)			
Inscribed: *Model of Wooden Shoe worn at Dinant.*			
Matching Arms: *DINANT*			
DONCASTER EWER	67mm	17.50	36.00
Inscribed: *Model of Ancient Ewer found during alterations at Elephant Hotel, Doncaster, 1914. Copyright.*			
Matching Arms: *DONCASTER*			
DONCASTER URN	39mm	9.50	36.00
Inscribed: *Model of Ancient Urn found in the Market Place Doncaster. Copyright.*			
Matching Arms: *DONCASTER*			
DONCASTER VASE	78mm	15.50	36.00
Inscribed: *Model of Ancient Vase found in High St., Doncaster. Copyright.*			
Matching Arms: *DONCASTER*			

Model		With any Arms £ p	With Matching Arms £ p
DORCHESTER JUG	50mm	5.50	17.00

DORCHESTER JUG
(Goss Record. 8th Edition: Page 20 and also see full
page advertisement on page 61)
Inscribed: *Model of Old Jug found in North Sq., Dorchester.*
Matching Arms: *DORCHESTER*

DORCHESTER ROMAN CUP	51mm	5.50	20.00
	82mm[1]	21.50	30.00

DORCHESTER ROMAN CUP
(Goss Record. 8th Edition: Page 21)
Inscribed: *Model of Roman Cup (Dorset Museum) found at
Dorchester.*

DOROTHY VERNON'S PORRIDGE POT	72mm[1]	15.50	28.00

DOROTHY VERNON'S PORRIDGE POT
(Goss Record. 8th Edition: Page 18)
Inscribed: *Model of Dorothy Vernon's Porridge Pot.*
The inscription is normally in Gothic script on the reverse, but
when the model carries two crests it can be found around the
rim or neck.
Matching Arms: *DOROTHY VERNON*

DOVER MORTAR (or Stone Vessel)	51mm	8.50	17.00

DOVER MORTAR (or Stone Vessel)
(Goss Record. 8th Edition: Page 26)
Inscribed: *Model of Ancient Stone Vessel from Dover Castle
in Dover Museum. Rd. No. 390788.*
This model is listed as DOVER MORTAR in the
8th Edition (page 26) and 9th Edition (page 20) of *The Goss Record.*
Matching Arms: *DOVER*

DUNGENESS LIGHTHOUSE	125mm		450.00

DUNGENESS LIGHTHOUSE
Inscribed: *Model of Dungeness Lighthouse*
This model is actually the Beachy Head Lighthouse
re-titled, presumably for the local agent. It is the rarest
version of this lighthouse, only one example being
known.
Matching Arms: *THE LORDS OF THE LEVEL OF
ROMNEY MARSH*

Model		With any Arms £ p	With Matching Arms £ p

DURHAM SANCTUARY KNOCKER
(Goss Record. 8th Edition: Page 21)
Inscribed: *(The) Durham Abbey Knocker.*
Inscribed (h): *Durham Abbey Knocker Cup Rd. No. 245459*

(a) Flower holder, or hair tidy, white glazed	Height 125mm	40.00†	
(b) Flower holder, or hair tidy, white unglazed	Height 125mm	40.00†	
(c) Flower holder, or hair tidy, brown	Height 125mm	47.50†	
(d) Flower holder, or hair tidy, gold front on brown. Probably an 1887 Golden Jubilee Edition.	Height 125mm	100.00†	
(e) Flower holder, or hair tidy, brown with green tingeing	125mm	115.00†	
(f) Night-light with base	83mm	95.00	117.50
(g) Mug or cup	52mm	40.00	65.00
(h) Mug or cup	80mm	56.50	82.50
(i) Mug or cup	118mm	82.50	110.00

A descriptive leaflet can also be found with the above
items and is worth £20.00. The brown example is
sometimes tinged with green to represent moss or
ageing.
Matching Arms: *DURHAM (CATHEDRAL)*

DUTCH SABOT	Length 82mm	19.50	40.00

(Goss Record. 8th Edition: Page 42)
Inscribed: *Model of Dutch Sabot.*
Matching Arms: *HOLLAND* OR *ANY DUTCH TOWN*

DUTCH MILK CAN and lid
Inscribed: *Model of Dutch Milk Can*

(identical to Boulogne Milk Can)	74mm	65.00	95.00

This model is incomplete without its lid, value £10.00
Matching Arms: *HOLLAND* OR *ANY DUTCH TOWN*

EDDYSTONE LIGHTHOUSE
Inscribed: *Model of Eddystone Lighthouse.*

Matching Arms: *PLYMOUTH* OR *STONEHOUSE*	125mm	26.00	40.00

for EDDYSTONE SPANISH JUG
see Plymouth Jug

for EDINBURGH CASTLE, MONS MEG
see Mons Meg, Edinburgh Castle

	With any Arms		With Matching Arms	
Model	£	p	£	p

THE EGYPTIAN MODELS

In order that the Egyptian models may be satisfactorily covered they have been listed in their chronological order of manufacture. According to the 8th Edition of *The Goss Record* (page 42) models of the Egyptian Water Jar and the Great Pyramid were in the course of preparation at the time of going to press in 1913, but the Water Jar must have been in production in 1911 as it has been found carrying the G & M Coronation decoration. By the time the 9th Edition was published in 1921 these two models had been on sale for some time (page 37) and ten other models of ancient shapes were listed as being in preparation.

The production of these models must arouse today's collectors' curiosity, but the discovery of the young King Tutankhamun's Tomb in 1922 was only the climax of many years aggressive investigation of the region by several teams of explorers. Indeed, from a commercial point of view, the Goss factory would have found it much more convenient had the tomb been discovered two or three years later as no sooner had the models made their appearance than interest in Egyptology began to wane.

The models 'in preparation' were given numbers and why 2, 3, 12, 13, 14 and 15 were not used can only be a matter for speculation. The most probable explanation is that around twenty designs were prepared for consideration by the Cairo Agent. He in turn selected the models thought to be most suitable, which he ordered and the rejected designs account for the missing numbers.

An Egyptian Lotus Vase was chosen in 1923 as the model for issue exclusively to members of the International League of Goss Collectors, and at around the same time two further models were issued by the Goss factory and these, together with the Wembley Lion, were put on sale at the 1924 and 1925 British Empire Exhibition.

CAIRO, PORT SAID OR *ALEXANDRIA* **may also be considered matching on any Egyptian piece.**

EGYPTIAN WATER JAR
(Goss Record. 9th Edition: Page 37)
Inscribed: *Model of Egyptian Water Jar. Rd. No. 569836.*
Matching Arms: *EGYPT* OR *ANY EGYPTIAN ARMS*

56mm   5.50   40.00

EGYPTIAN CANOPIC JAR WITH ANUBIS HEAD No.1
(Goss Record. 9th Edition: Page 37)
Inscribed: *Model of Ancient Egyptian Canopic Jar with Anubis Head. No. 1 Copyright.*
A most unusual model. The Anubis head is detachable and the model is incomplete without this lid, which is worth £40.00.
See also THIRD PERIOD (S) for a later one-piece model, and also one-piece version utilised as papper or salt cruets.
Matching Arms: *EGYPT* OR *ANY EGYPTIAN ARMS*

76mm   95.00   117.50

Durham Sanctuary Knocker Flower Holder, Brown

Durham Sanctury Knocker Cup, 118mm

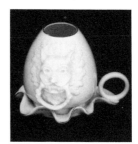

Durham Sanctuary Knocker Night-light with base

Durham Sanctuary Knocker Mug

Dutch Sabot

Eddystone Lighthouse

Egyptian Water Jar

Egyptian Canopic Jar with Anubis Head No. 1

Egyptian Kohl Pot No. 4

Egyptian Kohl Pot No. 5

Egyptian Kohl Pot No. 6

Egyptian Alabaster Vase No. 7

Model		With any Arms £ p	With Matching Arms £ p

EGYPTIAN KOHL POT No. 4   66mm   30.00   47.50
(Goss Record. 9th Edition: Page 37)
Inscribed: *Model of Egyptian Kohl Pot. No. 4 Copyright.*
Matching Arms: *EGYPT* OR *ANY EGYPTIAN ARMS*

EGYPTIAN KOHL POT No. 5   60mm   20.50   56.50
(Goss Record. 9th Edition: Page 37)
Inscribed: *Model of Ancient Egyptian Kohl Pot. No. 5 Copyright.*
Matching Arms: *EGYPT* OR *ANY EGYPTIAN ARMS*

EGYPTIAN KOHL POT No. 6   Dia. 70mm   19.50   47.50
(Goss Record. 9th Edition: Page 37)
Inscribed: *Model of Ancient Egyptian Kohl Pot. No. 6 Copyright.*
Matching Arms: *EGYPT* OR *ANY EGYPTIAN ARMS*

EGYPTIAN ALABASTER VASE No. 7   105mm   20.50   47.50
(Goss Record. 9th Edition: Page 37)
Inscribed: *Model of Ancient Egyptian Alabaster Vase. No. 7 Copyright.*
Matching Arms: *EGYPT* OR *ANY EGYPTIAN ARMS*

EGYPTIAN ALABASTER VASE No. 8   105mm   26.00   56.50
(Goss Record. 9th Edition: Page 37)
Inscribed: *Model of Ancient Egyptian Alabaster Vase. No. 8 Copyright.*
Matching Arms: *EGYPT* OR *ANY EGYPTIAN ARMS*

EGYPTIAN ALABASTER BOWL No. 9   58mm   16.00   56.50
(Goss Record. 9th Edition: Page 37)
Inscribed: *Model of Ancient Egyptian Alabaster Bowl. No. 9 Copyright.*
Matching Arms: *EGYPT* OR *ANY EGYPTIAN ARMS*

EGYPTIAN WOODEN EWER No. 10   66mm   20.50   47.50
(Goss Record. 9th Edition: Page 37)
Inscribed: *Model of Ancient Egyptian Wooden Ewer. No. 10 Copyright.*
Matching Arms: *EGYPT* OR *ANY EGYPTIAN ARMS*

EGYPTIAN PORCELAIN EWER No. 11   58mm   21.50   47.50
(Goss Record. 9th Edition: Page 37)
Inscribed: *Model of Ancient Egyptian Porcelain Ewer. No. 11 Copyright.*
Matching Arms: *EGYPT* OR *ANY EGYPTIAN ARMS*

Egyptian Alabaster Vase
No. 8

Egyptian Alabaster Bowl
No. 9

Egyptian Wooden Ewer
No. 10

Egyptian Porcelain Ewer
No. 11

Egyptian Porcelain Bottle
No. 16

Egyptian Lotus Vase
League Model, 1923

Egyptian Mocha Cup
(Bowl Shaped)

Egyptian Mocha Cup
(Egg-cup Shaped)

Elizabethan Jug

Ellesmere Ancient British
Canoe

Eton Vase

Exeter Flemish Goblet

Model		With any Arms £ p	With Matching Arms £ p

EGYPTIAN PORCELAIN BOTTLE No. 16   68mm   43.00   65.00
(Goss Record: 9th Edition: Page 37)
Inscribed: *Model of Ancient Egyptian Bottle. No. 16 Copyright.*
This is the rarest of the Egyptian models.
Matching Arms: *EGYPT* OR *ANY EGYPTIAN ARMS*

EGYPTIAN LOTUS VASE   80mm   185.00
Inscribed: *Model of Ancient Egyptian Lotus Vase. Copyright.*
Issued to members only & cannot be bought. 1923.
International League Model for 1923
Correct Arms: *INTERNATIONAL LEAGUE OF*
     GOSS COLLECTORS

EGYPTIAN MOCHA CUP (Bowl Shaped)   Named 40mm   9.00   41.50
Inscribed: *Model of Egyptian Mocha Cup.*   Unnamed 40mm   6.00   40.00
Rd. No. 572083
This model is not listed in any edition of *The Goss
Record*. It is described as Bowl shaped so as to distinguish
it from the Egg Cup shaped variety, also named
Egyptian Mocha Cup. This piece always appears to be
particularly finely modelled, the porcelain being very
thin and delicate. It is found both named and un-named.
Matching Arms: *EGYPT* OR *ANY EGYPTIAN ARMS*

EGYPTIAN MOCHA CUP (Egg Cup Shaped)   Named 52mm   12.50   41.50
Inscribed: *Model of Egyptian Mocha Cup.*   Unnamed 52mm   9.00   40.00
Rd. No. 572083.
This model is not listed in any edition of *The Goss
Record*. It is described as Egg Cup shaped so as to
distinguish it from the Bowl shaped version, also
named Egyptian Mocha Cup. It is found both named
and unnamed.
Matching Arms: *EGYPT* OR *ANY EGYPTIAN ARMS*

for EGYPTIAN ANCIENT LAMP
see Bournemouth Ancient Egyptian Lamp

for EGYPTIAN PYRAMID
see Great Pyramid

for ELIZABETHAN BUSHEL MEASURE
see Appleby Elizabethan Bushel Measure

Model			With any Arms £　p	With Matching Arms £　p
ELIZABETHAN JUG		95mm[1]	25.00	43.00

(Goss Record. 8th Edition: Page 43)
Inscribed: *The Elizabethan Jug.*
This model is listed as Miscellaneous in *The Goss Record*
under the heading at the end of the listing of special
historical shapes, that is, it was available to any agent
but was stocked with matching arms by the Stratford-
on-Avon agent. It is difficult to find this model in fine
condition as it is First Period; indeed it was one of the
first models issued and the gilding and enamels of the
coats of arms are invariably worn. Few large size
models can have been manufactured after 1895 when
the newer models with specific local connections
became so much more popular. Frequently found
impressed W.H. GOSS only, i.e. without the
Goshawk.
Matching Arms: *QUEEN ELIZABETH*

ELLESMERE ANCIENT BRITISH CANOE
(Goss Record. 8th Edition: Page 31)

(a) White glazed	Length 149mm		56.50	75.00
(b) Brown†	Length 149mm		220.00	

Inscribed: *Model of Ancient British Canoe dug out of
Whattall Moss near Ellesmere in 1864. Now in
Ellesmere Museum. Rd. No. 559521.*
This model is listed as bearing no arms in the 9th
Edition of *The Goss Record.* After 1921, a white glazed
version of this model was issued and it is more
commonly seen bearing a coat of arms.
Matching Arms: *ELLESMERE*

for ENGLISH WINE FLAGON
see London Christ's Hospital English Wine Flagon

ETON VASE		86mm	9.50	21.50

(Goss Record. 8th Edition: Page 16)
Inscribed: *Model of Ancient Vase dredged out of the Thames
near Eton. Rd. No. 539422.*
This model is identical to the Greenwich Vase
Matching Arms: *FLOREAT ETONA* OR *WINDSOR*

Model		With any Arms £ p	With Matching Arms £ p

EXETER FLEMISH GOBLET (a) 130mm — 19.50 — 49.50
(Goss Record. 8th Edition: Page 20) (b) 130mm — 35.00 — 56.50
Inscribed: *16th Century Goblet found in well in Cathedral Close Exeter.*
Matching Arms: *EXETER* (a)
It can also rarely be found inscribed: *Similar ones are to be seen in the Steen Museum, Antwerpen*
Matching Arms: *ANTWERPEN* OR *PROVINCIE ANTWERPEN (b)*

EXETER VASE — 63mm — 7.00 — 15.50
(Goss Record. 8th Edition: Page 20) — 101mm — 19.50 — 26.00
Inscribed: *The Exeter Vase from the original in the Museum.*
Matching Arms: *EXETER*

for FARM LABOURER'S BOTTLE
see Luton Bottle

for FEEDING BOTTLE
see Wilderspool Roman Tetinae

FELIXSTOWE ROMAN EWER — 73mm — 7.00 — 26.00
(Goss Record. 8th Edition: Page 34) — 114mm — 22.00 — 31.50
Inscribed: *Model of Roman Ewer found at Felixstowe, now in Ipswich Museum.*
Matching Arms: *FELIXSTOWE*

FELIXSTOWE ROMAN CINERARY URN — 47mm — 7.00 — 26.00
(Goss Record. 8th Edition: Page 34)
Inscribed: *Model of Roman Cinerary Urn circa A.D. 200. Found at Felixtowe From the original in the possession of S.D. Wall, Walton, Felixstowe. Rd. No. 638375.*
Matching Arms: *FELIXSTOWE*

FENNY STRATFORD POPPER — 58mm — 15.50 — 35.00
(Goss Record. 9th Edition: Page 11)
Inscribed: *Model of one of the six Fenny Stratford Poppers which are fired annually on the Patronal Festival St. Martin's Day, November 11th. Founded about 1730. Copyright.*
Matching Arms: *FENNY STRATFORD*

Exeter Vase

Felixstowe Roman Ewer

Felixstowe Roman Cinerary Urn

Fenny Stratford Popper

Fimber Ancient British Cinerary Urn League Model, 1928

Old Flemish Melk Pot

Folkestone Saltwood Roman Ewer

Fountains Abbey Abbot's Cup

Fourshire Stone

Fraser Cuach

Froxfield Roman Bronze Drinking Bowl

Gibraltar Alcaraza or Spanish Carafe

Model		With any Arms £ p	With Matching Arms £ p
FIMBER ANCIENT BRITISH CINERARY URN	106mm		195.00
FISH BASKET			
MODEL OF FISH BASKET	63mm		26.00
(OLD) FLEMISH MELK POT	Max. Dia. 118mm	19.50	35.00
FOLKESTONE SALTWOOD ROMAN EWER	88mm[1]	11.00	21.50
FOUNTAINS ABBEY, ABBOT'S CUP	44mm	6.50	16.00
	76mm[1]	14.50	30.00

FIMBER ANCIENT BRITISH CINERARY URN
Inscribed: *Model of Ancient British Cinerary Urn found at Fimber. Copyright 1928. This model is only issued to Members of the League and cannot be bought.*
International League Model for 1928
Correct Arms: *INTERNATIONAL LEAGUE OF GOSS COLLECTORS*

FISH BASKET
Early versions uncrested and without usual flat surface on front to receive Arms. Simply named
MODEL OF FISH BASKET
See also Alderney, Guernsey, Jersey, Sark, and Welsh Fish Basket

for FLEMISH GOBLET
see Exeter Flemish Goblet

(OLD) FLEMISH MELK POT
(Goss Record. 8th Edition: Page 42)
Inscribed: *Model of old Flemish Melk Pot. Rd. No. 574598.*
The name of this model is spelt as above in the 8th Edition of *The Goss Record* (page 42) and on every model produced from the Goss factory. This being Flemish for milk, it is obviously correct. However, it is incorrectly spelt milk in the 9th Edition (page 37).
Matching Arms: *ANTWERPEN*

for FLOATING MINE
see Contact Mine

FOLKESTONE SALTWOOD ROMAN EWER
(Goss Record. 8th Edition: Page 27)
Inscribed: *From original found at Saltwood, now in Folkstone Museum.*
Matching Arms: *FOLKESTONE* OR *SANDGATE*

FOUNTAINS ABBEY, ABBOT'S CUP
(Goss Record. 8th Edition: Page 38)
Inscribed: *The Abbots Cup from the original at Fountains Abbey.*
Also see POSTCARDS Chapter 5.
Matching Arms: *FOUNTAINS ABBEY*

German Smoking Pipe

Gerrans Celtic Cinerary Urn

Glastonbury (Abbot Beere's) Jack

Glastonbury Bronze Bowl

Glastonbury Vase (or Urn)

Glastonbury Roman Ewer

Glastonbury Ancient Salt Cellar

Glastonbury Terracotta Bowl

Gloucester Jug

Gnossus Ashmolean Vase League Model, 1920

Godalming Ancient Ewer

Gravesend Oriental Water Cooler

Model		With any Arms £ p	With Matching Arms £ p

FOURSHIRE STONE   118mm   35.00   70.00
(Goss Record. 8th Edition: Page 31)
Impressed on front: *The Fourshire Stone, Worcestershire.*
Impressed on left side: *Gloucestershire.* Impressed on right
side: *Oxfordshire.* Impressed on back: *Warwickshire.* Inscribed
on back: *Model of the Fourshire Stone near Chipping Norton.*
This stone marks the spot where the counties of Gloucester,
Oxford, Warwick and Worcester meet.
This model has a delicate finial particularly prone to damage.
Matching Arms: *CHIPPING NORTON*

FRASER (FORT AUGUSTUS) CUACH   Length 104mm   17.50   35.00
(Goss Record. 9th Edition: Page 35)
Inscribed: *Model of Highland Cuach in possession of the*
Frazers at Fort Augustus. Rd. No. 633433.
Matching Arms: *LORD LOVAT*, who is Head of the Fraser Clan,
or other Highland Arms are considered matching.

for FRID STOL
see Hexham Abbey Frid Stol

FROXFIELD ROMAN BRONZE
DRINKING BOWL   Dia. 72mm   40.00   45.00
(Goss Record. 8th Edition: Page 36)
Inscribed: *Model of Roman Bronze Drinking Bowl found at*
Rudge near Froxfield, Wilts. A.D. 1725.
This model was originally sold without arms and
subsequently with those of **MARLBOROUGH** which are
considered matching.

for GERMAN INCENDIARY BOMB
see Maldon (Essex) German Incendiary Bomb

GERMAN SMOKING PIPE   Overall
(*The Goss Record* 7th Edition 1910-11, page 56)   Length
Although manufactured as an ornamental object, it   252mm   70.00   100.00
merits inclusion in this section as an historic object or
special shape.
It consists of a wooden stem with a black Bakelite
mouthpiece, a porcelain bowl and separate porcelain
pipe, which bears the coat of arms. All these parts are
joined by push-fitting into cork rings.
Matching Arms: *FRANCO-BRITISH EXHIBITION 1908* for which
it was first made. Also *GERMAN* arms could be considered
appropriate.

Model		With any Arms £ p	With Matching Arms £ p

for GERMAN ZEPPELIN BOMB
see Bury St. Edmunds German Bomb

GERRANS CELTIC CINERARY URN
(Goss Record. 8th Edition: Page 18)
Inscribed: *Model of Celtic Cinerary Urn found at Gerrans,*
Cornwall.

With 1 coat of arms	57mm	6.50	14.00
With 1 coat of arms	127mm[1]	14.00	30.00
With 3 coats of arms	57mm	15.50	23.00
With 3 coats of arms	127mm[1]	23.00	30.00

Matching Arms: *FALMOUTH*

GIBRALTAR ALCARAZA or
SPANISH CARAFE   68mm   7.00   25.00
(Goss Record. 8th Edition: Page 42)
Inscribed: *Model of Spanish Alcaraza from Gibraltar.*
Rd. No. 449120.
This model can also be found inscribed Gibraltar
Carafe and is identical to the Canary Porron
Matching Arms: *GIBRALTAR* OR *SPAIN*

Glastonbury collectors should see the impressive
two-page advertisement in the Goss Record. 8th Edition:
Pages 80-81

Where Glastonbury models carry matching arms, they are
almost always inscribed on the base of the piece: *Arms of Glastonbury*
or *Borough of Glastonbury* under the same arms.

GLASTONBURY (ABBOT BEERE'S) JACK   56mm   6.50   21.50
(Goss Record. 8th Edition: Page 32)
Inscribed: *Model of Abbot Beere's Jack from carving on*
St. Benedict's Church, Glastonbury. Rd. No. 382436.
Matching Arms: *GLASTONBURY*

GLASTONBURY ANCIENT SALT CELLAR   82mm   17.00   28.00
(Goss Record. 8th Edition: Page 32)
Inscribed: *Model of Ancient Salt Cellar in Glastonbury*
Museum. Rd. No. 605731.
Matching Arms: *GLASTONBURY*

Model		With any Arms £ p	With Matching Arms £ p

GLASTONBURY BRONZE BOWL
(Goss Record. 8th Edition: Page 31)
Inscribed: *Model of Bronze Bowl from the Ancient British Lake-Village near Glastonbury.*
The larger version can be found with or without three ball feet, and earlier models can be found uncrested.

Dia. (overall) 65mm Height 73mm		14.00	26.00
Dia. (overall) 127mm Height 80mm [1]		40.00	56.50

Matching Arms: *GLASTONBURY*

GLASTONBURY ROMAN EWER
71mm 5.50 20.50
(Goss Record. 8th Edition: Page 32)
Inscribed: *Model of Ancient Roman Ewer found near Glastonbury. Rd. No. 382438.*
Matching Arms: *GLASTONBURY*

GLASTONBURY TERRACOTTA BOWL
36mm 5.50 16.00
(Goss Record. 8th Edition: Page 31)
Inscribed: *Model of Bowl from the Ancient Briitsh Lake-Village near Glastonbury.*
Matching Arms: *GLASTONBURY*

GLASTONBURY VASE
45mm 5.50 16.00
(Goss Record. 8th Edition: Page 31)
Inscribed: *Model of Vase from the Ancient Briitsh Lake Village near Glastonbury.*
Matching Arms: *GLASTONBURY*

for GLEN DORGAL CINERARY URN
see Truro Glen Dorgal Cinerary Urn

GLOUCESTER JUG
44mm 5.50 15.50
(Goss Record. 8th Edition: Page 22)
95mm[1] 19.50 28.00
Inscribed: *The Gloucester Jug from original in Museum.*
Matching Arms: *GLOUCESTER*

GNOSSUS ASHMOLEAN VASE
60mm 85.00
(Goss Record. 9th Edition: Pages 22, 41 and Plate C)
Inscribed: *Model of Ancient Vase from Gnossus No. 110 in Ashmolean Museum. Issued to Members only & cannot be purchased. Copyright.*
International league model for 1920.
Correct Arms: *INTERNATIONAL LEAGUE OF GOSS COLLECTORS*

Goodwin Sands Carafe

*Greek Amphora Vase
League Model, 1921*

The Great Pyramid

Greenwich Vase

Grinlow Tower

Guernsey Fish Basket

Guernsey Milk Can and Lid

Guildford Roman Vase

*Guillemot Egg, pointed end
and closed*

*Guy's Porridge Pot, named
on base*

*Guy's Porridge Pot (identical
to small Irish Bronze Pot)*

Haamoga Amaui, Tonga

Model		With any Arms £ p	With Matching Arms £ p

GODALMING ANCIENT EWER   55mm   17.00   28.00
(Goss Record. 8th Edition: Page 34)
Inscribed: *Model of Ancient Ewer found on Charterhouse Hill,*
Godalming, 31/3/1904, now in the museum. Rd. No. 630511.
Matching Arms: *GODALMING*

for GOGARTH ANCIENT VASE
see Llandudno (Gogarth) Ancient Vase

GOODWIN SANDS CARAFE   61mm   5.50   12.50
(Goss Record. 8th Edition: Page 27)
Inscribed: *Model of Ancient Carafe dredged off Goodwin Sands.*
Matching Arms: *BROADSTAIRS, DEAL, MARGATE,*
RAMSGATE, OR *WALMER*

GRAVESEND ORIENTAL WATER COOLER   72mm   21.50   30.00
Inscribed: *Model of Ancient Water Cooler found at*
Gravesend, from the original in Gravesend Public Library.
Copyright.
Matching Arms: *GRAVESEND*

(THE) GREAT PYRAMID   60mm   75.00   87.00
(Goss Record. 8th Edition: Page 42)
Inscribed: *Model of the Great Pyramid at Gizeh, Near Cairo,*
Egypt. Rd. No. 602907.
Could be considered as a Monument or Building -
often found chipped at the corners.
Matching Arms: *EGYPT* OR *ANY EGYPTIAN ARMS*, particularly
SAKKARA

GREEK AMPHORA VASE   138mm   117.50
(Goss Record 9th Edition: Page 40 and Plate A)
Inscribed: *Model of Greek Amphora Vase (circa 350 B.C.)*
which was given filled with oil as a prize in the
Panathenaic Games. This model is only issued to Members of the
League and cannot be bought.
International league model for 1921.
Correct Arms: *INTERNATIONAL LEAGUE OF*
    GOSS COLLECTORS

GREENWICH VASE   86mm   30.00   47.50
Inscribed: *Model of Ancient Vase found in Greenwich Park*
and of a similar one dredged out of the Thames, near Eton.
Rd. No. 539422.
This model, which is uncommon, is exactly the
same as the Eton Vase as stated on the base.
Matching Arms: *GREENWICH*

Model			With any Arms £ p	With Matching Arms £ p

GRINLOW TOWER   95mm   160.00   260.00

Inscribed: *Model of Grinlow Tower (known as Soloman's Temple). The building was erected by public subscription and stands on the site of a prehistoric barrow explored in 1894. Copyright.*
Probably the rarest white glazed Tower.
Matching Arms: *BUXTON*

GUERNSEY FISH BASKET

(Goss Record. 8th Edition: Page 17)		45mm	14.50	34.50
Inscribed: *Guernsey Fish Basket.*		58mm	29.00	40.00
(With outpressed shield)	Length 116mm	58mm[1]	35.00	90.00
Matching Arms: *GUERNSEY*				

GUERNSEY MILK CAN and lid

	70mm		23.00
(Goss Record. 9th Edition: Page 11)	108mm	17.50	30.00
Inscribed: *Model of Guernsey Milk Can*	140mm	22.50	35.00

This model is incomplete without its lid, value £10.00.
Matching Arms: *GUERNSEY*

GUILDFORD ROMAN VASE   63mm   12.50   24.50

(Goss Record. 8th Edition: Page 34)
Inscribed: *Model of Roman Vase in Surrey Archaeological Museum, Guildford. Rd. No. 602904.*
Matching Arms: *GUILDFORD*

GUILLEMOT EGG

	(a) Coloured, Open	83mm	75.00
Found closed, or open as	(b) Coloured, Closed	93mm	75.00
hanging posy vase either	(c) White, unglazed, Closed	96mm	82.50

with or without arms, none of which may be considered matching. It is however preferable to have the arms of a coastal town. Found in different speckled colours with the ground usually of blue, brown or green.
See also BIRD'S EGG, FIRST PERIOD 9C ORNAMENTAL

GUY'S PORRIDGE POT

	(a) 50mm	12.50	22.00
(Goss Record. 8th Edition: Page 35)	(b) 50mm	40.00	

Inscribed, usually on the side together with the Goshawk:
Model of Guy's Porridge Pot in Warwick Castle Rd. No. 413579.
for version (a), *Model of Guy's Porridge Pot* in Gothic script on the side of version (b).
Matching Arms: *WARWICK*

GUY'S PORRIDGE POT   40mm   70.00

Better known as a small Irish Bronze Pot but named *Guy's Porridge Pot* in large Gothic script on side. Only one example has been seen with the arms of Stratford-on-Avon.

Model		With any Arms £ p	With Matching Arms £ p

HAAMOGA AMAUI, TONGA   82mm   400.00   1300.00

Inscribed: *Model of Haamoga Amaui Tonga. Copyright. Made in England.*
This trilithon has a bowl-shaped depression on the top of the lintel stone to catch the sun's rays. Correctly, it is the locally named Ha'amonga-'a-Maui, believed to date from 1200 A.D.
The model was made for the Goss agent in Tonga, and only two examples with the Tonga crest are now known to exist.
An example has been seen with the Blackpool arms and the base glazed, and shards have been found in the factory spoilheap.
Matching Arms: *TONGA*

HAFOD GREEK VASE and lid   82mm   60.00   82.50

Inscribed: *Model of Greek Vase in Hafod Church near Devil's Bridge. Copyright.*
The lid has a knob on top which tends to get chipped.
Can be found also with a brown or black transfer of DEVIL'S BRIDGE - the matching arms value of which is given here as there are no correct arms.
An undated leaflet gave Goss souvenir china among the list of items available at "the picturesque little rustic hut" at the exit from the waterfalls, so that perhaps the proprietor of Devil's Bridge Hotel held the Goss agency, some time after 1902 when the railway was built.
Both the lid and the base are worth £30.00 each.

HAMBLEDON CRICKET STONE   Grey 80mm†   830.00

(Goss Record. 8th Edition: Page 16)
Inscribed on front: *This Stone marks the site of the Ground of the Hambledon Cricket Club circ. 1760-1787.*

HAMWORTHY LAMP   Length 100mm   11.00   21.50
                    Width 65mm

(Goss Record. 8th Edition: Page 21)
Inscribed: *Model of Ancient Lamp found at Lake Clay Pits, Hamworthy, Poole. Rd. No. 489579.*
Matching Arms: *POOLE*

HARROGATE ANCIENT EWER   62mm   6.00   21.50

(Goss Record. 8th Edition: page 38)
Inscribed: *Model of Ancient Ewer found at Aldborough Park, Harrogate. Rd. No. 639837.*
Matching Arms: *HARROGATE*

Hafod Vase and Lid

Hambledon Cricket Stone

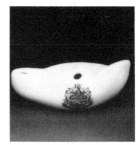

Hamworthy Lamp

Harrogate Ancient Ewer

Hastings Kettle

Hawes Ancient British Urn

Hawkins Henley Sculls in Presentation Box

Hereford Terracotta Kettle and Lid

Herne Bay Reculver Towers

Herne Bay Ancient Ewer

Hertford Ancient Ewer

Hexham Abbey Frid Stol

Model		*With any Arms* £ p	*With Matching Arms* £ p

HASTINGS KETTLE   51mm   6.50   16.00
(Goss Record. 8th Edition: Page 34)
Inscribed: *Model of Ancient Kettle dredged up off Hastings, 1873. In Hastings Museum.*
Matching Arms: *HASTINGS*

HAWES ANCIENT BRITISH URN   Dia. 95mm   16.00   26.00
(Goss Record. 8th Edition: Page 38)
Inscribed: *Model of Ancient British Urn found near Aysgill Force, Hawes, 1897. Rd. No. 517520.*
This model has two pairs of small holes on its underside.
Matching Arms: *HAWES*

HAWKINS HENLEY SCULL   Length 152mm   Each   75.00
(Goss Record. 9th Edition: Page 25)
Inscribed: *Hawkins Famous Henley Scull as used in the Diamonds Henley Royal Regatta. Rd. No. 636992.*
The sculls have never been seen other than with either of the two Henley coats of arms. The local agent had presentation boxes made to sell them individually, or, more commonly, in pairs.
The correct box is worth an additional £30.00
Matching Arms: *HENLEY-ON-THAMES ANCIENT* OR *HENLEY-ON-THAMES 1624*

for HEN CLOUD LEEK URN
see Leek Urn

for HENLEY HAWKINS SCULL
see Hawkins Henley Scull

HEREFORD TERRACOTTA KETTLE and lid   70mm   19.50   40.00
(Goss Record. 8th Edition: Page 24 and   121mm[1]   31.50   57.50
advertisement page 66)
Inscribed: *Model of Old Terra Cotta Kettle in Hereford Museum.*
This model is incomplete without its lid, worth £8.00
Matching Arms: *HEREFORD*

HERNE BAY RECULVER TOWERS
(Goss Record. 8th Edition: Page 27)
Inscribed: *Model of Reculver Towers.*
Rd. No. 639536.

(a) White glazed	101mm	82.50	125.00
(b) Grey†	101mm	220.00	
(c) Brown†	101mm	200.00	

Matching Arms: *HERNE BAY*

Model			With any Arms £ p	With Matching Arms £ p
HERNE BAY ANCIENT EWER		78mm	6.50	17.00

(Goss Record. 8th Edition: Page 27)
Inscribed: *Model of Ancient Ewer found in Brickfield, Herne Bay.*
Rd. No. 559523.
Matching Arms: *HERNE BAY*

HERTFORD ANCIENT EWER		69mm	12.50	25.00

(Goss Record. 8th Edition: Page 24)
Inscribed: *Model of Ancient Ewer in Hertford Museum.*
Rd. No. 617574.
Matching Arms: *HERTFORD*

HEXHAM ABBEY FRID STOL	(a) White unglazed	60mm	26.00	32.50
(Goss Record. 8th Edition: Page 30)	(b) White glazed	60mm	26.00	32.50
	(c) Brown	60mm	40.00	56.50
	(d) Brown, two-piece as pin box and lid	60mm	85.00	120.00

Inscribed: *Model of Ancient Frid Stol in Hexham Abbey,*
Northumberland.
Each of the three basic versions of this model can be
found both with and without a coat of arms, and
occasionally in the original box in which they were
sold labelled: *Model of Saxon Sanctuary Chair in Hexham Abbey,* and
the Agent's name: *Gibson & Son Hexham.*
Matching Arms: HEXHAM ABBEY

for HIGHLAND CUACH or WHISKEY CUP
see National Highland Cuach or Whiskey Cup

for HIGHLAND MILK CROGAN
see Stornoway Highway Milk Crogan

HITCHIN POSSET CUP		51mm	11.00	26.00

(Goss Record. 8th Edition: Page 24)
Inscribed: *Model of Ancient Posset Cup found at Hitchin.*
Rd. No. 521971.
Matching Arms: *HITCHIN*

HORNSEA ATWICK ROMAN VASE		51mm	10.00	30.00

(Goss Record. 8th Edition: Page 38)
Inscribed: *Model of Roman Vase found at Atwick near*
Hornsea. Rd. No. 500864.
Matching Arms: *HORNSEA*

Model		With any Arms £ p	With Matching Arms £ p

(THE OLD) HORSE SHOE   115mm   21.50
(Goss Record. 8th Edition: Page 43)
Inscribed on front: *The Old Horse Shoe*
May the good old shoe bring luck to you!
Good health and sweet content:
And may your path be ever blessed.
With peace from Heaven sent. Jno. Crowther.
The Legend. The Horse Shoe has long been regarded
as of great potency against evil. All Europe believes,
in a more or less degree, that the hanging up of a Horse
Shoe in the home is significant of Good Luck.
All the Kings of old up to the 13th Century carried out
the custom of having a Horse Shoe hung on the entrance
of the Palace. When the great St. Dunstan was asked to
shoe the hoof of Evil the One, he bound him up so fast, and
so tortured him, that he had to promise he would never
enter a doorway over which a Horse Shoe was hung.
Lord Nelson, England's greatest Admiral, had a Horse
Shoe nailed to the Victory. Copyright.

This model is classified under the heading Miscellaneous at the end
of the special historical shapes list in the 9th Edition of *The Goss
Record*. If the decoration is large, the descriptive matter is printed
on the reverse.
It has no matching arms, but those of PORTSMOUTH or
ADMIRAL LORD NELSON are preferable.

HORSHAM JUG   60mm   7.00   22.50
(Goss Record. 8th Edition: Page 34)
Inscribed: *Model of Mediaeval Jug in Brighton Museum
found at Horsham.*
Matching Arms: *HORSHAM*

HUNSTANTON EWER   65mm   7.00   26.00
(Goss Record. 8th Edition: Page 29)
Inscribed: *Model of Ancient Ewer found on Hunstanton Estate.
Rd. No. 495669.*
Matching Arms: *HUNSTANTON*

HYTHE CROMWELLIAN MORTAR   38mm   9.00   16.00
(Goss Record. 8th Edition: Page 27)
Inscribed: *Model of Cromwellian Mortar found at Hythe.
Rd. No. 590790.*
Matching Arms: *HYTHE*

Hitchin Posset Cup

Hornsea Atwick Roman Vase

(The Old) Horse Shoe

Horsham Jug

Hunstanton Ewer

Hythe Cromwellian Mortar

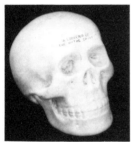

Hythe Crypt Skull

Ilkley Roman Ewer

Ipswich Ancient Ewer

Ipswich Roman Ewer

Irish Bronze Pot

*(Ancient) Irish Cruisken
League Model, 1929*

Model		With any Arms £ p	With Matching Arms £ p

HYTHE CRYPT SKULL
(Goss Record. 9th Edition: Page 20)
Inscribed: *A Souvenir of the Hythe Crypt.*

(a) Small pale yellow†	38mm	75.00	
(b) Large white†	72mm	110.00	
(c) Large pale yellow†	72mm	170.00	

ILKLEY ROMAN EWER — 60mm 5.50 23.00; 132mm 21.50 29.00
(Goss Record. 8th Edition: Page 38)
Inscribed: *Model of Roman Ewer in Ilkley Museum.*
Rd. No. 489582.
Matching Arms: *ILKLEY*

IPSWICH ANCIENT EWER — 60mm 7.50 18.50
(Goss Record. 8th Edition: Page 34)
Inscribed: *Model of Ancient Ewer dug up in Ipswich now in Museum. Rd. No. 553188.*
Matching Arms: *IPSWICH*

IPSWICH ROMAN EWER — 98mm 18.50 40.00
(Goss Record. 8th Edition: Page 34)
Inscribed: *Model of Roman Ewer dug up in Ipswich now in Museum.*
Matching Arms: *IPSWICH*

IRISH BRONZE POT — 43mm 5.50 23.00; 72mm 14.50 30.00
(Goss Record. 8th Edition: Page 40)
Inscribed: *Model of Ancient Irish Bronze Pot.*
Matching Arms: *ARMS OF IRELAND* OR *ANY IRISH ARMS*

(ANCIENT) IRISH CRUISKEN — 95mm 190.00
Inscribed: *Model of Ancient Irish Cruisken. Copyright 1929. This model is issued to Members of the League and cannot be bought.*
International League Model for 1929
Correct Arms: *INTENATIONAL LEAGUE OF GOSS COLLECTORS*

Irish Mather 152mm

Irish Wooden Noggin

*Italian Krater
League Model, 1922*

Itford Lewes Urn

Japan Ewer

Jersey Fish Basket

Jersey Milk Can and Lid

Kendal Jug

Kettering Urn

King Richard's Well Cover

*King's Newton Anglo-Saxon
Cinerary Urn, League Model*

*Kininmonth Moss Ancient
Pot*

Model		With any Arms £ p	With Matching Arms £ p

IRISH MATHER   76mm   10.00   22.50
(Goss Record. 8th Edition: Page 40 and   152mm   47.50   75.00
advertisement page 61)
Inscribed: *Model of Irish Mather or Wooden Drinking Cup in*
Dorset County Museum.
See also chapter 5 POSTCARDS
The large size is usually multi-crested and often carries a verse.
Matching Arms: *ARMS OF IRELAND* OR *ANY IRISH ARMS*

IRISH WOODEN NOGGIN   63mm   10.00   15.00
(Goss Record. 8th Edition: Page 40)
Inscribed: *Model of Ancient Irish Wooden Noggin. Rd. No.*
489580.
Matching Arms: *ARMS OF IRELAND* OR *ANY IRISH ARMS*

for ISLE OF WIGHT ROMAN EWER
see Brading Roman Ewer

ITALIAN KRATER   100mm   117.50
Inscribed: *Model of Italian Krater from the original*
in British Museum. This model is only issued to Members
of the League and cannot be bought.
International League Model for 1922.
Correct Arms: *INTERNATIONAL LEAGUE OF*
    GOSS COLLECTORS

ITFORD LEWES URN   66mm   7.00   23.00
(Goss Record. 8th Edition: Page 35)   111mm[1]   22.50   34.50
Inscribed: *Model of British Urn found at Itford near*
Lewes. Rd. No. 573577.
Matching Arms: *LEWES*

JAPAN EWER   90mm   12.50   30.00
(Goss Record. 8th Edition: Page 42)   200mm[1]   34.50   56.50
Inscribed: *The Japan Ewer.*
Both sizes are found named and unnamed,
same price
Matching Arms: *JAPAN*
See also FIRST PERIOD 9C ORNAMENTAL

Model		With any Arms £ p	With Matching Arms £ p
JERSEY FISH BASKET	45mm	14.50	24.50
(Goss Record. 8th Edition: Page 17)	60mm[1]	22.50	34.50
Inscribed: *Jersey Fish Basket*			
This model can be found without a coat of arms and			
no flat area to receive a decoration, but this has little or no			
bearing on the price.			
Matching Arms: *JERSEY*			
JERSEY MILK CAN and lid	70mm		23.00
(Goss Record. 9th Edition: Page 11)	108mm	17.00	30.00
Inscribed: *Model of Jersey Milk Can*	136mm	21.50	40.00
This model is incomplete without its lid			
which is worth £10.00			
Matching Arms: *JERSEY*			

for JOHN BARROW'S MONUMENT
see Sir John Barrow's Monument, Ulverston

KENDAL JUG	86mm	10.50	21.50
(Goss Record. 8th Edition: Page 36)	145mm[1]	26.00	47.50
Inscribed: *Model of Jug in Kendal Museum dated 1602.*			
Matching Arms: *KENDAL*			
KETTERING URN	43mm	5.50	23.00
(Goss Record. 8th Edition: Page 30)			
Inscribed: *Model of Ancient Urn found at Kettering now in*			
Northampton Museum. Rd. No. 543008.			
Matching Arms: *KETTERING*			
KING ALFRED'S STATUE	170mm	82.50	
KING RICHARD'S WELL COVER	100mm	155.00	240.00

(Goss Record. 9th Edition: Page 21)
Inscribed: *Model of structure covering King Richard's Well on Bosworth Field. Copyright.*
Translation of inscription: With water drawn from this well Richard III, King of England, assuaged his thirst (when) fighting in the most desperate and hostile manner with Henry, Earl of Richmond, and about to lose before night his life, together with his sceptre. August 22. (O.S.) A.D. 1485.
Matching Arms: *MARKET BOSWORTH*

Model		With any Arms £ p	With Matching Arms £ p
KING'S NEWTON ANGLO-SAXON			
CINERARY URN	(a) 60mm		35.00
(Goss Record. 9th Edition: Pages 22, 41 and	(b) 60mm		95.00
Plate B)			

Inscribed: *Model of Anglo-Saxon Urn found at King's Newton. Copyright. This is only issued to Members of more than 6 years standing & cannot be purchased.* This model was first introduced bearing THE LEAGUE OF GOSS COLLECTORS motif (a), and re-introduced later bearing the INTERNATIONAL LEAGUE OF GOSS COLLECTORS motif (b).

KININMONTH MOSS ANCIENT POT	49mm	17.00	35.00

(Goss Record. 9th Edition: Page 35 and Plate M)
Inscribed: *Model of Ancient Moss Pot dug out of Kininmonth Moss near Old Deer in 1855. Copyright*
Matching Arms: *OLD DEER*

for KIRKPARK URN
see Musselburgh Urn

LANCASHIRE CLOG	Length 93mm	47.50	65.00

(Goss Record. 9th Edition: Page 21)
Inscribed: *Model of Lancashire Clog. Copyright.*
Matching Arms: *LANCASHIRE*

LANCASTER JUG	68mm	6.50	30.00

(Goss Record. 8th Edition: Page 27)
Inscribed: *Model of Ancient Jug in Lancaster Museum. Rd. No. 500863.*
Matching Arms: *LANCASTER*

for LANDGATE CANNON BALL
see Rye Cannon Ball

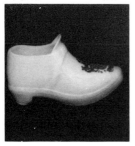

Lancashire Clog

Lancaster Jug

Lanlawren Celtic Sepulchral Urn

(Battle of) Largs Memorial Tower

Las Palmas Ancient Covered Jarra and Lid

Las Palmas Ancient Earthen Jar

Las Palmas Ancient Jarra

Laxey Gretch-Veg Urn

Leek Urn

Leicester Tyg

Leiston Abbey Pitcher

Lewes Roman Vase

Model				With any Arms £ p	With Matching Arms £ p

LANLAWREN CELTIC SEPULCHRAL URN   50mm   6.50   17.00
(Goss Record. 8th Edition: Page 18)   102mm[1]   19.50   28.00
Inscribed: *Model of Celtic Sepulchral Urn, found at*
Lanlawren, Cornwall.
There are no correct arms for this model, but any
Cornish arms would be considered as local. Lanlawren is
near Fowey and this must, therefore, be considered
the correct arms, although *The Goss Record* does not give
any particular agency as being stockists of this model.
Matching Arms: *FOWEY OR POSSIBLY FALMOUTH*

(BATTLE OF) LARGS MEMORIAL TOWER
(Goss Record. 8th Edition: Page 40)   (a)   White glazed   128mm   37.50   47.50
                                    (b)   Grey glazed   128mm   305.00
Inscribed: *Model of Battle of Largs*
Memorial Tower. Rd. No. 610012.
Matching Arms: *LARGS*

LAS PALMAS ANCIENT COVERED JARRA and lid   58mm   14.50   34.50
(Goss Record. 8th Edition: Page 42)
Inscribed: *Model of Ancient Covered Jarra in Museum*
Las Palmas Grand Canary. Rd. No. 572205.
This model is incomplete without its lid, value £6.00
Matching Arms: *LAS PALMAS*

LAS PALMAS ANCIENT EARTHEN JAR   58mm   12.50   26.00
(Goss Record. 8th Edition: Page 42)
Inscribed: *Model of Ancient Earthan Jar in Museum*
Las Palmas Grand Canary. Rd. No. 610010.
Matching Arms: *LAS PALMAS*

LAS PALMAS ANCIENT JARRA   53mm   9.00   25.00
(Goss Record. 8th Edition: Page 42)
Inscribed: *Model of Ancient Jarra in Museum Las Palmas*
Grand Canary. Rd. No. 572204.
Matching Arms: *LAS PALMAS*

for LAS PALMAS CANARY PORRON
see Canary Porron

Model of Roman Cinerary Urn 120-140 AD. in Letchworth Museum Copyright 83mm Very rare

Model			With any Arms £ p	With Matching Arms £ p
LAXEY GRETCH-VEG URN		Dia. 55mm	9.00	15.50

(Goss Record. 9th Edition: Page 19)
Inscribed: *Model of Ancient Urn found on Gretch-Veg near Laxey I.O.M. Rd. No. 489581.*
This model can be found bearing arms on the base (on the inside) or in the usual position on the outside.
Matching Arms: *LAXEY, ISLE OF MAN.*

for LEEK
see Welsh Leek

LEEK URN		63mm	9.00	28.00

(Goss Record. 8th Edition: Page 32)
Inscribed: *Model of British Urn found at Hen Cloud Near Leek. Rd. No. 500865.*
Matching Arms: *LEEK*

LEICESTER TYG	(a) 1 coat of arms	59mm	8.50	17.50
(Goss Record. 8th Edn: Page 28)	(b) 3 coats of arms	59mm	16.00	28.50

Inscribed: *Model of Tyg found in Highcross Street 1867 now in Leicester Museum. Rd. No. 495670.*
Matching Arms: *LEICESTER*

LEISTON ABBEY PITCHER		61mm	6.50	19.00
(Goss Record. 8th Edition: Page 34)		107mm	21.50	30.00

Inscribed: *Model of Pitcher in Ipswich Museum found at Leiston Abbey.*
Matching Arms: *LEISTON ABBEY*

LETCHWORTH CELTIC CINERARY URN		97mm	40.00	70.00

(Goss Record. 9th Edition: Page 19 and Plate J)
Inscribed: *Model of late Celtic Cinerary Urn in Letchworth Museum found in 1912 Copyright.*
Matching Arms: *LETCHWORTH*

LETCHWORTH ROMAN CARINATED VASE		60mm	65.00	150.00

Inscribed: *Model of Roman Carinated Vase 120-140 A.D. in Letchworth Museum. Copyright.*
Matching Arms: *LETCHWORTH*

LETCHWORTH ROMAN CINERARY URN		83mm	375.00	550.00

Inscribed: *Model of Roman Cinerary Urn 120-140 AD. in Letchworth Museum Copyright*
Matching Arms: *LETCHWORTH*

*Letchworth Carinated
Roman Vase*

*Letchworth Celtic Cinerary
Urn*

Letchworth Roman Vase

Lichfield Jug

*Lincoln Leather Jack, small
with City Ringers Decoration*

Lincoln Vase

Littlehampton Roman Ewer

*Llandudno (Little Orme)
Roman Vase*

*Llandudno (Gogarth)
Ancient Vase*

Llangollen Coracle

Lobster Trap

*London Christ's Hospital
English Wine Flagon*

Model		With any Arms £ p	With Matching Arms £ p

LETCHWORTH ROMAN VASE   86mm   375.00   550.00
Inscribed: *Model of Roman Vase, late first century in*
Letchworth Museum Copyright
Matching Arms: *LETCHWORTH*

LEWES ROMAN VASE   35mm[1]   5.50   17.00
(Goss Record. 8th Edition: Page 35)
Inscribed: *Model of Roman Vase in Lewes Castle.*
Matching Arms: *LEWES*

for LEWES URN
see Itford Urn

for LHANNAN SHEE CUP
see Ballafletcher (Cup of)

LICHFIELD JUG   60mm   5.50   19.50
(Goss Record. 8th Edition: Page 32)   121mm[1]   19.50   30.00
Inscribed: *Model of Ancient Jug dug out of the*
foundations of Lichfield Museum.
Matching Arms: *LICHFIELD*

for LIMPET SHELL
see SECOND PERIOD 10K5 ORNAMENTAL and
    FIRST PERIOD 9C ORNAMENTAL Chapters.

LINCOLN LEATHER JACK
(Goss Record. 8th Edition: Page 28)
Inscribed: *Model of Lincoln Jack. This Jack was the gift of*
Alderman Bullen to the Company of Ringers. (a) and (c), with
the addition of: *1782 City Ringers* on (b),(d) and (e)
   (a) White glazed   56mm   9.00   21.50
   (b) Correct marking-coloured bell and shield, no arms   56mm   56.50
   (c) White glazed   153mm   24.50   32.50
   (d) White glazed, brown trim, blue and red shields
       on white glazed ground   153mm   800.00
   (e) Matt black with multi-coloured bells, no arms   153mm   875.00
Matching Arms: *LINCOLN*

LINCOLN VASE   67mm   6.50   23.00
(Goss Record. 8th Edition: Page 28)   88mm   15.00   28.00
Inscribed: *The Lincoln Vase, from Original at Cathedral.*
Matching Arms: *LINCOLN*

Model		With any Arms £ p	With Matching Arms £ p

LITTLEHAMPTON ROMAN EWER   73mm   9.00   23.00
(Goss Record. 8th Edition: Page 35)
Inscribed: *Model of Roman Ewer found when pulling down
houses in Arundel Road, Littlehampton. Rd. No. 521977.*
Matching Arms: *LITTLEHAMPTON*

LLANDUDNO (LITTLE ORME) ROMAN VASE   82mm   16.00   28.00
(Goss Record. 9th Edition: Page 34 and Plate K)
Inscribed: *Model of Roman Vase found on the Little Orme,
Llandudno 17/Dec/19. Copyright.*
Matching Arms: *LLANDUDNO*

LLANDUDNO (GOGARTH) ANCIENT VASE   84mm   17.00   26.00
(Goss Record. 9th Edition: Page 34 and Plate K)
Inscribed: *Model of Vase found at Gogarth, Marine Drive
Llandudno. Copyright.*
Matching Arms: *LLANDUDNO*

LLANGOLLEN CORACLE   Length 77mm   21.50   37.50
(Goss Record. 8th Edition: Page 39 and advertisement,
page 101)
Inscribed on base or on seat: *Model of Llangollen Coracle. Survival of
Ancient British wicker and hide boats.*
Matching Arms: *LLANGOLLEN*
Up until 1903, the Welsh Coracle was so called and
listed in *The Goss Record* as a national model having no
particular town or city arms. From 1904 onwards, it
was re-named The Llangollen Coracle, with Llangollen
given as the matching arms, which explains the
confusion of the two descriptions that can be found on
the same piece.
See also WELSH CORACLE

LOBSTER TRAP   51mm   15.50   30.00
(Goss Record. 8th Edition: Page 17)   84mm[1]   34.50   47.50
Inscribed: *Model of Lobster Trap.*
Matching Arms: *ANY OF THE CHANNEL ISLANDS
(ALDERNEY, GUERNSEY, JERSEY, SARK) OR
BOGNOR.*
The large size has a flat background to receive the
coat of arms, but earlier First Period examples have the
decoration applied directly to the moulded surface.

		With any Arms £ p	With Matching Arms £ p
Model			

LONDON CHRIST'S HOSPITAL ENGLISH WINE FLAGON 90mm 11.50 21.50
(Goss Record. 8th Edition: Page 29)
Inscribed: *Model of Early English Wine Flagon found under the foundations of Christ's Hospital, London. Rd. No. 539425.*
Matching Arms: *CHRIST'S HOSPITAL* OR *CITY OF LONDON*

LONDON STONE   (a) White†   109mm   125.00
                          (b) Brown†   109mm   170.00
Inscribed on base: *Model of the London stone near Staines*
Inscribed Side One Top: *To perpetuate and preferve this ancient Monument of the jurifdiction of the Citizens of London The fame was raifed on this Pedestal A.D. 1781 S^R Watkin Lewis KN^T Lord Mayor*
Base: *The Conservators of the River Thames 1857 Samuel Wilson ESQ^{RE} Lord Mayor 27th July 1859 John Johnson ESQ^{RE} Lord Mayor 8th August 1846*
Side Two Top: *The ceremony of claiming the jurifdiction of the City of London was repeated at this ftone by the R^T Hon^{BLE} Clau^{DS} Step. Hunter Lord Mayor A.D. 1812.*
Base: *The Right Hon^{BLE} Thomas Quested Finnis Lord Mayor Warren Stormes Hale ESQ^{RE} Alderman John Humphery ESQ^{RE} Alderman Jonathan Thorp ESQ^{RE}*
Side Three Top: *The ancient stone above this infcription is raifed upon this pedeftal exactly over the spot where it formerly ftood infcribed God preferveye City of London A.D. 1285.*
Base: *Commodore John Shepherd Captain B.J. Sulivan R.N.C.B. Captain John Shepherd Deputy Master of the Trinity House Captain William Pigott.*
Side Four Top: *The Right Honourable William Venables Lord Mayor of the City of London and Conservator of the River of Thames viewed the weftern boundary of the City's Jurisdiction in the said river marked by the ancient stone raised upon this pedestal erected A.D. 1285 on the 29th day of July A.D. 1826 God preferve the City of London*
Base: *Joseph Turner ESQ^{RE} Thomas Henry Fry ESQ^{RE} Thomas Dakin ESQ^{RE} Deputy Captain Horatio Thomas Austin R.N.C.B.*

LONGSHIPS LIGHTHOUSE, LAND'S END   122mm   40.00   75.00
(Goss Record. 8th Edition: Page 18)
Inscribed: *Model of the Longships Lighthouse Land's End.*
Matching Arms: *LAND'S END*

London Stone

Longships Lighthouse,
Land's End

Looe Ewer

Louth Ancient Ewer

Ludlow Sack Bottle

Luton Bottle or Costrel

Lyme Regis Ammonite

Madeira Bullock Car
(restored)

Maidstone Roman Ewer

Maldon (Essex) German
Incendiary Bomb

Maltese Carafe

Maltese Double-mouthed
Vase

Model		With any Arms £ p	With Matching Arms £ p

LOOE EWER   65mm   7.50   21.50
(Goss Record. 8th Edition: Page 18)
Inscribed: *Model of Ancient Ewer in St. Nicholas Church Looe.*
Rd. No. 450629.
Matching Arms: *LOOE OR EAST LOOE OR WEST LOOE EAST*

for LOTUS VASE
see Egyptian Lotus Vase

LOUTH ANCIENT EWER   43mm   7.50   22.50
(Goss Record. 8th Edition: Page 28)   113mm   24.50   40.00
Inscribed: *Model of Ancient Ewer found at Louth.*
Rd. No. 449119.
Matching Arms: *LOUTH*

LUDLOW SACK BOTTLE   75mm[1]   15.50   27.50
(Goss Record. 8th Edition: Page 31)
Inscribed: *Model of Sack Bottle dug up at Castle Mount,*
Ludlow, now in Ludlow Museum.
Matching Arms: *LUDLOW*

LUTON BOTTLE OR COSTREL   Length 65mm   14.50   30.00
(Goss Record. 8th Edition: Page 16)
Inscribed: *Model of "Costrell" or Farm Labourers Water Bottle,*
circa 16th century. Made of local clay at St. Mary's Pottery,
Skimpot. Dug up on the site of the London & County Bank,
Luton, May 1898. Rd. No. 630308.
Matching Arms: *LUTON*

LYME REGIS AMMONITE   73mm   34.50   56.50
(Goss Record. 9th Edition: Page 14)
Inscribed: *Model of Lyme Regis Ammonite. Rd. No. 513063.*
This model is identical to the Whitby Ammonite
Matching Arms: *LYME REGIS*

MADEIRA BULLOCK CAR   58mm   1800.00
Inscribed: *Model of Madeira Bullock Car. Copyright 778.*
One model only has been found, with the delicate trace pole and
the front and rear ring bars all missing. Even in that condition, it
remains an extremely rare and desirable collector's piece.
The model has now been restored with the aid of photographs of
the originals.
Matching Arms: *FUNCHAL, MADEIRA*

Maltese Fire Grate

Maltese Funereal Urn

Maltese Twin Vase

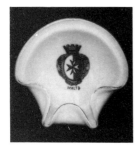

Maltese Two-wick Lamp

Maltese Vase à Canard

Manx Lobster Trap

Manx Peel Pot

*Ancient Manx Spirit
Measure*

*The Maple Leaf of Canada
813*

*Mary, Queen of Scots
Nightlight*

Melrose Cup

Minster Ancient Ewer

Model		With any Arms £ p	With Matching Arms £ p
MAIDSTONE ROMAN EWER	82mm	7.50	19.50
(Goss Record. 8th Edition: Page 27)	130mm	27.50	33.50

Inscribed: *Roman ewer. From the original in Maidstone Museum.*
Matching Arms: *MAIDSTONE*

MALDON (ESSEX) GERMAN INCENDIARY BOMB	75mm	26.00	40.00

(Goss Record. 9th Edition: Page 16)
Inscribed: *Model of Indendiary Bomb dropped at Maldon 16 April 1915 from a German zeppelin. Copyright.*
This model has a delicate handle which is frequently found broken, in which condition it is of little value.
Matching Arms: *MALDON*

Either MALTA or VALLETTA would be considered matching on any Maltese Model

MALTESE CARAFE	105mm	21.50	40.00

(Goss Record. 8th Edition: Page 42)
Inscribed: *Model of Maltese Carafe. Rd. No. 539424.*
Matching Arms: *MALTA*

MALTESE DOUBLE-MOUTHED VASE	60mm	23.00	37.50

(Goss Record. 9th Edition: Page 36 and Plate P)
Inscribed: *Model of Double-mouthed Vase of Bronze Age period, from Tarxien Sanctuary.*
Matching Arms: *MALTA*

MALTESE FIRE GRATE	53mm	17.00	24.50

(Goss Record. 8th Edition: Page 42)
Inscribed: *Model of Maltese Fire Grate.*
Matching Arms: *MALTA*

MALTESE FUNEREAL URN	61mm	9.00	25.00

(Goss Record. 8th Edition: Page 42)
Inscribed: *Model of Maltese Funereal Urn (circa 600 B.C.) found in Rock Tombs, Malta. Rd. No. 559525.*
Matching Arms: *MALTA*

MALTESE TWIN VASE	50mm	40.00	56.50

(Goss Record. 9th Edition: Page 36 and Plate P)
Inscribed: *Model of Maltese Twin Vase from Tarxien Sanctuary. Bronze Age period.*
Matching Arms: *MALTA*

Model		With any Arms £ p	With Matching Arms £ p

MALTESE TWO-WICK LAMP — Length 81mm — 17.00 — 27.50
(Goss Record. 8th Edition: Page 42)
Inscribed: *Model of Maltese Two-wick Lamp
(circa 600 B.C.) found in Rock Tombs, Malta.
Rd. No. 562738.*
Matching Arms: *MALTA*

MALTESE VASE à CANARD — 45mm — 20.50 — 22.00
(Goss Record. 9th Edition: Page 36)
Inscribed: *Model of Maltese Vase à Canard of Bronze Age
period from Tarxien Sanctuary.*
Matching Arms: *MALTA*

MANX LOBSTER POT — Dia. 67mm — — 45.00
Inscribed: *Model of Manx Lobster Trap.*
This model is identical to the Lobster Trap, but
specifically named.
Matching Arms: *ISLE OF MAN*

MANX PEEL POT — 49mm — 9.00 — 25.00
(Goss Record. 8th Edition: Page 26)
Inscribed: *Model of old Manx Pot at Peel. Rd. No. 390789.*
This model is identical to The Devon Cooking Pot.
Matching Arms: *CITY OF PEEL, ISLE OF MAN*

(ANCIENT) MANX SPIRIT MEASURE — 68mm — 14.00 — 30.00
(Goss Record. 8th Edition: Page 26)
Inscribed: *Model of Ancient Manx Spirit Measure. Rd. No. 578695.*
Matching Arms: *CITY OF PEEL, ISLE OF MAN*

(THE) MAPLE LEAF OF CANADA — 118mm — 70.00 — 145.00
Inscribed: *813 The Maple Leaf of Canada Copyright*
Matching Arms: CANADA OR ANY CANADIAN COAT OF ARMS

MARY QUEEN OF SCOTS
Face in high relief on (a) two-piece night-light — 78mm — 130.00 — 160.00
  (b) two or three-handled mug — 118mm — 87.50 — 145.00
Inscriptions:
(a) *Mary Queen of Scots Night Light
    Rd. No. 273298*
(b) *Mary Queen of Scots Cup
    Rd. No. 273244*
Correct Arms: *MARY QUEEN OF SCOTS*

Model		With any Arms £ p	With Matching Arms £ p

MELROSE CUP   128mm   47.50   65.00
(Goss Record. 8th Edition: Page 40 and advertisement
page 101)
Inscribed: *The Melrose Cup*
Not really a model in the true sense of the word, it was
designed by and made expressly for William Dick, the Melrose
Agent and first marketed exclusively by him. The bowl of the cup
incorporates the same leaf design that can be found at the top of the
pillars in Melrose Abbey.
Matching Arms: *MELROSE ABBEY OR MELROSE*

for MILK CROGAN
see Stornoway Highland Milk Crogan

MINSTER ANCIENT EWER   88mm   23.00   31.50
Inscribed: *Model of Ancient Ewer found at Minster,*
Thanet. Copyright.
Matching Arms: *MINSTER*

MINSTER ANCIENT URN   65mm   11.50   35.00
Inscribed: *Model of Ancient Urn found at Minster,*
(or Thanet), Kent. Copyright.
Matching Arms: *MINSTER*

for MONMOUTH MASK
See FIRST PERIOD 9C ORNAMENTAL Chapter

for MONNOW GATE
see Old Gateway on Monnow Bridge

MONS MEG, EDINBURGH CASTLE   Length 122mm   34.50   45.00
(Goss Record. 8th Edition: Page 40)
Inscribed: *Model of "Mons Meg" Edinburgh*
Castle. Rd. No. 605732.
Matching Arms: *EDINBURGH*

MUNICH BEER SEIDEL   52mm   75.00   125.00
Inscribed: *Model of Munich Beer Seidel.*
Matching Arms: *MUNICH (MÜNCHEN)*

Minster Ancient Urn

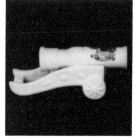

Mons Meg, Edinburgh Castle

Munich Beer Seidel

Musselburgh Kirkpark Ancient Urn

National Highland Cauch or Whiskey Cup

Newbury Leather Bottle, small

Newbury Leather Bottle, (large) with Stopper

Newcastle (Staffordshire) Cup

Newcastle Castle

Newcastle Roman Jug

North Foreland Lighthouse

Northwich Sepulchral Urn League Model 1930

Model		With any Arms £ p	With Matching Arms £ p

MUSSELBURGH KIRKPARK ANCIENT URN   51mm   7.50   26.00
(Goss Record. 8th Edition: Page 40)
Inscribed: *Model of Ancient Urn found in Kirkpark*
Musselburg N.B. Rd. No. 448431.
N.B. Inscription misspelt Musselburg; the arms correctly
captioned Musselburgh.
Matching Arms: *MUSSELBURGH*

for MYCENAEAN VASE
see Cyprus Mycenaean Vase

NATIONAL HIGHLAND CUACH or WHISKEY CUP
(Goss Record. 8th Edition: Page 40)   Width 94mm   11.00   16.00
Inscribed: *Model of Highland Cuach or Whiskey Cup.*
Any Highland Arms are considered matching.

for NAUTILUS SHELL
see SECOND PERIOD 10K5 ORNAMENTAL and
     FIRST PERIOD 9C ORNAMENTAL chapters.

NEWBURY LEATHER BOTTLE

(Goss Record. 8th Edition: Page 16)	(a)	58mm	7.50	16.00
	(b)	114mm[1]	19.50	32.50
	(c) With Stopper	125mm[1]	40.00	56.50

Inscribed: *Model of Leather Bottle found on Battle-field of Newbury, 1644.*
Now in Museum.
First Period examples of the larger size have a thicker rim to take a
porcelain and cork stopper, whilst Second Period models are
thinner and no stopper was included, nor indeed will fit.
Matching Arms: *NEWBURY*

NEWCASTLE (STAFFORDSHIRE) CUP   70mm[1]   23.00   33.50
(Goss Record. 8th Edition: Page 32)
Inscribed: *Model of an Ancient Black-&-brown Cup dug*
up at the south side of Red Lion Sq., Newcastle, Staffs.
in 1882: now in the possession of Messrs. Chapman &
Snape.
Matching Arms: *NEWCASTLE-UNDER-LYME*

Model			With any Arms £ p	With Matching Arms £ p
NEWCASTLE CASTLE	(a) White glazed	88mm	130.00	190.00
	(b) Brown†	88mm	525.00	525.00

Inscribed: *Newcastle on Tyne. Robert Curthose eldest son of the Conqueror, built a fortress here in 1080, which, in contradistinction to the old Roman Castrum of Pons Aelii, was called The New Castle, whence the present name of the town. Copyright.*
Matching Arms: *NEWCASTLE*

NEWCASTLE ROMAN JUG		63mm	5.50	16.00

(Goss Record. 8th Edition: Page 27)
Inscribed: *Model of Roman Jug in the Museum Newcastle on Tyne. Rd. No. 392069.*
Matching Arms: *NEWCASTLE*

for NORMAN TOWER, CHRISTCHURCH
see Christchurch Priory Church Norman Tower

NORTH FORELAND LIGHTHOUSE		108mm	56.50	75.00

(Goss Record. 8th Edition: Page 27)
Inscribed: *Model of the North Foreland Lighthouse. Rd. No. 639537.*
Matching Arms: *BROADSTAIRS OR RAMSGATE OR MARGATE*

NORTHWICH SEPULCHURAL URN		85mm		285.00

Inscribed: *Model of Britano-Romam Sepuchural Urn found near Northwich (Salinæ) now in Warrington Museum. Copyright 1930. This model is only issued to Members of the League and cannot be bought.*
International League Model for 1930
Correct Arms: *INTERNATIONAL LEAGUE OF GOSS COLLECTORS*

NORWEGIAN BUCKET		58mm	14.50	56.50

(Goss Record. 8th Edition: Page 42)
Inscribed: *Model of Norwegian Bucket. Rd. No. 599332.*
Can be found with either plain or gilded rim.
Matching Arms: *NORWAY (NORGE)*

Model		With any Arms £ p	With Matching Arms £ p

NORWEGIAN DRAGON-SHAPED BEER BOWL

(Goss Record. 8th Edition: Page 42)

Inscribed: *Model of Norwegian Dragon-shaped Beer Bowl. Rd. No. 526382.*

Can be rarely found (b) with the following inscription in Norwegian: *Model of Norsk Ølbolle (Kjenge) med Draghoved. Rd. No. 526382.*

Matching Arms: *NORWAY (NORGE)*

	With any Arms	With Matching Arms
(a) Length 155mm	28.00	56.50
(b) Length 155mm		75.00

NORWEGIAN HORSE-SHAPED BEER BOWL

(Goss Record. 8th Edition: Page 42)

Inscribed: *Model of Norwegian Horse-shaped Beer Bowl. Rd. No. 526383.*

Two varieties with joined or separate ears.

Can rarely be found (b) with the following inscription in Norwegian: *Model of Norsk Ølbolle (Kjenge) med Hesthoved Rd. No. 526383.*

Matching Arms: *NORWAY (NORGE)*

	With any Arms	With Matching Arms
(a) Length 115mm	25.00	56.50
(b) Length 115mm		75.00

NORWEGIAN WOODEN SHOE

(Goss Record. 8th Edition: page 42)

Inscribed: *Model of Norwegian Shoes.*

Matching Arms: *NORWAY (NORGE)*

	With any Arms	With Matching Arms
Length 103mm	25.00	47.50

The Arms of any Norwegian Town would also be considered matching. BERGEN is the most common, followed by Trondheim with the Norwegian spelling TRONDHJEM

NORWICH URN

(Goss Record. 8th Edition: page 29)

Inscribed: *Model of the Norwich Urn from the original in the Museum.*

Matching Arms: *NORWICH*

	With any Arms	With Matching Arms
51mm	5.50	15.50
62mm	9.50	19.50
90mm[1]	14.50	31.50

for NOSE OF BRASENOSE

see (The Nose of) Brasenose

NOTTINGHAM EWER

(Goss Record. 8th Edition: Page 30)

Inscribed: *Model of Ancient Ewer found during excavations top of Long Stairs High Pavement, now in Castle Museum. Rd. No. 472576.*

Matching Arms: *NOTTINGHAM*

		With any Arms	With Matching Arms
(a) 1 crest	63mm	6.50	21.00
(b) 2 crests	63mm	7.50	25.00

Norwegian Bucket

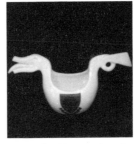

Norwegian Dragon-shaped Beer Bowl

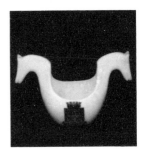

Norwegian Horse-shaped Beer Bowl

Norwegian Wooden Shoe

Norwich Urn

Nottingham Ewer

Nottingham Urn

Old Gateway on Monnow Bridge

Orkney Craisie

Ostend Flemish Bottle

Ostend Flemish Tobacco Jar

Ostend Vase

Model		With any Arms £ p	With Matching Arms £ p

NOTTINGHAM URN   40mm   5.50   20.50
(Goss Record. 8th Edition: Page 30 and advertisement
page 79)
Inscribed: *Model of Ancient Urn found during excavations in*
Nottingham. 1897. Now in Castle Museum. Rd. No. 472577.
Matching Arms: *NOTTINGHAM*

for OLD BRAZIER (ISLES OF SCILLY)
see Tresco Old Brazier

OLD GATEWAY ON MONNOW BRIDGE
(Goss Record. 9th Edition: Page 23
and Plate J)   (a) White glazed   95mm   85.00   170.00
                    (b) Brown†   95mm   215.00
Inscribed: *Model of Monnow Gate Monmouth.*
This model is the MONNOW GATE and not
MONMOW GATE as misspelt in the 9th Edition of
The Goss Record and usually on the model itself. The
side gates are found both open and closed.
Matching Arms: *MONMOUTH*

for OLD HORSE SHOE
see Horse Shoe (The Old)

for OLD PILLION STONE, FLOWERGATE, WHITBY
see Whitby Pillion Stone

for OLD SARUM KETTLE
see Salisbury Kettle

ORKNEY CRAISIE   80mm   19.50   40.00
(Goss Record. 9th Edition: Page 35)
Inscribed: *Model of Orkney Craisie. Rd. No. 559522.*
This model of the basket used in the Orkney Islands
has the description and mark on its inside and has a high
thin handle which can frequently be found either cracked
or completely broken off, in which condition it is of
little value.
Matching Arms: *COUNTY OF ORKNEY* or *KIRKWALL*

OSTEND FLEMISH BOTTLE   65mm   9.00   23.00
(Goss Record. 8th Edition: Page 42)
Inscribed: *Model of Flemish Bottle, Ostend Museum.*
Rd. No. 495673.
Matching Arms: *OSTENDE*

Oxford Ewer

Oxford Jug

Painswick Pot

Panama Vase

Penmaenmawr Urn

Perth Coronation Chair

Peterborough Tripod

Plymouth Spanish Jug

Pompeian Ewer

Portland Lighthouse

*Portland Vase
League Model*

Preston Old Bushel Measure

Model		With any Arms £ p	With Matching Arms £ p

OSTEND FLEMISH TOBACCO JAR — 54mm — 7.50 — 26.00
(Goss Record. 8th Edition: Page 42)
Inscribed: *Model of Flemish Tobacco Jar in Liebaert Museum at Ostend. Rd. No. 495674.*
Matching Arms: *OSTENDE*

OSTEND VASE — 57mm — 7.50 — 21.50
(Goss Record. 8th Edition: Page 42)
Inscribed: *Model of Ostend Vase A.D. 1617, found inside a fishing smack in the Fisherman's Dock at Ostend. Now in Ostend Museum. Rd. No. 495672.*
Matching Arms: *OSTENDE*

OXFORD EWER — 76mm — 6.50 — 15.50
(Goss Record. 8th Edition: Page 31) — 126mm[1] — 19.50 — 26.00
Inscribed: *The Oxford Ewer from the original in the Ashmolean Museum, found at Exeter Coll.*
Matching Arms: *OXFORD* with *EXETER* College Oxford perhaps being considered the next appropriate.

OXFORD JUG — 173mm[1] — 23.00 — 28.00
(Goss Record. 8th Edition: Page 31)
Inscribed: *The Oxford Jug from the original in the Ashmolean Museum, found at Trinity Coll.*
Matching Arms: *OXFORD* with *TRINITY* College Oxford perhaps being considered the next appropriate.

PAINSWICK POT — 50mm — 5.50 — 22.50
(Goss Record. 8th Edition: Page 22)
Inscribed: *Model of Roman Pot found at Ifold Villa Painswick 1902. Rd. No. 500869.*
Matching Arms: *PAINSWICK*

PANAMA VASE — 130mm — 26.00
Inscribed: *Panama Vase. Rd. No. 639532.*
Matching Arms: *PANAMA*, but not yet seen on this model.

PENMAENMAWR URN — 45mm — 5.50 — 19.50
(Goss Record. 8th Edition: Page 39)
Inscribed: *Model of Ancient Urn found at Penmaenmawr.*
Matching Arms: *PENMAENMAWR*

Model			With any Arms £ p	With Matching Arms £ p
PERTH CORONATION CHAIR	(a) White glazed	85mm	82.50	110.00
(Goss Record. 9th Edition: Page 36)	(b) Stone in brown	85mm	117.50	170.00
	(c) Brown†	85mm	285.00	

Inscribed: *Model of the Coronation Chair in Westminster
Abbey. Rd. No. 578694. The chair contains the Ancient
Stone on which the Kings and Queens of Scotland were
formerly crowned at Scone, Perthshire.*
This model is the same as the Westminster Abbey
Coronation Chair except that it carries the longer
inscription.
Earlier versions have an open space between the back
legs; later versions have a solid back, are 90mm high
and have the top of the back-rest gilded.
Matching Arms: *PERTH*

PETERBOROUGH TRIPOD	(a) 1 crest	47mm	11.00	16.00
(Goss Record. 8th Edition: Page 30)	(b) 3 crests	47mm	9.50	18.50

Inscribed: *Model of Bronze Roman Tripod in
Peterborough Museum found at Whittlesey Mere.*
This model is identical to the Witch's Cauldron
Example found named incorrectly as the Scarborough Jug.
Matching Arms: *PETERBOROUGH*

for **PILGRIM'S BOTTLE**
see Ancient Costril

for **PINE CONE**
see Bournemouth Pine Cone

for **PIPES**
see German Smoking Pipe and Twickenham Antique Pope's Pipe

PLYMOUTH (SPANISH) JUG	55mm	5.50	20.00

(Goss Record. 8th Edition: Page 20)
Inscribed: *Model of Old Spanish Jug dredged up near
Eddystone now in Athenaeum Plymouth.*
Matching Arms: *PLYMOUTH or STONEHOUSE*

POMPEIAN EWER	91mm	10.00	
(Goss Record. 8th Edition: Page 42)	208mm	34.50	

Inscribed: *Model of Pompeian Ewer*
Both sizes are also found unnamed - same price.
Italian Arms have yet to be recorded on this model, but
they would certainly be considered matching were they to exist.

Model			With any Arms £ p	With Matching Arms £ p

for POPE'S PIPE, TWICKENHAM
see Twickenham Antique Pope's Pipe

			With any Arms	With Matching Arms
PORTLAND LIGHTHOUSE	(a) Plain	120mm	26.00	
(Goss Record. 8th Edition: Page 21)	(b) Black band	120mm	100.00	140.00
	(c) Brown band	120mm	75.00	82.50
	(d) Orange band	120mm	100.00	140.00

Inscribed: *Model of the Portland Lighthouse. Rd. No. 622476.*
Matching Arms: *THE ISLAND & ROYAL MANOR OF PORTLAND URBAN DISTRICT COUNCIL*

			With any Arms	With Matching Arms
PORTLAND VASE	(a) 51mm		6.00	30.00
Inscribed: *Model of The Portland Vase in The*	(b) 51mm		26.00	65.00
British Museum.	(c) 51mm		47.50	

This is one of the most interesting models. All have the above inscription on the base (a), and some additionally have commemorative wording on the base, marking the anniversary of the death of Josiah Wedgwood, viz: *MEMORIAL OF JOSIAH WEDGWOOD* (b), and are thus much sought after: collectors picking up every Portland Vase could easily have a pleasant surprise. Mr. J.J. Jarvis, when starting The League of Goss Collectors, chose this as the first League model (c).
Collectors can read about the discovery and history of the original in *The Goss Record.* 8th Edition: page 28.
There are no correct town arms for this model as the Goss original is currently in the British Museum. As the original was purchased by the Duchess of Portland, the arms of the Duke of Portland could be considered matching, or perhaps also those of The Island & Royal Manor of Portland U.D.C.
Matching Arms: *(a) DUKE OF PORTLAND*
(b) JOSIAH WEDGWOOD
(c) THE LEAGUE OF GOSS COLLECTORS

	With any Arms £ p	With Matching Arms £ p
Model		

PRESTON OLD BUSHEL MEASURE   Dia. 58mm   75.00   150.00
(Goss Record. 9th Edition: Page 21 and Plate M)
Inscribed: *Model of The Old Bushel Measure made for Preston*
in 1670 and used by the Mayor and Clerk of the Markets under
the Old Charters granted to the Town. Copyright.
This model is the rarest of the small bushels, and is
embossed on the side: *For Preston in the County of*
Lancashire 1670.
Matching Arms: *PRESTON*

for PRINCESS VICTORIA'S FIRST SLIPPER
see Queen Victoria's First Shoe

for PYRAMID
see Great Pyramid (The)

for QUEEN CHARLOTTE'S KETTLE
see Windsor Kettle

QUEEN ELIZABETH'S RIDING SHOE   Length 105mm   85.00   117.50
(Goss Record. 9th Edition: Page 16 and Plate L)
On page 16 of *The Goss Record* it is referred to as a
slipper and under Plate L as a shoe.
Inscribed: *Model of Queen Elizabeth's Riding Shoe*
formerly at Horham Hall, Thaxted. Copyright.
This model is by far the rarest of the Goss shoe models.
Matching Arms: *THAXTED*

QUEEN PHILIPPA'S RECORD CHEST
(Goss Record. 8th Edition: Page 33)   Length (a) 80mm   30.00   40.00
Inscribed: *Model of Queen Phillipa's Record Chest*   (b) 94mm   30.00   40.00
found in Knaresborough Castle. Rd. No. 643868.
Matching Arms: *KNARESBOROUGH (ABBEY)*

Model			With any Arms £ p	With Matching Arms £ p

QUEEN VICTORIA'S FIRST SHOE

	(a) Without Arms	102mm	35.00†	
(Goss Record. 8th Edition: Page 20)	(b) Pre-1901	102mm	26.00	35.00
	(c) Post-1901	102mm	26.00	35.00

Inscribed on Pre 1901 examples: *Model, exact size of
first shoes worn by Princess Victoria - H.M. The Queen -
Made at Sidmouth 1819.*
Inscribed on Post 1901 examples: *Model, exact size,
of first shoes worn by Princess Victoria - H.M. late Queen -
(who died Jan. 22nd. 1901) made at Sidmouth in 1819.*
Can sometimes be found with a hole in the back
of the shoe for hanging.
A descriptive leaflet was issued with this model and
is valued at £15.00.
Matching Arms: *H.M. QUEEN VICTORIA* OR *SIDMOUTH*

RAMSEY CRONK AUST CINERARY URN   59mm   9.00   22.50
(Goss Record. 8th Edition: Page 26)
Inscribed: *Model of Cinerary Urn from Cronk Aust,
Ramsey. Rd. No. 521975.*
Matching Arms: *RAMSEY, ISLE OF MAN*

RAMSGATE ROMANO-BRITISH EWER   47mm   23.00   46.00
Inscribed: *Model of Romano British 1st Century Ewer
found at Ramsgate. 794 Copyright.*
Matching Arms: *RAMSGATE*

RAMSGATE ROMANO-BRITISH JUG   70mm   14.50   36.00
Inscribed: *Model of Romano-British 1st Century Jug found at
Ramsgate 795 Copyright.*
Matching Arms: *RAMSGATE*

RAMSGATE URN   75mm   15.00   36.00
Inscribed: *Model of Ancient Urn found at Ramsgate 787
Copyright*
Matching Arms: *RAMSGATE*

An example of each of the three Ramsgate models, all unglazed and unmarked, and
without decoration have recently been found in rooms above a Ramsgate shop. The
dimensions, and quality of the porcelain render them unmistakably Goss prototypes of
the actual models in Ramsgate museum, or factory samples.

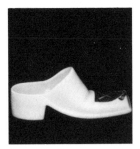

Queen Elizabeth's Riding Shoe

Queen Philippa's Record Chest

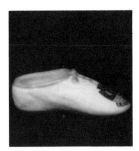

Queen Victoria's First Shoe

Ramsey Cronk Aust Cinerary Urn

Ramsgate Romano-British Ewer

Ramsgate Romano-British Jug 795

Ramsgate Urn

Rayleigh Ancient Cooking Pot

Reading Jug

Reading (Silchester) Urn

Reading (Silchester) Vase

Rochester Bellarmine Jug

Model		With any Arms £ p	With Matching Arms £ p
RAYLEIGH ANCIENT COOKING POT	33mm	6.50	30.00

RAYLEIGH ANCIENT COOKING POT
(Goss Record. 8th Edition: Page 22)
Inscribed: *Model of Ancient Cooking Pot found at Rayleigh Castle Essex. Rd. No. 602903.*
Matching Arms: *RAYLEIGH*

READING JUG — 82mm — 5.50 — 14.00
140mm — 19.50 — 27.50
(Goss Record. 8th Edition: Page 16)
Inscribed: *Model of 15th Cent. Jug dug up in Minster St. Reading. Now in Museum.*
Matching Arms: *READING*

READING (SILCHESTER) URN — 50mm — 5.50 — 14.00
(Goss Record. 8th Edition: Page 16)
Inscribed: *Model of Roman Urn from Silchester in Reading Museum. Rd. No. 573577.*
Matching Arms: *READING*

READING (SILCHESTER) VASE — 50mm — 5.50 — 15.50
(Goss Record. 8th Edition: Page 16)
Inscribed: *Model of Vase from Silchester in Reading Museum.*
Matching Arms: *READING*

for RECULVER TOWERS
see Herne Bay Reculver Towers

ROCHESTER BELLARMINE JUG — 65mm — 5.50 — 19.50
(Goss Record. 8th Edition: Page 27)
Inscribed: *Model of Bellarmine Jug 17th Century found in Rochester. Rd. No. 403421.*
The effigy of a bearded man is embossed on the neck of this model, also known as a Greybeard
Matching Arms: *ROCHESTER*

for ROMAN EWER
see Cirencester Roman Ewer

ROMAN MORTARIUM   (a) Named — Dia. 95mm — 50.00
(Goss Record. 8th Edition: Page 43) (b) Unnamed — 30.00
Inscribed: *Model of Ancient Roman Mortarium.*
This model has no matching arms.

for ROMAN TETINAE
see Wilderspool Roman Tetinae

Roman Mortarium

Roman Vase, 783

Romsey Bushel

Rothesay Stone

Rufus Stone

Russian Shrapnel Shell

Rye Cannon Ball with Plinth

Rye Cannon Ball without Plinth

Saffron Walden Covered Urn and lid

St. Albans Ancient Cooking Pot

St. Mary's Lighthouse, Whitley Bay

St. Neots Ancient Urn

Model			With any Arms £ p	With Matching Arms £ p
ROMAN VASE	(a) White glazed	160mm	47.50	
Inscribed: *The Roman Vase 783 Copyright*	(b) Lustre†	160mm		75.00
It has no matching arms.				
ROMSEY BUSHEL		Dia. 68mm	14.00	34.50
(Goss Record. 8th Edition: Page 23)				
Inscribed: *Model of Ancient Romsey Bushel in the*				
possession of the Corporation. Rd. No. 489663.				
Inscribed on side: *Winchester Bushel-Romsey Joseph*				
Mortimer Mayor 1792. Corcoran Fecit London				
Matching Arms: *ROMSEY*				
ROTHESAY STONE	Brown†	Length 95mm	1250.00	
(Goss Record. 9th Edition: Page 35		Width 25mm		
and Plate G) Only two examples of this rare model are				
known to exist and only in brown, 6mm thick.				
RUFUS STONE		94mm	12.00	19.50
(Goss Record. 8th Edition: Page 23 and advertisement				
page 64)				
Occasionally appears with no arms			10.00	

Inscribed with its history and legend on all three faces of
this triangular-shaped model as follows: *Here stood the*
oak tree, on which an arrow shot by Sir Walter Tyrrell at
a Stag, glanced and struck King William the Second,
surnamed Rufus, on the breast, of which he instantly died,
on the second day of August ANNO 1100.
King William the Second surnamed Rufus being slain as
before related was laid in a cart belonging to one Purkis
and drawn from hence to Winchester and buried in the
Cathedral Church of that City.
That the spot where an event so memorable might not
hereafter be forgotten, the enclosed stone was set up by
John, Lord Delaware who had seen the tree growing in this
place. This stone having been much mutilated and the
inscriptions on each of its three sides defaced this more
durable memorial with the original inscriptions was
erected in the year 1844. By Wm Sturges Bourne Warden.
The nearest Agency to the Rufus Stone is Lyndhurst and
this may also be considered matching, as is New Forest.
Matching Arms: *KING WILLIAM RUFUS*

Model		With any Arms £ p	With Matching Arms £ p
RUSSIAN SHRAPNEL SHELL	110mm	25.00	56.50

(Goss Record. War Edition: Page 5 [illustrated] and 7)
Inscribed: *Model of Russian Shrapnel Shell. The original was captured by the Huns & fired by them at the British. Copyright.*
Matching Arms: *RUSSIA* OR *ANY ARTILLERY REGIMENT*

RYE CANNON BALL, Multi-coloured
(Goss Record. 8th Edition: Page 35)
Inscribed: *Model of Cannon Ball excavated at Landgate, Rye 1907. This ball was probably fired by the French who twice burnt Rye to the ground (1377 & 1448)*

	(a) On plinth	106mm	75.00	125.00
	(b) Without plinth	68mm	40.00	65.00

Matching Arms: *RYE*

SAFFRON WALDEN COVERED URN and lid	70mm	19.50	30.00
(Goss Record. 8th Edition: Page 22)	121mm	28.50	36.50

Inscribed: *Model of Covered Urn found near site of Walden Abbey in 1878.*
This model has a lid that looks very like an Egyptian Mummy's Head without which it is incomplete, value £8.00
Matching Arms: *SAFFRON WALDEN*
With any Egyptian Arms add £10.00

ST. ALBANS ANCIENT COOKING POT	58mm	16.00	28.00

(Goss Record. 8th Edition: Page 24)
Inscribed: *Model of Ancient Cooking Pot in St. Albans Museum. Rd. No. 633430.*
Matching Arms: *ST. ALBANS*

ST. MARY'S LIGHTHOUSE, WHITLEY BAY	135mm	550.00	750.00

Inscribed: *Model of St. Mary's Lighthouse Whitley Bay. Copyright.*
This model is not listed in any edition of *The Goss Record* and is the second rarest lighthouse.
Matching Arms: *WHITLEY BAY*

ST. NEOTS ANCIENT URN	63mm	7.50	26.00

(Goss Record. 8th Edition: Page 24)
Inscribed: *Model of Ancient Urn found 1816 near St. Neot's, Hunts. Rd. No. 413576.*
Matching Arms: *ST. NEOTS*

ST. SIMON OF SUDBURY'S SKULL	(a) White†	72mm	175.00	
Inscribed: *Skull of St. Simon of Sudbury*	(b) Brown†	72mm	285.00	

Model		With any Arms £ p	With Matching Arms £ p
SALISBURY KETTLE	88mm	15.50	24.50
(Goss Record. 8th Edition: Page 36 and	133mm	17.50	32.50
advertisement page 114)			
Inscribed: *Model of Old Kettle in Salisbury Museum.*			
Also known as the Old Sarum Kettle			
Matching Arms: *SALISBURY*			
SALISBURY LEATHER JACK	44mm	5.50	19.50
(Goss Record. 8th Edition: Page 36)	80mm		300.00
Inscribed: *Model of the Royal Salisbury Jack from original*	140mm[1]	23.00	40.00
in Museum.			
The large size is always, and the small size is			
sometimes found with C R 1646 on the side under a			
crown. In addition, it appears both crested and			
uncrested. Same price.			
Matching Arms: *SALISBURY*			
SALISBURY LEATHER GILL	75mm	14.50	26.00
(Goss Record. 8th Edition: Page 36)			
Inscribed: *The Salisbury Leather Gill from original in*			
Museum. This model is always found with RSM 1658			
in red and blue letters on the side. It can be found			
both crested and uncrested. Same price.			
Matching Arms: *SALISBURY*			

The Salisbury Jack and Gill are thought to be the
inspiration for the popular nursery rhyme, with the
broken crown being that of Charles I. The initials C R
(Carolus Rex) 1646 on the Salisbury Jack is held to be
a commemoration of the visit by Charles I to the
neighbourhood, and the loyal owner of the Jack
marked it thus. 1658 on the Gill is the year of Oliver
Cromwell's death. R S M stands for Resurgam
meaning: I shall rise again, referring to the rising
hopes of the Loyalists on hearing of the death of
Cromwell. The originals should still be in
Salisbury Museum.

for SALTWOOD EWER
see Folkestone Roman Ewer

SARK FISH BASKET	45mm		30.00
(Goss Record. 8th Edition: Page 17)	58mm		37.50
Inscribed: *Sark Fish Basket.*			
Matching Arms: *SARK (SERCQ)*			

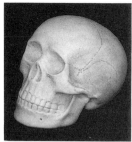

St. Simon of Sudbury's Skull | Salisbury (or Old Sarum) Kettle | Salisbury Leather Jack, Small

Salisbury Leather Gill | King Alfred's Statue | Salisbury Leather Jack, Large

The Southdown Sheep Bell, showing inscription and clapper

234

Model		With any Arms £　p	With Matching Arms £　p
SARK MILK CAN and lid	70mm	20.00	35.00
(Goss Record. 9th Edition: Page 11)	108mm		40.00
Inscribed: *Model of Sark Milk Can.*	140mm		47.50

This would be incomplete without its lid, value £10.00.
Matching Arms: *SARK (SERCQ)*

for SCALLOP SHELL
see SECOND PERIOD 10K5 ORNAMENTAL Chapter

SCARBOROUGH JUG	51mm	6.50	13.00
(Goss Record. 8th Edition: Page 38)	70mm	14.00	22.50

Inscribed: *Model of Jug about 600 years old found in the Ancient Moat of Scarborough.*
Matching Arms: *SCARBOROUGH*

SCARBOROUGH KETTLE	65mm	12.50	21.00
(Goss Record. 8th Edition: Page 38)	88mm	18.50	31.50

Inscribed: *Model of the Scarboro Kettle found near Ancient Pottery, North Side.*
This model can be found labelled as a *Scarborough Jug*, same price.
Matching Arms: *SCARBOROUGH*
Up until 1911-1916, the two Scarborough models were both known as Scarborough Jugs. The name of one was changed, probably to avoid confusion.
Originally one jug was named as follows:
Model of Jug found in Old Moat at the back of Huntress Row 600 years old
and the other:
Model of Jug found near Ancient Pottery.
It was the latter which was re-named a kettle between 1911 and 1916. *The Goss Record* prior to 1911 lists both as Scarborough Jugs. Both shapes were in production before 1900.

SEAFORD URN	48mm	9.00	17.50

(Goss Record. 8th Edition: Page 35)
First Period models inscribed: *Seaford Urn* or *The Seaford Urn* [1]
Second Period Models inscribed: *Model of Roman Urn found at Seaford 1825.* [2]
One of the first models to be introduced.
Matching Arms: *SEAFORD*

Sark Fish Basket

Sark Milk Can and Lid

Scarborough Jug

Scarborough Kettle

Seaford Urn

Shakespeare's Jug

Shrewsbury (Uriconium) Ewer

Shrewsbury Romano-Salopian Ewer

Sir John Barrow's Monument, Ulverston

Skegness Clock Tower

Southampton Ancient Pipkin

Southampton Bargate

Model		With any Arms £ p	With Matching Arms £ p
SHAKESPEARE'S JUG	58mm	11.00	17.50
(Goss Record. 8th Edition: Page 35)	76mm	12.00	23.00
Inscribed: *Model of Shakespeare's Jug, in the Museum,*	88mm	17.50	30.00

SHAKESPEARE'S JUG
(Goss Record. 8th Edition: Page 35)
Inscribed: *Model of Shakespeare's Jug, in the Museum, Stratford-on-Avon.*
Also named on the side: *Model of the Jug of William Shakespeare;* the title in illuminated Gothic script, and his name as a facsimile signature.
Matching Arms: *WILLIAM SHAKESPEARE* OR
 STRATFORD-ON-AVON

for SHEPHERD'S CROWN SEA URCHIN
see Steyning Shepherd's Crown

SHREWSBURY (URICONIUM) EWER 100mm 26.00 34.50
(Goss Record. 8th Edition: Page 31)
First Period models inscribed: *The Uriconium Ewer* [1]
Second Period models inscribed: *Model of Ewer, found in the Ancient Roman City of Uriconium, Nr. Shrewsbury.* [2]
One of the first models to be introduced.
Matching Arms: *SHREWSBURY*

SHREWSBURY ROMANO-SALOPIAN EWER 68mm 6.50 21.50
(Goss Record. 8th Edition: Page 31)
Inscribed: *Model of Romano-Salopian Ewer found at Uriconium. Now in Shrewsbury Museum.*
Matching Arms: *SHREWSBURY*

for SILCHESTER URN
see Reading (Silchester) Urn

for SILCHESTER VASE
see Reading (Silchester) Vase

for SIMON OF SUDBURY'S SKULL
see St. Simon of Sudbury's Skull

**SIR JOHN BARROW'S MONUMENT
ULVERSTON**   120mm 82.50 160.00
Inscribed: *Model of Sir John Barrow's Monument Ulverston. Copyright. "In Honour of Sir John Barrow Bart. Erected A.D. 1850".*
Matching Arms: *ULVERSTON*

SKEGNESS CLOCK TOWER   132mm 82.50 145.00
Inscribed: *Model of the Clock Tower Skegness.*
Matching Arms: *SKEGNESS*

Southport Vase

Southwold Ancient Gun

Southwold Jar

*Staffordshire Drinking Cup
League Model, 1926*

*(Staffordshire) One-handled
Tyg*

*(Staffordshire) Two-handled
Tyg*

Southdown Sheep Bell

*Staffordshire Tyg
League Model*

*Steyning Shepherd's
Crown Sea Urchin*

Stirling Pint Measure

Stockport Plague Stone

Stockton Ancient Salt Pot

238

Model		With any Arms £ p	With Matching Arms £ p

for SKULLS
see Hythe Crypt Skull, St. Simon of Sudbury's Skull
and Yorick's Skull

for SOLDIER'S WATER BOTTLE
see Waterlooville Soldier's Water Bottle

SOUTHAMPTON ANCIENT PIPKIN	56mm	5.50	13.00
(Goss Record. 8th EWdition: page 23)	76mm	17.50	28.00
Inscribed: *Model of Ancient Pipkin dug up at*	101mm[1]	23.00	35.00

N.P. Bank Southampton.
Matching Arms: *SOUTHAMPTON*

SOUTHAMPTON BARGATE
(Goss Record. 8th Edition: page 23)
Inscribed: *The Bargate Southampton. Of the seven gates which*
formerly gave entrance to Southampton only two now remain.
Of these the finest is the Bargate which contains Norman work.
It was originally defended by a drawbridge over a moat. On
the north side are two semicircular towers through which
side arches have been cut for the convenience of pedestrians,
and between which is a fine projecting front supposed to have
been added in the reign of Richard II. Rd. No. 594375

(a) Small, white glazed	55mm	47.50	82.50
(b) Small, grey†	55mm	87.50	
(c) Large, white glazed or unglazed†	87mm	65.00	145.00
(d) Large, grey†	87mm	130.00	
(e) Large, brown†	87mm	185.00	

Matching Arms: *SOUTHAMPTON*

SOUTHDOWN SHEEP BELL	54mm	65.00	95.00

Inscribed: *Model of Southdown Sheep Bell. Copyright.*
This model is identical to the Small Swiss Cow Bell and is
incomplete without the loose porcelain clapper suspended
inside it.
It has no correct arms - any Sussex Downland arms are to be
considered as matching

SOUTHPORT VASE	50mm	6.00	17.00

(Goss Record. 8th Edition: Page 27)
Inscribed: *Model of Vase at Botanic Gardens Southport.*
Rd. No. 403423.
Matching Arms: *SOUTHPORT*

Model		With any Arms £ p	With Matching Arms £ p
SOUTHWOLD ANCIENT GUN (Goss Record. 9th Edition: Page 28) Inscribed: *Model of Ancient Gun washed out of Gun Hill Cliff, Southwold, now in the Town Hall.* Matching Arms: *SOUTHWOLD*	Length 94mm	117.50	190.00
SOUTHWOLD JAR (Goss Record. 8th Edition: Page 34) Inscribed: *Model of Ancient Jar washed out of cliff near Southwold, now in Town Hall.* Matching Arms: *SOUTHWOLD*	88mm 140mm[1]	6.50 25.00	20.50 37.50
for SPANISH CARAFE see Gibraltar Alcaraza			
for SPANISH (EDDYSTONE) JUG see Plymouth (Spanish) Jug			
STAFFORDSHIRE DRINKING CUP Inscribed: *Model of Staffordshire Drinking Cup circa. 1650. Copyright. This model is only issued to Members of the League and cannot be bought.* International League Model for 1926 Correct Arms: *INTERNATIONAL LEAGUE OF GOSS COLLECTORS*	111mm		145.00
(STAFFORDSHIRE) ONE-HANDLED TYG (Goss Record. 8th Edition: Page 32) Inscribed: *Model of Ancient Tyg.* Matching Arms: *STAFFORDSHIRE*	65mm	5.50	24.50
(STAFFORDSHIRE) TWO-HANDLED TYG (Goss Record. 8th Edition: Page 32) Inscribed: *Model of Ancient Tyg.* Matching Arms: *STAFFORDSHIRE*	65mm	5.50	24.50
STAFFORDSHIRE TYG (Goss Record. 9th Edition: Pages 22 and 28 and Plate B) Inscribed: *Model of Ancient Staffordshire Tyg. Rd. No. 641312. The model is only issued to Members of more than 4 years standing and cannot be purchased.* This model was first introduced bearing THE LEAGUE OF GOSS COLLECTORS motif (a), and re-introduced later bearing the INTERNATIONAL LEAGUE OF GOSS COLLECTORS motif (b).	(a) 70mm (b) 70mm		87.50 110.00

		With any Arms £ p	With Matching Arms £ p
Model			

STEYNING SHEPHERD'S CROWN SEA URCHIN 50mm   30.00   52.00
(Goss Record. 9th Edition: page 29)
Inscribed: *Model of Fossil Sea Urchin found on The Downs at*
Steyning, locally known as Shepherds Crown. Copyright.
Matching Arms: *STEYNING*

STIRLING PINT MEASURE   61mm   9.00   30.00
(Goss Record. 8th Edition: Page 40)
Inscribed: *Model of the Stirling Pint Measure. One of the*
Ancient Standard Measures of Scotland deposited in Stirling by
Act of Parliament 1457. Rd. No. 543012.
Matching Arms: *STIRLING*

STOCKPORT PLAGUE STONE   Length 75mm   30.00   47.50
(Goss Record. 8th Edition: Page 17)
Inscribed: *Model of Plague Stone found during excavations in*
Stockport Market Place. Original now in Vernon Park Museum,
Stockport. The hollow was filled with vinegar, and when food
etc. was brought into the town, the money was placed in the
vinegar to prevent infection.
Matching Arms: *STOCKPORT*

STOCKTON ANCIENT SALT POT   73mm   10.00   26.00
(Goss Record. 8th Edition: Page 21)
Inscribed: *Model of Ancient Salt Pot found in bed of river at*
Stockton-on-Tees. Rd. No. 406301.
Matching Arms: *STOCKTON-ON-TEES*

STORNOWAY HIGHLAND MILK CROGAN   56mm   9.00   26.00
(Goss Record. 8th Edition: Page 40)
Inscribed: *Model of Highland Milk Crogan made by Crofters*
at Barvas, Isle of Lewis. Rd. No. 617576.
Matching Arms: *STORNOWAY*
Also found decorated in red overall with black and green drip,
similar in style to C.J. Noke's Sung pattern for Royal Doulton   300.00†
See illustration on jacket rear of *The Price Guide to Arms and*
Decorations on Goss China

STRATFORD-ON-AVON SANCTUARY KNOCKER
in high relief on two-handled mug   Height of detail 62mm   145.00   225.00
(Goss Record. 9th Edition: Page 30)
Inscribed: *Model of the Stratford-on-Avon Sanctuary*
Knocker. Copyright.
Matching Arms: *STRATFORD-ON-AVON*

Stornoway Highland Milk Crogan

Stratford-on-Avon Sanctuary Knocker

Stratford-on-Avon Toby Basin

Stratford-on-Avon Toby Jug

Sunderland Bottle

Swindon Vase

Swiss Cow Bell

Swiss Milk Bucket

Swiss Milk Pot and lid

Swiss Vinegar Bottle

Teignmouth Lighthouse

Tenby Gateway

Model		With any Arms £ p	With Matching Arms £ p

STRATFORD-ON-AVON TOBY BASIN
Multi-coloured   53mm   85.00†
(Goss Record. 8th Edition: Page 35)

STRATFORD-ON-AVON TOBY JUG
Multi-coloured   78mm   75.00†
(Goss Record. 8th Edition: Page 35)
Inscribed: *Model of the Stratford Toby Jug.*
Also, white glazed (Blackpool arms)   78mm   60.00

The above two models are a pair.

During the Goss family ownership of the pottery,
Stratford models could only be obtained from the
Stratford agency. This is why the Shakespeare's
Font is rarely found without matching arms.

SUNDERLAND BOTTLE   58mm   5.50   19.50
(Goss Record. 8th Edition: Page 21 and advertisement
page 65)
Inscribed: *Model of Ancient Bottle in Sunderland Museum.*
Rd. No. 392068. (One example found with *392089)*
Matching Arms: *SUNDERLAND*

SWINDON VASE   55mm   6.50   24.50
(Goss Record. 8th Edition: Page 36)   110mm[1] 14.00   28.00
Inscribed: *Model of Vase dug up near Swindon.*
Matching Arms: *SWINDON*

SWISS COW BELL   51mm   13.00   34.50
(Goss Record. 8th Edition: Page 43)   73mm   19.50   40.00
Inscribed: *Model of Old Swiss Cow Bell.*
Only the 73mm size listed in *The Goss Record.*
The small size is identical to the Southdown Sheep Bell.
This model is incomplete without the loose porcelain
clapper hanging inside it.
Matching Arms: *SWITZERLAND* or any Arms from that
country

SWISS MILK BUCKET   56mm   11.00   34.50
(Goss Record. 8th Edition: Page 43)   82mm   17.50   41.50
Inscribed: *Model of Swiss Milk Bucket. Rd. No. 526385.*
Matching Arms: *SWITZERLAND* or any Arms from that
country

Tewkesbury Saxon Urn

Tintern Ancient Water Bottle

Tonbridge Eastcheap Roman Ewer

Tresco Old Brazier

Tresvannack Ancient Urn

Tuscan Vase, 785, white

Truro Glen Dorgal Cinerary Urn

Twickenham Antique Pope's Pipe

Walmer Roman Vase

Wareham Bottle

Waterlooville Soldier's Water Bottle

Welsh Crochon

Model			With any Arms £ p	With Matching Arms £ p
SWISS MILK POT and lid		82mm	17.00	47.50

SWISS MILK POT and lid — 82mm — 17.00 — 47.50
(Goss Record. 8th Edition: Page 43)
Inscribed: *Model of Old Swiss Milk Pot. Rd. No. 500867.*
Often found cracked in the base.
This model is incomplete without its lid which is
valued at £7.00.
Matching Arms: *SWITZERLAND* or any Arms from that
country

SWISS VINEGAR BOTTLE — Length 75mm — 11.00 — 45.00
(Goss Record. 8th Edition: Page 43)
Inscribed: *Model of Old Swiss Vinegar Bottle. Rd. No. 496832.*
Matching Arms: *SWITZERLAND* or any Arms from that
country

for TEAR BOTTLE
see Caerleon Glass Lachrymatory

TEIGNMOUTH LIGHTHOUSE — 118mm — 65.00 — 82.50
(Goss Record. 8th Edition: Page 20)
Inscribed: *Model of Teignmouth Lighthouse. Rd. No. 622474.*
Matching Arms: *TEIGNMOUTH*

TENBY GATEWAY (a) White glazed — 65mm — 87.50 — 175.00
(b) Brown — 65mm — 175.00 — 275.00
(c) Brown — 65mm — 275.00†
Inscribed: *Model of South West Gateway (known as Five Arches)
in the Town Walls of Tenby. The walls date from the reign of
Edward III about 1328. Copyright.*
Matching Arms: *TENBY*

TEWKESBURY SAXON URN — 45mm — 5.50 — 23.00
(Goss Record. 8th Edition: Page 22)
Inscribed: *Model of Saxon Urn found at the Tolsey,
Tewkesbury. Rd. No. 411451.*
Matching Arms: *TEWKESBURY*

TINTERN ANCIENT WATER BOTTLE — 76mm — 10.50 — 30.00
(Goss Record. 8th Edition: Page 29)
Inscribed: *Model of Ancient Water Bottle found during
excavations for bridge at Brockweir, Tintern. 1907.
Rd. No. 626750.*
Matching Arms: *TINTERN ABBEY* OR *CHEPSTOW*

for TOBY BASIN
see Stratford-on-Avon Toby Basin

Model		With any Arms £ p	With Matching Arms £ p

for TOBY JUG
see Stratford-on-Avon Toby Jug

TONBRIDGE EASTCHEAP ROMAN EWER
63mm 6.50 23.00

(Goss Record. 8th Edition: Page 27)
Inscribed: *Model of Roman Ewer found in Eastcheap London now in Tonbridge Museum. Rd. No. 599334*
Matching Arms: *TONBRIDGE*

TRESCO OLD BRAZIER
69mm 16.00 35.00

(Goss Record. 8th Edition: Page 18)
Inscribed: *Model of the Old Brazier at Tresco formerly the Beacon Light at St. Agnes, Isles of Scilly. Rd. No. 589292.*
Matching Arms: *F ALGERNON DORRIEN-SMITH, LORD PROPRIETOR OF THE ISLES OF SCILLY*

TRESVANNACK ANCIENT URN
55mm 10.50 22.50

(Goss Record. 8th Edition: Page 18)
Inscribed: *Model of Ancient Urn found at Tresvannack, St. Paul, Cornwall. Rd. No. 594378.*
Matching Arms: *PENZANCE (PENSANS A.D.)*

TRURO GLEN DORGAL CINERARY URN
54mm 7.50 26.00

(Goss Record. 8th Edition: Page 18)
Inscribed: *Model of Cinerary Urn found at Glen Dorgal, now in Truro Museum. Rd. No. 594376.*
Matching Arms: *TRURO*

TUSCAN VASE (a) White glazed
150mm 125.00

    (b) Lustre (orange or yellow)
150mm 160.00

Inscribed: *The Tuscan Vase. 785 Copyright.*
It has no matching arms

TWICKENHAM ANTIQUE POPE'S PIPE
(Goss Record. 8th Edition: Page 29)   Length 118mm   30.00 45.00
Inscribed: *Model of Antique Pipe found among the debris of Pope's House at Twickenham.*
Matching Arms: *TWICKENHAM*

for TYG (ONE HANDLE)
see Staffordshire One-Handled Tyg

for TYG (TWO HANDLES)
see Staffordshire Two-Handled Tyg

Model		With any Arms £ p	With Matching Arms £ p

for ULVERSTON, SIR JOHN BARROW'S MONUMENT
see Sir John Barrow's Monument, Ulverston

for URICONIUM EWER (First Period models so marked)
see Shrewsbury Ewer

for WALDEN ABBEY COVERED URN
see Saffron Walden Covered Urn

WALMER ROMAN VASE	65mm	5.50	19.50

(Goss Record. 8th Edition: Page 27)
Inscribed: *Model of Roman Vase. Found at Walmer Lodge.*
Rd. No. 382437.
Matching Arms: *WALMER* OR *DEAL*

WAREHAM BOTTLE	67mm	6.00	19.50

(Goss Record. 8th Edition: Page 21)
Inscribed: *Model of Roman Bottle found at Wareham.*
Rd. No. 500866.
Matching Arms: *WAREHAM*

for WARWICK - GUY'S PORRIDGE POT
see Guy's Porridge Pot

WATERLOOVILLE SOLDIER'S WATER BOTTLE	83mm	17.00	30.00

(Goss Record. 8th Edition: Page 24)
Inscribed: *Model of Army Water Bottle used at the Battle of*
Waterloo. Waterlooville. When the troops came back after
"Waterloo" their first camp was at this place which thus
obtained its name. The original water bottle which is of oak,
bound with brass, was left behind by one of the soldiers.
Rd. No. 638373.
Matching Arms: *WATERLOOVILLE*

Any Welsh arms may be considered matching on Welsh models

WELSH CORACLE	Length 77mm	22.50	30.00

(Goss Record. 8th Edition: Page 39)
Inscribed: *Model of Welsh Coracle. Survival of Ancient*
British wicker and hide boats.
Matching Arms: *LLANGOLLEN* OR *ANY WELSH ARMS*
First Period version plain with inscription on base.
Second Period version with ribbed sides and
inscription on top of seat.
Up until 1903, the Welsh Coracle was called thus and

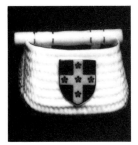

Welsh Fish Basket

Welsh Hat

Welsh Jack and Lid

Welsh Leek

Welsh Milk Can and Lid

Welsh Picyn

Wensleydale Leyburn Leather Jack

Westminster Abbey Coronation Chair, Brown

Weymouth Roman Vase

Whitby Ammonite

Whitby Pillion Stone

Whitstable Roman Patera

Model		With any Arms £ p	With Matching Arms £ p

listed in *The Goss Record* as a national model having no particular town or city arms. From 1904 onwards, it was re-named The Llangollen Coracle with Llangollen given as the matching arms, which explains the confusion of the two descriptions that can be found on the same piece.

WELSH CROCHON

(Goss Record. 8th Edition: Page 39)

Inscribed: *Model of Ancient Welsh Bronze Crochon, about A.D. 400, dug up at Caerhun (Conovium) in collection of W.H. Goss.*

Also see POSTCARDS Chapter 5.

(**N.B.** The Welsh word for cauldron is spelt Crochon)

Matching Arms: *CONWAY*

	50mm	12.50	22.50
	61mm	12.50	25.00
	76mm[1]	17.00	30.00
	107mm[1]	28.50	65.00
	115mm[1]	31.50	75.00

WELSH FISH BASKET   58mm   75.00

Inscribed: *Model of Welsh Fish Basket.*

Matching Arms: *ARMS OF WALES OR ANY WELSH ARMS*

WELSH HAT   (a) Plain brim   Dia. 74mm   17.50   30.00

                 (b) Llanfair P.G. on brim   30.00   45.00

Inscribed: *Model of Hat formerly worn by women in Wales.*

Matching Arms: *ARMS OF WALES OR ANY WELSH ARMS*

WELSH JACK and lid   120mm   19.50   45.00

(Goss Record. 8th Edition: Page 39)

Inscribed: *Model of Welsh Jack.*

This model is not complete without its lid, value £10.00.

Matching Arms: *ARMS OF WALES OR ANY WELSH ARMS*

WELSH LEEK   90mm   19.50   30.00

Inscribed on the base or more commonly, the side: *K. Henry V.*

"The Welshmen did goot servace (at Crecy) in a garden where leeks did grow". Shakespeare.

This model has six leaf tips each coloured green.

Matching Arms: *ARMS OF WALES OR ANY WELSH ARMS OR SHAKESPEARES ARMS*

WELSH MILK CAN and lid

(Goss Record. 8th Edition: Page 39)

Inscribed: *Model of Old Welsh Milk Can.*

The model is incomplete without its lid which is worth £10.00

Matching Arms: *ARMS OF WALES OR ANY WELSH ARMS*

	70mm	15.00	30.00
	108mm	30.00	47.50
	130mm	30.00	56.50
	140mm	30.00	56.50

Model		With any Arms £ p	With Matching Arms £ p

WELSH PICYN   62mm   14.50   30.00
(Goss Record. 8th Edition: Page 39)
Inscribed: *Model of Welsh Picyn or Porridge Bowl.*
Rd. No. 543010.
Matching Arms: *ARMS OF WALES OR ANY WELSH ARMS*

for WELSH PORRIDGE BOWL
see Welsh Picyn

WENSLEYDALE LEYBURN LEATHER JACK   67mm   7.50   30.00
(Goss Record. 8th Edition: Page 38)
Inscribed: *Model of Wensleydale Jack date about 1500 in*
Hornes Museum Leyburn. Rd. No. 521972.
Matching Arms: *LEYBURN*

WESTMINSTER ABBEY CORONATION CHAIR
(Goss Record. 8th Edition: Page 29)
Inscribed: *Model of The Coronation Chair in Westminster*
Abbey. Rd. No. 578694.
See also Perth Coronation Chair
Two varieties, one with hole in rear;
one without and gilded

(a) White	85mm	34.50	56.50
(b) Stone in brown	85mm	82.50	117.50
(c) Brown	85mm	250.00†	285.00
(d) Blue	85mm		unpriced

A blue version is thought to exist, but has not yet been seen.
Matching Arms: *WESTMINSTER ABBEY*

WEYMOUTH ROMAN VASE   56mm   7.50   19.50
(Goss Record. 8th Edition: Page 21   94mm[1]   20.50   32.50
and advertisement page 61)
Inscribed: *Model of Roman Vase found at Jordan Hill,*
Weymouth, now in Dorset Museum.
Matching Arms: *WEYMOUTH*

for WHISKEY CUP
see National Highland Cuach or Wiskey Cup

WHITBY AMMONITE   73mm   34.50   56.50
(Goss Record. 7th Edition: Page 52-Illustrated)
Inscribed: *Model of the Whitby Ammonite. Rd. No. 513063.*
Identical to the rarer Lyme Regis Ammonite
Matching Arms: *WHITBY*

Model		With any Arms £ p	With Matching Arms £ p

WHITBY PILLION STONE Length 72mm 30.00 47.50
(Goss Record. 9th Edition: Page 33)
Inscribed: *Model of Old Pillion Stone Flowergate,*
Whitby. Rd. No. 641311.
Matching Arms: *WHITBY*

for WHITEHALL, CENOTAPH
see (The) Cenotaph, Whitehall

for WHITLEY BAY, ST. MARY'S LIGHTHOUSE
see St. Mary's Lighthouse, Whitley Bay

WHITSTABLE ROMAN PATERA Dia. 88mm 16.00 40.00
(Goss Record. 8th Edition: Page 27)
Inscribed: *Model of Roman Patera about 1600 years old*
dredged up off Whitstable.
Matching Arms: *THE SEAL OF THE CORPORATION*
OF THE DREDGERS OF WHITSTABLE, 1793

WILDERSPOOL ROMAN TETINAE 105mm 95.00
Inscribed: *Model of Roman Tetinae or Feeding Bottle*
found at Wilderspool - Copyright 1924. This model is only
issued to Members of the League and cannot be bought.
International League Model for 1924
Correct Arms: *INTERNATIONAL LEAGUE OF*
  GOSS COLLECTORS.

GOSS IN WINCHESTER
William Savage opened a shop in Winchester in 1839 selling fancy needlework. He was a most enterprising man, typical of many in the Victorian era. His shop was near the Cathedral and when the tourist trade blossomed with the advent of cheap railway travel in the 1850s he began to sell a whole range of Winchester china. This was decorated with transfer prints of local scenes from photographs taken by himself, crests of the Hospital of St. Cross and William of Wykeham, and The Trusty Servant. This china was "published" by himself and produced by the great firm of Copeland. In addition to a wide range of domestic china he stocked models of the Winchester Cathedral Font, the Winchester Bushel and the Leathern Jack (from Winchester College). The last item we now know as the Winchester Flagon.
It must have been through this business that W.H. Goss got to know William Savage. It is probable that William Savage inspired W.H. Goss in the possibilities for the production of souvenir ware. He was one of the first in the country to offer models of "ancient artifacts" and china with local crests and views to the expanding tourist trade.
Although William Savage continued to do business with Copeland after W.H. Goss started up on his own, it is apparent that Goss was producing items for William Savage from a very early date. Copies of the Copeland style Jacks can be found; these are very rare and usually unmarked, but recognisably Goss. This early period also saw the production of the William of Wykeham and St. Cross parian plates, designed by

Wilderspool Roman Tetinae
League Model, 1924

Winchester Bushel

Winchester Flagon

Winchester Jack

Winchester Pot

Winchester Quart

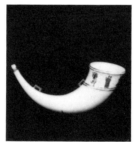

Winchester Castle
Warden's Horn on plinth

Winchester Castle
Warden's Horn

Windsor Round Tower
Two-piece Nightlight

Windsor Urn

Windsor Kettle and Lid
(Queen Charlotte's)

Windleshaw Chantry

252

William Savage himself. The W.H. Goss prizewinning entry in the International Exhibition of 1862 shows a William of Wykeham plate and a Winchester Bushel. Gradually over the years the design of the "Jacks" changed to the one typical of W.H. Goss, and more models were introduced. New models of the Warder's Horn, Cardinal Beaufort's Salt Cellar and Candlestick, the Elizabethan Quart and the magnificent model of the Trusty Servant were introduced.

William Savage died on the 6th April 1887. The contents of his shop were auctioned in July of that year - what an auction to have attended! His niece, Mrs. Fieldwick, took over the Goss agency in July. She only stayed in business for about a year, advertising QUEEN VICTORIA IVORY PORCELAIN as well as the Winchester Memorial China in the local paper.

Although A.L. Henty bought the shop at 58, High Street on the death of William Savage in 1887, he did not become the Goss agent until the middle of 1888 when Mrs. Fieldwick closed. William Savage had catered to the expensive end of the souvenir trade. Henty went more "down market". He introduced more (and cheaper) new models - the Winchester College Black Jacks, the Winchester Pot, the small size Bushel and a wide range of domestic and miniature shapes. It seems probable that the Winchester Flagon was dropped out of production during the Henty period, accounting for its relative rarity. In 1893 he introduced the second Winchester figure, William of Wykeham, to celebrate the Quincentenary (500th anniversary) of Winchester College. Up until 1903 the Winchester models were only available from Henty; after that time they were available to other agents to order with their own crests.

In 1915 Henry closed and Prouten and Dugen, next door, took over the agency and held it until they, in turn, closed in 1926. They had sold cheap, poorer quality crested china for many years before they started to sell Goss china. They do not appear to have introduced any new models during their time as Goss agent.

The agency then passed to Watson and Sons London Bazaar Stores at the other end of the High Street. This was an old established business that had stocked the better ranges of crested ware (Arcadian, Carlton, etc.) A new Goss model that appears about this time is that of King Alfred's Statue. This model does seem to be from a different pattern to the corresponding Willow and Arcadian models (which Watson and Sons had been selling for many years). It was probably produced towards the end of the Second Period at their request. The fine Goss Trusty Servant was also available from Watson and Sons up until the end of the Second Period. It was then replaced by the Arcadian model marked *Goss England*. Watson and Sons were still advertising Goss china in 1939 right up to the closure of the factory.

The story of Goss in Winchester mirrors the Goss story itself. It is very probable that the idea of "Winchester Memorial China" as William Savage called it, was the inspiration for the models, crests and transfers that made W.H. Goss famous. Every period is represented in Winchester Goss, from the earliest, relatively crude parian ware, through the very high quality Second Period pieces and on up to the poorer Third Period. Winchester probably has more varieties of models and more decorations than any other single place, illustrating the rich history of the city.

Model		With any Arms £ p	With Matching Arms £ p

WINCHESTER BUSHEL
(Goss Record. 8th Edition: Page 24)
Decorated with red and blue lettering
in relief, and various symbols.

	100mm across Height 38mm	155.00†	190.00
	Height 51mm	125.00†	265.00
	145mm across Height 65mm[1]	400.00†	500.00

Inscribed: *Reduced Model of Winchester Bushel.*
The largest size is normally unmarked.
Matching Arms: *WINCHESTER*
There is also a rare First Period example, unglazed,
with pale blue legs, brushed gilding, red and blue
lettering in relief. Published by A.L. Henty, and also
a black unglazed version, similarly coloured.

	Both 170mm across Height 70mm[1]		500.00

WINCHESTER FLAGON
This model is not listed in any edition of *The Goss
Record*. It is an unnamed historical shape and tradi-
tional to the first Winchester Agent, W. Savage, who
stocked this model manufactured by the Copeland
works until Goss set up on his own and was able to
meet his requirements.

100mm[1]	26.00	45.00
130mm[1]	26.00	65.00
152mm[1]	36.00	85.00

Characteristics of Goss examples include typical Goss body,
hatched gilding, hollow base; verse lettering type is specific to
Goss, and the lettering style on the base is typical Goss, i.e. upper
case serif italics.
See also FIRST PERIOD 9C ORNAMENTAL WARE
Matching Arms: *WINCHESTER*

WINCHESTER FLAGON   150mm[1]†   250.00
Overall surface decoration representing crinkled leather.
Row of dots in relief around top, base and handle, turquoise blue
line to rim and base. Gilded rim and handle.

for WINCHESTER BLACK JACK
see Winchester Jack

WINCHESTER JACK
(Goss Record. 8th Edition: Page 23)
Inscribed: *Model of the Black Jack at Winchester
College.*
Matching Arms: *WINCHESTER*

32mm	17.50	28.50
44mm	6.50	17.50
83mm	14.00	25.00
121mm[1]	21.50	40.00

WINCHESTER POT   74mm   19.50   26.00
(Goss Record. 8th Edition: Page 24)
Inscribed: *Model of Pot dug up at George Hotel, Winchester.*
Matching Arms: *WINCHESTER*

Model			With any Arms £ p	With Matching Arms £ p
WINCHESTER QUART	92mm†[1]		650.00	

(Goss Record. 8th Edition: Page 24)
Inscribed: *Model of The Winchester Quart Temp. Q. Elizabeth.*
This model is not known bearing a coat of arms, but carries
an embossed crown and 16 01 E.R on its side. It is a
most impressive piece - rare and desirable.

WINCHESTER CASTLE WARDER'S HORN		Length		
(Goss Record. 8th Edition: Page 24)	(a) on plinth†	152mm[1]	565.00	
	(b) without plinth†	152mm[1]	400.00	

Inscribed: *Warder's Horn, Winchester Castle, A.D. 1300.*
Found named as Warder's or Warden's Horn
A magnificent model in either form which carries no arms.

WINDLESHAW CHANTRY		128mm	85.00	160.00

Inscribed in Gothic script around the four edges on the
base:
A Present From Lowe House New Church Bazaar 1920.
surrounding the further inscription:
Model of Windleshaw Chantry, in St. Helens Catholic Burial
Ground. Founded by Sir Thomas Gerard of Bryn, after the Battle
of Agincourt (A.D. 1415), for a Priest to celebrate Mass there for
the souls of his ancestors for ever. The last Priest was Richard
Frodsham, of Wyndle (A.D. 1548).
Matching Arms: *EN DIEU EST MON ESPERANCE*
(Sir Thomas Gerard of Kingsley & Bryn)

WINDSOR KETTLE and lid		170mm	125.00	170.00

(Goss Record. 8th Edition: Page 17)
Inscribed: *Model of Queen Charlotte's Windsor Favourite now*
in William H. Goss's Collection.
This model should have a circular lid with a flat top
surmounted by a round knob. Value £35.00
Matching Arms: *WINDSOR*

WINDSOR ROUND TOWER	(a) Large white†	145mm	430.00	
Two-piece, unglazed night-light	(b) Large brown†	145mm	650.00	
	(c) Large grey†	145mm	525.00	

(This model is illustrated in the
Goss Record. 9th Edition: Page 40, Plate I)
Inscribed: *Round Tower Windsor Rd. No. 209991.*

Wisbech Jug

Winsford Salt Lump

Witch's Cauldron

Worcester Jug

Wymondham Ancient Jar

Yarmouth Ewer

Yarmouth Jug

York Roman Ewer

York Roman Urn

York Roman Vessel

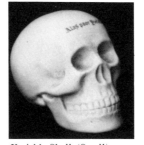

Yorick's Skull (Small)

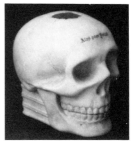

Yorick's Skull (Large)
Two-piece Nightlight

256

Model		With any Arms £ p	With Matching Arms £ p
WINDSOR URN (Goss Record. 8th Edition: Page 16) Inscribed: *Urn found at Old Windsor, from original in Museum.* Matching Arms: *WINDSOR* OR *ETON (FLOREAT ETONA)*	45mm 82mm	7.50 19.50	12.50 26.00
WINSFORD SALT LUMP Inscribed: *Model of Salt Lump as made at Winsford, Cheshire.* This is identical to the Cheshire Salt Block, and appears with the Arms of Winsford either glazed or unglazed (a). A rare variety (b) has been seen with holes for pouring in the top and SALT in Gothic script on the front. Matching Arms: *WINSFORD*	(a) 80mm (b) 80mm		82.50 100.00
WISBECH JUG (Goss Record. 8th Edition: Page 17) Inscribed: *Model of Ancient Jug found at Wisbech River, 1848, in Museum.* Matching Arms: *WISBECH*	82mm[1]	26.00	56.50
WITCH'S CAULDRON (Goss Record. 9th Edition: Page 30) This model is identical to the Peterborough Tripod and carries the following quotation in Gothic Script, with illuminated initial letter D:- *Double double toyle and trouble, Fyre burne and caldrone bubble, Macbeth.* Matching with Scottish, Shakespeare's arms or *STRATFORD-ON-AVON*	47mm	23.00	35.00
WORCESTER JUG (Goss Record. 8th Edition: Page 38) Inscribed: *The Worcester Jug from the original in the Museum, found at Castle Hill.* Matching Arms: *WORCESTER*	64mm 101mm[1]	8.50 14.50	17.50 26.00
WYMONDHAM ANCIENT JAR (Goss Record. 8th Edition: Page 29) Inscribed: *Model of Ancient Jar found in the Abbey ruins Wymondham. Rd. No. 617572.* Matching Arms: *WYMONDHAM*	61mm	12.50	30.00

Model		With any Arms £　p	With Matching Arms £　p

YARMOUTH EWER　　　　　　　　　　62mm　　　5.50　　　15.50
(Goss Record. 8th Edition: Page 29 and advertisement
page 77)
Inscribed: *Model of Early English Ewer dredged up in River
Yare now in Yarmouth Museum. Rd. No. 495671.*
Matching Arms: *GREAT YARMOUTH*

YARMOUTH JUG　　　　　　　　　　132mm　　56.50　　　75.00
(Goss Record. 8th Edition: Page 29 and
advertisement page 77)
Inscribed: *Model of Ancient Jug dredged from the sea off
Great Yarmouth, now in the Museum. Rd. No. 500870.*
Matching Arms: *GREAT YARMOUTH*

YORICK'S SKULL
(Goss Record. 8th Edition: Page 35)
Usually inscribed: *Alas poor Yorick*

(a) Pale yellow†	38mm	75.00	
(b) White unglazed†	75mm	95.50	
(c) Pale yellow†	75mm	170.00	
(d) White unglazed†	102mm	125.00	
(e) Pale yellow†	102mm	175.00	
(f) White glazed†	102mm	130.00	

The 102mm version is in two pieces
and is designed for use as a night-light,
the base modelled as three books.

YORK ROMAN EWER　　　　　　　　63mm　　　5.50　　　20.50
(Goss Record. 8th Edition: Page 38)　127mm[1]　14.50　　30.00
Inscribed: *From original in Hospitium. Found at York.*
see also POSTCARDS Chapter 5
Matching Arms: *YORK*

YORK ROMAN URN　　　　　　　　　51mm　　　5.50　　　15.00
(Goss Record. 8th Edition: Page 38)　101mm[1]　14.50　　30.00
Inscribed: *Roman Urn, from original in Hospitium. Found
at York.*
Matching Arms: *YORK*

YORK ROMAN VESSEL　　　　　　　73mm[1]　16.00　　30.00
(Goss Record. 8th Edition: Page 38)
Inscribed: *Roman Vessel. From original in Hospitium.
Found at York.*
Matching Ams: *YORK*

The Goss China stall at the British Empire Exhibition, Wembley 1925. The shelf of lustre wares shows the factory moving with the times.

William H. Goss, Stoke-on-Trent. England

Manufacturer of the original heraldic and Armorial Ivory ..... Porcelain .....

No. 1 Ancient Jar found in the Abbey ruins, Wymondham. Rd. No. 617572.
No. 2 Leaden Measure, *circa* 1682, found in the old lock up in the Town Hall, Amersham. Rd. No. 626749.
No. 3 Ancient Water Bottle found during excavations for bridge at Brockwier. Rd. No. 626750.
No. 4 Norwegian Bucket. Rd. No. 599332.

No. 5 Coronation Chair in Westminster Abbey. Rd. No. 578694.
No. 6 Orkney Craisie. Rd. No. 559522
No. 7 Ancient Bronze Kettle dug up near Bettws-y-Coed, 1877. Rd. No. 543011.
No. 8 Ancient Vase dredged out of the Thames, near Eton. Rd. No. 539422.

MARK
W.H. GOSS.

There is an Agent in every town, and when asking for this China see it is marked.

A rare advertisement placed by W.H. Goss

F   Cottages and Coloured Buildings

In 1893 Adolphus introduced a new range that was to prove highly successful. These were reproductions in miniature of historic buildings, famous cottages and churches of an exact likeness and colouring. The first seven models were night-lights and those surviving today can often be found with candlewax still inside or with heat cracks as they were sold to be used at bedtime. The smoke came out of hollow chimneys and the light shone out through extra thin porcelain windows and half-open doors when a candle was placed inside. Initially, the three most popular were the famous Shakespeare's Birthplace and Ann Hathaway's Cottage, both at Stratford-on- Avon, and Burns' Cottage, Ayrshire.

Heavy demand for these coloured houses led to the range being gradually extended to 42 buildings with a variety of sizes, some half-size versions and night-light burners. In the latter half of the firm's life, some cottages were glazed and this intensifies the colouring. £20.00 should be added to values for glazed varieties.

Other changes in the moulds occurred when the original buildings that the models were produced from were altered in any significant way. For example, the extensions to The First and Last House at Land's End and Lloyd George's Home, both of which appear in the original and extended forms.

Charles Dickens' House at Gads Hill in Rochester was originally moulded with no porch windows due to ivy completely covering the walls. When the Goss artists discovered that there was a small window either side of the front door after the ivy had been cut away, future models incorporated these windows. Keen collectors of cottages would probably like to have an example of each variation. The coloured houses were not normally crested, but The First and Last House in England can be found with a glass or enamel badge containing the Arms of Cornwall affixed to one end wall. Plain white cottages are rare, and were possibly examples taken home by employees.

There were slight differences in the colours used over the years: hardly surprising with some models like the two Stratford cottages which were in production for over 40 years, and having regard to a succession of different paintresses, new batches of enamels being mixed every week, and differences in firing temperatures. Generally, however, the sizes, colours and moulds were consistent. Most of the cottages were made up from sketches by Adolphus Goss, then later his son, Clarence Richard (Dick), Noel and John Goss (Dick's cousins), and a few of the pottery's best workmen.

The Cat and Fiddle Inn at Buxton was measured up by Noel Goss and a workman Alfred Mollart in 1925, modelled by John Goss and in production all in the same year. John also modelled Isaac Walton's cottage, Shallowford, between 1925 and 1928 using photographs, the original building having burned down completely long before. During the 1920's Noel and Alfred measured up several buildings including the pretty John Knox's House in Edinburgh in 1929.

Several new models were in preparation towards the end, such as the An Clachan in 1938., and the later smaller sizes of Shakespeare's and Hathaway's cottages, which are all Third Period Goss and can be found listed in that section. Designs have been found for Plas Newydd, Llangollen, and Atlantic View Hotel, Lands End, but these have never been seen and it is not now thought that even one example of each exists.

Some of the white glazed buildings, for example, Massachusetts Hall, the Abbot's Kitchen, and the Newquay Huers's House with the Blackpool crest are seconds, although no other variation of the latter piece has been found to date. It has been established that Massachusetts Hall did not go into production in coloured form, but small fragments of it have been unearthed at the site of the factory. Perhaps this model and the Atlantic View Hotel, or maybe even Plas Newydd, will appear in colour in the future, but it is now thought to be doubtful.

Cottages and Buildings in this section have been listed alphabetically by person, town or title. Buildings that are not recorded in this section will appear under SECOND PERIOD 10E or THIRD PERIOD 11.O Chapters.

All sizes are given by length unless otherwise stated.

Old Toll Bar, Gretna Green, over 10,000 marriages performed in the marriage room. Est. 1830. Copyright.
Unglazed, sometimes found not marked W.H. Goss

John Bunyan's Cottage,
Elstow

Robert Burns' Cottage,
Ayrshire, small

Robert Burns' Cottage,
Ayrshire, nightlight

Buxton, Cat and Fiddle Inn

Christchurch, Old Court
House

Charles Dickens' House,
Rochester, no Porch Windows

First and Last House in
England with Annexe

First and Last House, Land's
End

Charles Dickens' House,
Rochester, with Porch Windows

First and Last Post Office, in
England, Sennen

Glastonbury, Church of Joseph
of Arimathoea

Goss Oven, Stoke-on-Trent

£   p

Exceptionally, all dimensions given in this chapter are the length

for ABBOT'S KITCHEN, GLASTONBURY ABBEY
see Glastonbury Abbey, Abbot's Kitchen

for AN CLACHAN COTTAGE
see THIRD PERIOD 11.O BUILDINGS AND MONUMENTS

for ANN HATHAWAY'S COTTAGE, SHOTTERY
see Hathaway's Cottage, Shottery

for ARIMATHŒA, JOSEPH OF
see Glastonbury, Church of

for ATLANTIC VIEW HOTEL, LAND'S END
see Land's End, Atlantic View Hotel

for BEDDGELERT, PRINCE LLEWELYN'S HOUSE
see Prince Llewelyn's House, Beddgelert

for BOURNEMOUTH, PORTMAN LODGE
see Portman Lodge, Bournemouth

(JOHN) BUNYAN'S COTTAGE, ELSTOW	60mm	850.00

Inscribed: *John Bunyan's Cottage, Elstow, Bedfordshire. John Bunyan was born in this Parish in 1628, not far from this spot and lived in this cottage after his marriage in 1649. Copyright.*
Unglazed

(ROBERT) BURNS' COTTAGE, AYRSHIRE
(Goss Record. 8th Edition: Page 40) glazed or unglazed
Inscribed: *Model of Burns' Cottage. Robert Burns the Ayrshire Poet was born on the 25th January A.D. 1759 died 21st July A.D. 1796 aged 37½ years. Rd. No. 211037.*

(a) Small	62mm	105.00
(b) Night-light, blue windows with brown glazing bars	145mm	160.00
(c) as (b) but with no windows, unglazed only	145mm	330.00
(d) Night-light, white, unglazed	150mm	150.00

BUXTON, CAT AND FIDDLE INN	68mm	190.00

Inscribed: *Model of the Cat-and-Fiddle Inn. Nr. Buxton, 1690 feet above sea level, the highest Licensed House in England. Copyright.*
Unglazed

for CHARLES DICKENS' HOUSE, GADS HILL PLACE
see (Charles) Dickens' House, Gads Hill, Rochester

£   p

CHRISTCHURCH, OLD COURT HOUSE   76mm   325.00
(Not listed in any edition of *The Goss Record*, but advertised by
Ritchie & Co. on the back cover of the Eighth Edition.)
Inscribed: *Model of the Old House built 1511 Castle
Street Christchurch, Hants. Copyright.*
Unglazed.

for COCKERMOUTH, WORDSWORTH'S HOUSE
see Wordsworth's Birthplace, Cockermouth

for COURT HOUSE, CHRISTCHURCH
see Christchurch Old Court House

(CHARLES) DICKENS' HOUSE, GADS HILL,
ROCHESTER   65mm   160.00
(Goss Record. 8th Edition: Page 27)
Inscribed: *Model of Charles Dickens' House Gad's Hill,
Rochester. Rd. No. 630367.*
There are two varieties of this model - with and without small
windows on either side of the front door. The value is unaffected.
Unglazed.

for DOVE COTTAGE, GRASMERE
see (William) Wordsworth's Home, Dove Cottage, Grasmere

for ELLEN TERRY'S FARM, TENTERDEN, KENT
see (Miss Ellen) Terry's Farm, Tenterden, Kent.

for FEATHERS HOTEL
see Ledbury, The Feathers Hotel

FIRST AND LAST HOUSE IN ENGLAND
(Goss Record. 8th Edition: Page 18)
Inscribed: *First and Last House in England. Rd. No. 521645.*
Can be found with the badge of Cornwall on one end for which
£20.00 should be added. The small model can be found with either a
green or black door.
This model can be found glazed or unglazed and sometimes
bears the Penzance agent's name, Stevens and Sons, Western
Esplanade, on the base. A box of these cottages was sold from this
shop for 7/6d in the 1960s!

(a) Small, cream or brown roof, green door	64mm	115.00
(b) Small, grey roof, black or green door	64mm	115.00
(c) Night-light, cream roof, green door	117mm	300.00
(d) Night-light, grey roof, black door	117mm	255.00
(e) Night-light, white, green door, brown chimney	117mm	325.00

£   p

FIRST AND LAST HOUSE IN ENGLAND - WITH ANNEXE
Inscribed: *First and Last House in England. Rd. No. 521645.*
Unglazed   140mm   850.00
Can be found with the matching arms of *LAND'S END* on
roof for which £50.00 should be added.

FIRST AND LAST POST OFFICE IN ENGLAND, SENNEN
(Goss Record. 8th Edition: Page 18   73mm   160.00
Inscribed: *Model of the First and Last Post Office in England at*
Sennen, Cornwall. Rd. No. 618950.
Unglazed
Sometimes has the badge of Cornwall on one end for which
£20.00 should be added.

GLASTONBURY ABBEY - THE ABBOT'S KITCHEN
(Goss Record. 9th Edition: Page 26 & 27)
                          Height 88mm Length   70mm
Inscribed: *Model of Abbot's Kitchen Glastonbury Abbey.* (a) Coloured   650.00
Copyright.   (b) White Glazed   110.00
Can be found with either black or brown doors.
Unglazed. The white glazed version has been found with
Blackpool coat of arms applied

GLASTONBURY - CHURCH OF JOSEPH OF
ARIMATHŒA   70mm   800.00
Inscribed: *Model of Church built by Joseph of Arimathoea A.D.*
63 at Glastonbury. The first Christian Church in England. Built
of willows and thatched with rushes, it stood on the site now
occupied by St. Joseph's Chapel, Glastonbury Abbey. From a
drawing in the British Museum. Copyright.
Unglazed

GOSS OVEN
(Goss Record. 9th Edition: Page 27 & 28) (Plate G).
There are two varieties: (a) Orange chimney unglazed   75mm   325.00
                         (b) Brown chimney part-glazed   75mm   325.00
Inscribed: *Model of Oven in which Goss porcelain is fired.*
Copyright.
A descriptive leaflet entitled "The Potter's Oven" was issued
with this model and is valued at £25.00
The ovens were situated in Sturgess Street, Stoke-on-Trent and
are still standing today.

GRETNA GREEN, OLD TOLL BAR   125mm 2200.00
Inscribed in script: *Old Toll Bar, Gretna Green, Over 10,000*
Marriages Performed in the Marriage Room. E$^{ST.}$ 1830.
Copyright.
Unglazed, sometimes found not marked W.H. Goss,
a factor which does not affect the price.

£ p

GULLANE, THE OLD SMITHY   75mm   600.00
(Goss Record. 9th Edition: Page 35 and advertisement
in the 8th Edition: Page 98)
Inscribed: *Model of The Old Smithy, Gullane, N.B. Copyright.*
Unglazed

(THOMAS) HARDY'S BIRTHPLACE, DORCHESTER
(Goss Record. 9th Edition: Page 14)   100mm   350.00
Inscribed: *Model of Birthplace of Thomas Hardy*
"The Wessex Poet" Dorchester. Copyright.
Unglazed

(ANN) HATHAWAY'S COTTAGE, SHOTTERY
Goss Record. 8th Edition: Page 35)
Inscribed: *Model of Ann Hathaway's Cottage Shottery Near*
Stratford-on-Avon. Rd. No. 208047.
Glazed or unglazed
                           (a) Small   64mm   87.50
                           (b) Night-light   148mm   170.00
                           (c) Night-light white unglazed only   148mm   265.00
This model was in constant production from the mid-1890's and
minor variations occurred as moulds were replaced.
Such variations do not affect values. The above are the only models
produced from Goss moulds.
For later examples see THIRD PERIOD 11.O BUILDINGS
AND MONUMENTS.

for HEADCORN HOP KILN
see Hop Kiln, Headcorn, Kent

HOLDEN CHAPEL, HARVARD UNIVERSITY,
CAMBRIDGE, MASSACHUSETTS, USA
(Goss Record. 8th Edition: Page 43)   137mm 2200.00
Inscribed: *Model of Holden Chapel, Built 1744,*
Harvard University. Cambridge, Mass. Rd. No. 643867.
Jones, McDuffee & Stratton Co. 33, Franklin St., Boston, Mass.
Unglazed Night-light.

HOP KILN, HEADCORN, KENT   Height   89mm 1575.00
(Goss Record. 9th Edition: Page 20)
Inscribed: *Model of Hop Kiln, Headcorn, Kent. Copyright.*
Unglazed

for HUER'S HOUSE
see Newquay Huer's House

£   p

for ISAAC WALTON'S COTTAGE or BIRTHPLACE, SHALLOWFORD
see Walton's Cottage, (Birthplace), Shallowford

for JOHN BUNYAN'S COTTAGE, ELSTOW
see Bunyan's Cottage, Elstow

(DR. SAMUEL) JOHNSON'S HOUSE, LICHFIELD   Height   75mm   170.00
(Goss Record. 8th Edition: Page 32)   Length   47mm
Inscribed: *Model of the House at Lichfield in which Dr.*
Samuel Johnson was born. Born 1709 died 1784. Educated at
Lichfield Grammar School Buried in Westminster Abbey.
Rd. No. 605733.
Glazed or unglazed

for JOHN KNOX'S HOUSE, EDINBURGH
see THIRD PERIOD 11.O. BUILDINGS AND MONUMENTS

for JOSEPH OF ARIMATHŒA'S CHURCH
see Glastonbury - Church of

LAND'S END, ATLANTIC VIEW HOTEL   Unpriced
(Goss Record. 8th Edition: Page 18)
Although this model was listed as being in the course of
preparation in the Eighth Edition, it was apparently never
produced, and was omitted from the Ninth Edition of *The Goss*
Record

LEDBURY, THE FEATHERS HOTEL   114mm   800.00
Inscribed: *Model of Feathers Hotel, Ledbury, Copyright.*
Unglazed.
Rumour has it that the Hotel owner purchased the entire
remaining output of this model when the Ledbury agency closed,
and presented them to couples honeymooning at the Hotel.

LEDBURY, OLD MARKET HOUSE   68mm   305.00
(Goss Record. 9th Edition: Page 18. Plate H)
Inscribed: *Model of Ye Old Market House, Ledbury. Copyright.*
Unglazed.

for LLANGOLLEN, PLAS NEWYDD
see Plas Newydd, Llangollen

for LLEWELYN'S HOUSE, BEDDGELERT
see Prince Llewelyn's House, Beddgelert

Glastonbury Abbey, The Abbot's Kitchen

Gullane, The Old Smithy

Thomas Hardy's Birthplace, Dorchester

Ann Hathaway's Cottage, Shottery, small

Ann Hathaway's Cottage, Shottery Night-light

Holden Chapel, Harvard University Cambridge, USA

Hop Kiln, Headcorn, Kent

Dr. Samuel Johnson's House, Lichfield

Ledbury, The Feathers Hotel

Ledbury, Old Market House

(Rt. Hon.) Lloyd George's Early Home without Annexe,

(Rt. Hon.) Lloyd George's Early Home with Annexe,

£   p

(RT.HON.) LLOYD GEORGE'S EARLY HOME   62mm   160.00
Llanystymdwy, Criccieth
(Goss Record. 8th Edition: Page 39)
Inscribed: *Rt. Hon. D. Lloyd George's Early Home*
Llanystymdwy, Criccieth. Rd. No. 617573.
Glazed or unglazed

(RT.HON.) LLOYD GEORGE'S EARLY HOME   102mm   140.00
- WITH ANNEXE, Llanystymdwy, Criccieth
Inscribed: *Rt. Hon. D. Lloyd George's Early Home*
Llanystymdwy, Criccieth. Rd. No. 617573.
Unglazed

for LOOK-OUT HOUSE
see Newquay Look-Out House

MANX COTTAGE	(a) Small	62mm	125.00
(Goss Record. 8th Edition: Page 26)	(b) Night-light	122mm	170.00

Inscribed: *Model of Manx Cottage. Rd. No. 273243.*
Glazed or unglazed

MASSACHUSETT'S HALL, HARVARD UNIVERSITY,
CAMBRIDGE, USA   175mm   2500.00
(Goss Record. 8th Edition: Page 43)
Inscribed: *Massachusetts Hall 1718-1720. Harvard University*
Cambridge, Mass. Rd. No. 647235.
Jones, McDuffee & Stratton Co. 33, Franklin St.,
Boston, Mass.
The only varieties known to exist are white glazed night-lights and
bear the Blackpool arms. Shards of a coloured variety have been
found on the factory spoil heap, but to date a perfect coloured
example has not come to light.
Found with the Goshawk mark and inscription in blue.

NEWQUAY, HUER'S HOUSE
(Goss Record. 8th Edition: Page 18)	(a) Grey	70mm	170.00
	(b) White	70mm	105.00

Inscribed: *Model of Huer's House*
Newquay Cornwall. Rd. No. 610011.
Glazed and unglazed.

NEWQUAY, LOOK-OUT HOUSE	(a) 4 windows	Height	65mm	125.00
(Goss Record. 8th Edition: Page 18)	(b) 5 windows	Height	65mm	125.00

Inscribed: *Model of Look Out House Newquay, Cornwall.*
Rd. No. 605735.
Glazed only

for OLD COURTHOUSE, CHRISTCHURCH
see Christchurch, Old Courthouse

Manx Cottage

Newquay, Huer's House

Newquay, Look-out House

Old Maids' Cottage, Lee, Devon

Old Thatched Cottage, Poole

Gretna Green, Old Toll Bar

Portman Lodge, Bournemouth

Priest's House, Prestbury

Prince Llewellyn's House, Beddgelert

St. Catherine's Chapel, Abbotsbury

St. Nicholas Chapel, Lantern Hill, Ilfracombe

St. Nicholas Chapel, St. Ives, white glazed

                                                 £   p

OLD MAIDS' COTTAGE, LEE, DEVON   73mm   145.00
(Goss Record. 8th Edition: Page 20)
Inscribed: *Model of Old Maid's Cottage at Lee, Devon.*
Rd. No. 622406.
Glazed or unglazed

for OLD MARKET HOUSE, LEDBURY
see Ledbury - Old Market House

for OLD SMITHY, GULLANE
see Gullane, The Old Smithy

OLD THATCHED COTTAGE, POOLE   68mm   565.00
(Goss Record. 9th Edition: Page 14)
Inscribed: *Model of The Old Thatched Cottage Poole. Copyright.*
Unglazed

for OLD TOLL BAR, GRETNA GREEN
see Gretna Green, Old Toll Bar

PLAS NEWYDD, LLANGOLLEN
(Goss Record. 8th Edition: Page 39)   Unpriced
It is said that seven of these models were produced, and sold by
the local agent. Apparently no more were made, and none have
as yet been discovered.

for POOLE, OLD THATCHED COTTAGE
see Old Thatched Cottage, Poole

PORTMAN LODGE, BOURNEMOUTH   84mm x   72mm   350.00
Inscribed: *Portman Lodge the Second House built in*
Bournemouth. Copyright. Built by Squire Tregonwell about
1810 & called "Tregonwell House". Name altered to "Portman
Lodge" when it was occupied by Lord Portman.
Appears with either open or closed door, or rarely
an aperture.
Unglazed.

PRIEST'S HOUSE, PRESTBURY   Height   71mm   1100.00
Inscribed: *786 Model of the Priests House Prestbury,*   Length   90mm
Cheshire. Copyright.
Unglazed

PRINCE LLEWELYN'S HOUSE, BEDDGELERT   63mm   155.00
(Goss Record. 8th Edition: Page 38)
Inscribed: *Model of Prince Llewelyn's house Beddgelert.*
Rd. No. 594374.
Glazed or unglazed

Shakespeares's House,
Stratford-on-Avon, small

Shakespeare's House,
Half-length

Shakespeare's House, Two-
piece Night-light

Southampton Tudor House

Sulgrave Manor,
Northamptonshire

Miss Ellen Terry's Farm,
Tenterden, Kent

Isaac Walton's Cottage
(Birthplace), Shallowford

A Window in Thrums Night-
light

A Window in Thrums small

William Wordsworth's
Birthplace, Cockermouth

William Wordsworth's Home,
Dove Cottage, Grasmere

Massachusetts Hall, Harvard
University Cambridge, USA

		£ p

ST. CATHERINE'S CHAPEL, ABBOTSBURY   87mm   450.00
(Goss Record. 9th Edition: Page 14)
Inscribed: *Model of St. Catherine's Chapel, Abbotsbury.*
Dorset. Copyright.
Unglazed

for ST. IVES, ANCIENT CHAPEL OF ST. NICHOLAS
see St. Nicholas Chapel, St. Ives

ST. NICHOLAS CHAPEL, LANTERN HILL,
ILFRACOMBE
(Goss Record. 8th Edition: Page 20)   74mm   170.00
Inscribed: *Model of St. Nicholas Chapel, Lantern Hill,*
Ilfracombe, which up to the time of Henry VIII was used
as a Place of Worship for Sailors. Rd. No. 613770.
Glazed or unglazed

ST. NICHOLAS CHAPEL, ST. IVES
(Goss Record. 8th Edition: Page 18)
Inscribed on gable end: *Model of the Ancient Chapel of*
St. Nicholas, St. Ives, Cornwall. Partially destroyed by Order
of the War Office, 1904. Rebuilt & restored by Sir Edward
Hain 1911. Rd. No. 602905.
             (a) White, glazed   55mm   170.00
             (b) Coloured, glazed or unglazed   55mm   220.00

SHAKESPEARE'S HOUSE, STRATFORD-ON-AVON
(Goss Record. 8th Edition: Page 35)
Inscribed: *Model of Shakespeare's House. Rd. No. 225833.*
Many variations in size may be found, both glazed and un-
glazed. These are the only models made from Goss moulds: for
all other sizes see THIRD PERIOD 11.O BUILDINGS AND
MONUMENTS

(a)	Small. Full-length	65mm	87.50
(b)	Small. Full-length	78mm	75.00
(c)	Medium. Full-length	110mm	95.00
(d)	Medium. Full-length	140mm	105.00
(e)	Night-light. Full-length. Coloured	185mm	160.00
(f)	Night-light. Full length. White unglazed	185mm	180.00
(g)	Small. Half-length open door.	70mm	95.00
(h)	Small. Half-length closed door.	70mm	140.00
(i)	Large. Half-length closed door	83mm	140.00
(j)	Night-light. Half-length. Separate base. Coloured	105mm	120.00
(k)	Night-light, Half-length. Separate base. White unglazed	105mm	110.00
(l)	Night-light, two piece, First Period impressed mark only so obviously a trial piece [1]	115mm	150.00
(m)	Night-light, half length, separate base, coloured (no threshold at base of door opening)	122mm	220.00

£   p

SOUTHAMPTON TUDOR HOUSE   83mm   350.00
(Goss Record. 8th Edition: Page 23)
Inscribed: *Tudor House, Southampton, Built 1535. Its Royal Visitors.*
If only the old house itself could speak what stories it could tell of the doings
of the dozen generations who have dwelt within its walls or have passed
athwart the Square beneath its windows. Tradition associates it doubtfully
with two Royal visits. Henry VIII is said to have brought Anne Boleyn
beneath its roof. Philip of Spain is supposed to have made it his lodging
during his three days sojourn in Southampton (20th to 23rd July, 1554)
prior to his marriage with Queen Mary at Winchester. It is impossible at
this late day either to confirm or disprove these legends. There is nothing
impossible or even improbable in either of them. Copyright.
Unglazed

SULGRAVE MANOR, NORTHAMPTONSHIRE
(Goss Record. 8th Edition: Page 30)   Overall length   125mm   1100.00
Inscribed: *Model of Sulgrave Manor, Co. Northampton, England.*
Rd. No. 638372. Lawrence Washington had A Grant of Sulgrave 30 Hen.
VIII. His great-grandson John Washington went to America about 1657
and was the great-grandfather of George Washington.
There are many restored and few perfect examples of this model,
which means that sub-standard models are worth less than half of
the perfect price.
Unglazed.

(MISS ELLEN) TERRY'S FARM, TENTERDEN, KENT.
(Goss Record. 8th Edition: Page 27)   70mm   325.00
Inscribed: *Model of Miss Ellen Terry's Farm near Tenterden,*
Kent. Rd. No. 641313.
This cottage is unglazed with a glazed, brown roof.

for THOMAS HARDY'S HOUSE
see Hardy's Birthplace.

(ISAAC) WALTON'S COTTAGE (BIRTHPLACE), SHALLOWFORD
Inscribed: *Model of Isaac Walton's Birthplace, Shallowford.*
There are two sizes of this model, but the variations   (a)   86mm   400.00
in size are minimal. The larger size is numbered 834.   (b)   95mm   700.00
Unglazed

A WINDOW IN THRUMS   (a) Small   60mm   155.00
(Goss Record. 8th Edition: Page 40)   (b) Night-light   130mm   300.00
Inscribed: *"A Window in Thrums". Rd. No. 322142.*
Both varieties found glazed and unglazed.
This cottage in Kirriemuir was the subject of a novel by
author J.M. Barrie

£   p

(WILLIAM) WORDSWORTH'S BIRTHPLACE, COCKERMOUTH

(Goss Record. 8th Edition: Page 18)   81mm   225.00
Inscribed: *Model of Wordsworth's Birthplace Cockermouth.*
Rd. No. 639535.
Unglazed

(WILLIAM) WORDSWORTH'S HOME, DOVE COTTAGE, GRASMERE

(Goss Record. 9th Edition: Page 31)   Overall length   102mm   425.00
Inscribed: *Model of Dove Cottage, Grasmere. The Home of*
Wordsworth 1799 to 1808. Now the Wordsworth Memorial
Copyright.
Unglazed

Model of Dove Cottage, Grasmere. The Home of Wordsworth 1799 to 1808. Now the Wordsworth Memorial. Copyright.

G   Crosses

The unglazed brown crosses are nearly all pre-1900. Possibly the first cross was the Sandbach model, which was made in three parts, the two crosses being held to the base with large corks. William Henry Goss himself was very fond of the Sandbach crosses and often paid them a visit. The chosen originals were usually in the country and well off the beaten track. This inaccessability to the potential customer may account for their rarity, although they could be obtained at the Stoke Agency of Ritchie and Co as well as agencies local to the site of the original. They were somewhat expensive at up to 4/-, when small crested models sold for between 1/- and 1/6d. each. No brown crosses bore arms, and their colouring was as natural as the artists could make them, with green tinges of moss and brown shading.

The Richmond Market Cross was introduced much later, in 1916, with the St Buryan, St Columb Major and Buxton, being introduced after the Great War. The white glazed and unglazed varieties are also post 1900. Another of Mr Goss's favourite crosses was the St Martin's Cross, Iona, a large stone replica of which was used as his memorial in Hartshill Cemetery, Stoke-upon-Trent.

All crosses are uncrested with the exception of the Richmond Market Place Cross.

Model			With any Arms £ p	With Matching Arms £ p

BAKEWELL ANCIENT CROSS   (a) White 145mm 190.00
(Goss Record. 8th Edition: Page 18) (b) Brown 145mm 255.00
Impressed on front: *Bakewell.*

for BANBURY CROSS
See THIRD PERIOD 11.O - BUILDINGS AND MONUMENTS

BUXTON, OLD MARKET CROSS   Grey 88mm 1350.00
Inscribed: *Old Market Cross, Buxton*

CAMPBELTOWN ANCIENT CROSS   Brown 152mm 615.00
(Goss Record. 8th Edition: Page 40)
Inscribed: *Model of The Campbeltown Cross*

CAREW ANCIENT CROSS
(Goss Record. 9th Edition: Page 34)
Impressed on front: *Carew Near Pembroke.* Inscribed on
front step: *Model of Ancient Cross at Carew, Near Pembroke,*
with inscription in unknown Literature Restored.

(a) White unglazed	150mm	95.00
(b) Brown	150mm	125.00
(c) White glazed	216mm	135.00
(d) Brown	216mm	255.00

EYAM ANCIENT CROSS
(Goss Record. 8th Edition: Page 18)
Impressed on front: *Eyam*

(a) White glazed	168mm	155.00
(b) White unglazed	168mm	185.00
(c) Brown	168mm	300.00

INVERARY - ANCIENT CROSS OF THE NOBLES
(Goss Record. 8th Edition: Page 40)   Brown 145mm 1100.00
Impressed on front: *Inverary Cross.* Inscribed on back:
This is the Cross of the Nobles, viz:- Duncan, McComyn,
Patrick his son and Ludovick the son of Patrick who caused
the Cross to be erected.

for IONA CROSS
see St. Martin's Cross, Iona

Bakewell Ancient Cross

Buxton Old Market Cross

Campbeltown Ancient Cross

Carew Ancient Cross

Eyam Ancient Cross

Llandaff Ancient Cross

St. Martins Cross, Iona

Kirk Braddan Cross

Inverary Ancient Cross of the Nobles

Richmond Market Place Cross

St. Buryan Ancient Cross

St. Columb Major Ancient Cross

278

Model	With any Arms £ p	With Matching Arms £ p

KIRK BRADDAN CROSS
(Goss Record. 8th Edition: Page 26)
Inscribed on back: *Model of Cross at Kirk Bradden I. of Man probably more than 1000 years old.*

(a) Brown	84mm	90.00	
(b) White unglazed	84mm	185.00	
(c) White glazed (Blackpool arms)	84mm	47.50	

LLANDAFF ANCIENT CROSS
(Goss Record. 8th Edition: Page 39)
Impressed on front: *Llandaff.*

(a) White unglazed	147mm	285.00	
(b) Brown	147mm	565.00	

RICHMOND MARKET PLACE CROSS
(Goss Record. 8th Edition: Page 38)
Inscribed: *Model of the Cross in the Market Place, Richmond, Yorkshire. Rebuilt 1771.*

(a) White glazed	130mm	52.50	82.50
(b) Brown	130mm	325.00	

Matching Arms: *RICHMOND (YORKS)*

ST. BURYAN ANCIENT CROSS
Inscribed: *Model of Ancient Cross in St. Buryan Churchyard near Lands-End Cornwall.*

(a) White glazed	43mm	65.00	
(b) White unglazed	43mm	82.50	
(c) Brown	43mm	125.00	

ST. COLUMB MAJOR ANCIENT CROSS
(Goss Record. 8th Edition: Page 18)
Impressed on back: *Model of Ancient Cross in St. Columb Major Churchyard.*

(a) White glazed	90mm	56.50	
(b) White unglazed	90mm	70.00	
(c) Brown	90mm	145.00	

Versions (a) and (b) can be found with the Blackpool arms which would halve their values.

Model		With any Arms £ p	With Matching Arms £ p

ST. IVES ANCIENT CROSS
(Goss Record. 8th Edition: Page 18)
Impressed, bottom front:
St. Ives Cornwall.

(a) White glazed	140mm	285.00	
(b) White unglazed	140mm	190.00	
(c) Brown	140mm	295.00	
(d) White	204mm	220.00	
(e) Brown	204mm	330.00	

ST. MARTIN'S CROSS, IONA
(Goss Record. 8th Edition: Page 40)
Impressed, bottom front:
St. Martin Iona.

(a) White glazed, flat back	142mm	100.00	
(b) Brown, detailed back	142mm	170.00	
(c) White glazed, flat back	216mm	165.00	
(d) White unglazed	216mm	170.00	
(e) Brown, detailed back	216mm	220.00	

SANDBACH CROSSES
(Goss Record. 8th Edition: Page 17)   260mm   1300.00
Impressed on plinth front and back: *Sandbach*
Inscribed underneath: *The Sandbach Crosses*
or, more rarely, in addition *The Great Cross shows the chief truths of Christianity. The small cross is supposed to depict the return of Peada (son of Penda King of Mercia 626 - 656) from Northumbria with his bride Alchfleda, after having embraced Christianity.*
This model is made in three sections, the two crosses being held in place by cork plugs and each section bearing the W H Goss impressed mark.

(a) White unglazed	200mm	1300.00	
(b) Brown	200mm	1500.00	

Sandbach Crosses

St. Ives Ancient Cross

H Fonts

Twelve fonts were produced, none in great numbers, and are highly prized by collectors. Like crosses, the bulk of the fonts were made before 1900 in brown unglazed form. After 1900 other varieties were introduced including white glazed and glazed crested. Between 1904 and 1916 the Avebury, St Iltyd's and St Ives were produced, with the Buckland Monachorum following later in the 1920s.

Shakespeare's Font could only be obtained from the Stratford agency up until 1929 which explains why that particular model is almot always found with matching arms.

Those fonts which were also produced during the First Period are denoted thus: [1]

Hereford Cathedral Font, Brown 96mm

Avebury Ancient Saxon Font (Calne)

Buckland Monachorum Font

Haddon Hall Norman Font

Hereford Cathedral Font

St. Iltyd's Church Font, Llantwit Major

St. Ives Church Ancient Font

St. Martin's Church Font, Canterbury, lidded

St. Martin's Church Font, Canterbury, Dished

St. Martin's Church Font, Canterbury, Open

St. Tudno's Church Font, Llandudno

Southwell Cathedral Font

Stratford-on-Avon Church Font

Model		With any Arms £ p	With Matching Arms £ p

AVEBURY ANCIENT SAXON FONT (CALNE)

(Goss Record. 8th Edition: Page 36 and Page 91
photograph and advertisement)
Inscribed: *Model of Ancient Saxon Font in Avebury Church Near Calne, Wilts. Rd. No. 617575.*

(a) White glazed	86mm	115.00	175.00
(b) Brown†	86mm	350.00	

Matching Arms: *CALNE*

for BARMOUTH, ST. JOHN'S CHURCH FONT

see FIRST PERIOD 9B FIGURES, Angel, kneeling

BUCKLAND MONACHORUM FONT

Inscribed: *Model of Ancient Saxon Font about 1000 years old discovered in foundations of Buckland Monachorum Church in 1857 after being buried 400 years now in St. Paul's Church. Yelverton. Copyright.*

(a) White glazed	75mm	525.00	
(b) White glazed(Blackpool arms)	75mm	435.00	

Matching Arms: *BUCKLAND ABBEY, NR. YELVERTON*

for CALNE FONT

see Avebury Ancient Saxon Font

for CANTERBURY FONT

see St Martin's Church Font, Canterbury

HADDON HALL NORMAN FONT [1]

(Goss Record. 8th Edition: Page 18)
Inscribed: *Model of Norman Font found at Haddon Hall.*

(a) White glazed	92mm	65.00	82.50
(b) Brown†	92mm	305.00	

On the white version, the inscription is in Gothic script on the side, whilst on the brown coloured variety it is printed on the base.
Matching Arms: *BAKEWELL OR DUKE OF RUTLAND,*who once owned the Hall, or *DOROTHY VERNON* (77966 Design) might be considered appropriate, she having inherited Haddon Hall from her father in 1567

Model	With any Arms £ p	With Matching Arms £ p

HEREFORD CATHEDRAL FONT
(Goss Record. 8th Edition: Page 24 and Page 66 photograph)
Inscribed: *Model of Font in Hereford Cathedral. The figures of 12 Apostles were partly erased by the Puritans.*

(a) White glazed	96mm	130.00	155.00
(b) White unglazed†	96mm	300.00	
(c) Brown	96mm	285.00	300.00

Matching Arms: *HEREFORD CATHEDRAL*
OR *SEE OF HEREFORD A.D. 1275*

for LLANTWIT MAJOR NORMAN FONT IN ST. ILTYD'S CHURCH
see St. Iltyd's Church Font (Llantwit Major)

for MONMOUTH FONT
see Warwick Font, Troy House, Monmouth

ST. ILTYD'S CHURCH FONT (LLANTWIT MAJOR)
(Goss Record. 8th Edition: Page 39)
Inscribed: *Model of Norman Font in St. Iltyd's Church, Llantwit Major. Rd. No. 599335*

(a) Brown†	88mm	435.00	
(b) White unglazed†	88mm	830.00	
(c) White glazed, Blackpool Arms	88mm	300.00	
(d) White glazed with Matching Arms of *LLANTWIT MAJOR*	88mm		875.00

ST. IVES CHURCH ANCIENT FONT
(Goss Record. 8th Edition: page 18)
Inscribed: *Model of Ancient Font in St. Ives Church, Cornwall. Rd. No. 594379*

(a) White glazed	88mm	47.50	65.00
(b) White unglazed†	88mm	110.00	
(c) Brown†	88mm	170.00	

Matching Arms: *ST. IVES (CORNWALL)*

ST. MARTIN'S CHURCH FONT, CANTERBURY [1]
(Goss Record. 8th Edition: Page 26)
Inscribed: *Model of Font (Restored) in which King Ethelbert was Baptized by St. Augustine in St. Martin's Church Canterbury.*
The quotation of the inscription can be found to vary from model to model. There are three varieties of this font: Lidded, dished, and open.

Model			With any Arms £ p	With Matching Arms £ p
(a) lidded, white glazed†	75mm	60.00		
(b) lidded, white unglazed†	75mm	75.00		
(c) lidded, brown†	75mm	115.00		
(d) dished, white glazed	69mm	47.50		65.00
(e) open, white glazed†	74mm	52.50		
(f) open, brown†	74mm	115.00		

Matching Arms: *CITY* or *SEE OF CANTERBURY*

ST. TUDNO'S CHURCH FONT, LLANDUDNO
(Goss Record. 8th Edition: Page 91 photograph and advertisement)
Inscribed: *Model of Ancient Font in St. Tudno's Church
Llandudno. Rd. No. 546713.*

(a) White glazed	95mm	47.50		75.00
(b) White unglazed†	95mm	75.00		
(c) Brown†	95mm	215.00		

Matching Arms: *LLANDUDNO*

for SHAKESPEARE'S FONT
see Stratford-on-Avon Church Font

SOUTHWELL CATHEDRAL FONT
(Goss Record. 8th Edition: Page 30)
Inscribed: *Model of Font in Southwell Cathedral.*

(a) White glazed†	95mm	82.50		
(b) White unglazed†	95mm	115.00		
(c) Brown	95mm	300.00		300.00

Matching Arms: *SEE OF SOUTHWELL*

STRATFORD-ON-AVON CHURCH FONT
(Goss Record. 8th Edition: Page 35)

(a) White unglazed	54mm	28.00		30.00
(b) White glazed and gilded (Blackpool)	54mm	20.00		
(c) Brown†	54mm	350.00		

The following inscription appears inside bowl in
Gothic lettering surrounding arms:
Model of Font in which Shakespeare was Baptized
Matching Arms: *STRATFORD-ON-AVON,
SHAKESPEARE'S ARMS* or *SHAKESPEARE'S CHURCH*
During the Goss family ownership of the pottery, the Stratford
models could only be obtained from the Stratford agency. This is
why the Shakespeare's Font is rarely found without matching
arms.

Model	With any Arms £ p	With Matching Arms £ p

for TROY HOUSE FONT
see Warwick Font, Troy House, Monmouth

WARWICK FONT, TROY HOUSE, MONMOUTH [1]
(Goss Record. 8th Edition: Page 36)
Inscribed: *Model of Ancient Font at Troy House, Monmouth.*

(a) White glazed†	55mm	65.00
(b) White unglazed†	55mm	75.00
(c) White glazed but with coloured shields†	55mm	95.00
(d) Brown†	55mm	220.00

WINCHESTER CATHEDRAL FONT [1]

(a) White glazed†	115mm	300.00
(b) White unglazed†	115mm	300.00
(c) Black†	115mm	300.00
(d) White glazed	135mm	350.00
(e) White unglazed	135mm	350.00
(f) Black†	135mm	350.00

Impressed around three sides: *Model of Font in the Cathedral at Winchester.*
This model was made in two sizes: Height 115mm and 135mm
It was produced from a mould originally used by Copeland.

Winchester Cathedral Font large, white, 135mm

Winchester Font, Black, small, 115mm

Warwick Font, Troy House, Monmouth

I   Animals and Birds

The majority of animals were produced during the latter half of the Second Period, mainly in the 1920's. John Goss, youngest son of Huntley, designed most of these, including the lion, rhino, hippo, and a dog lying on a plinth. They were exhibited and sold at the British Empire Exhibition held at Wembley, Middlesex in 1924 and 1925. Of particular interest would have been the Wembley Lion, produced especially for the exhibition and sold bearing the 1925 B.E.E. Motif. Matching Arms are given where known, in the absence of which B.E.E. Wembley are considered correct.

With only four exceptions, Goss animals are not inscribed or named. First Period animals and birds include the Bear and Ragged Staff, Bird on tree stump, Bullock and two sheep group, Cockatoo, Dolphin inkwell, Elephant with howdah, Falcon inkwell, Fox and its prey, House Martins on wall vase nest, Humming Bird wall vase, Lion and Mouse group, Sheep, Squirrel, Swan, and Wren resting on nest. These will be found listed in the FIRST PERIOD 9C ORNAMENTAL AND DOMESTIC Chapter.

After the sale of the Goss pottery in 1929, animals continued to be manufactured during the Third Period until 1934, but not in great numbers. These include Budgerigar, Cats (Black, Cheshire and others), Chicken, Crow (Royston), Dogs (Scottie and others), Fish (plaice), Frog, Hippopotamus, Lion, Monkeys, Owl, Pig, Penguin, Ponies (New Forest and Shetland), Rabbit, Racehorse, Rhinoceros, Swan and Toucan, which will be found listed in the THIRD PERIOD 11R FIGURES AND ANIMALS Chapter.

Aylesbury Duck

Model			With any Arms £ p	With Matching Arms £ p
AYLESBURY DUCK		Length 100mm	220.00	265.00

Inscribed: *Model of the Aylesbury Duck. Copyright.*
Matching Arms: *AYLESBURY*

| **BEAR, POLAR** | (a) Glazed | Length 125mm | 375.00 | |
| | (b) Unglazed | | 375.00 | |

Matching Arms: *B.E.E. WEMBLEY*

for BEAR AND RAGGED STAFF
see FIRST PERIOD 9C ORNAMENTAL Chapter

for BIRD ON TREE STUMP
see FIRST PERIOD 9C ORNAMENTAL Chapter

| **BULL** | Length 135mm | 400.00 | 435.00 |

Matching Arms: *B.E.E. WEMBLEY OR ANY SPANISH ARMS*

for BULLOCK AND TWO SHEEP GROUP
see FIRST PERIOD 9C ORNAMENTAL Chapter

| **CALF** | Length 117mm | 285.00 | 325.00 |

Matching Arms: *B.E.E. WEMBLEY OR COWES*

CHESHIRE CAT
(Goss Record. 9th Edition: Page 1, Plate M)

	(a) Glazed	Length 83mm	160.00	215.00
	(b) Unglazed		160.00	
	(c) Unglazed on glazed base		160.00	

Inscribed *He grins like a Cheshire Cat Chewing Gravel.*
Sometimes marked *Copyright.*
Can be found with red and green colour to eyes and
mouth, for which £20.00 should be added. This cat
often has a firing flaw in one or both ears, which
reduces the price by around one-third.
Matching Arms: *CHESHIRE*

for COCKATOO
see FIRST PERIOD 9C ORNAMENTAL Chapter

| **COW** | Length 135mm | 350.00 | 400.00 |

Matching Arms: *B.E.E. WEMBLEY OR COWES*

| **DOG** | Length 133mm | 475.00 | 495.00 |

See also Prince Llewellyn's Dog
Matching Arms: *B.E.E. WEMBLEY*

Model	With any Arms £ p	With Matching Arms £ p

for ELEPHANT with Howdah
see FIRST PERIOD 9C ORNAMENTAL Chapter

for FOX AND ITS PREY
see FIRST PERIOD 9C ORNAMENTAL Chapter

HIPPOPOTAMUS	Length 127mm	375.00	400.00

Matching Arms: *B.E.E. WEMBLEY*

for HOUSE MARTINS ON WALL VASE NEST
see FIRST PERIOD 9C ORNAMENTAL Chapter

for HUMMING BIRD WALL VASE
see FIRST PERIOD 9C ORNAMENTAL Chapter

KANGAROO	Height 94mm	700.00	800.00

Matching Arms: *B.E.E. WEMBLEY*

for LION AND MOUSE GROUP
see FIRST PERIOD 9C ORNAMENTAL Chapter

LION, STANDING	Length 135mm	350.00	400.00

Matching Arms: *B.E.E. WEMBLEY*

LION, LUCERNE
(Goss Record. 9th Edition: Page 38)
Inscribed: *The Lion of Lucerne. Rd. No. 589059.*

	Length		
(a) White glazed and crested (at front or rear, usually Blackpool)	114mm	47.50	160.00
(b) White glazed with Latin wording	114mm	120.00†	
(c) White unglazed with Latin wording	114mm	110.00	175.00
(d) Brown unglazed with Latin wording	114mm	285.00†	

This model should have a spear protruding 7mm out of
the centre of the back. Often the spear is broken off
level with the lion's back in manufacture and is glazed
over. Beasts without the 7mm spear are worth some
50% less than the varieties priced here.
Latin scription: *Die X Augusti II et III Septembris MDCCXCII*
And on back: *Helvetiorum Fidei Ac Virtuti. Haec sunt nomina eorum
qui ne sacramenti fidem fallerent fortissime pugnantes
ceciderunt soerti amicorum cura cladi superfuerunt.*

(For the origin of the model, and the English translation,
see *The Price Guide to Arms and Decorations on Goss China,* section K2)
(Milestone Publications)
Matching Arms: LUCERNE

Model		With any Arms £ p	With Matching Arms £ p

for LION (SCOTTISH)
see THIRD PERIOD 11R FIGURES AND ANIMALS Chapter

for LION (WEMBLEY)
see Wembley Lion

for LUCERNE LION
see Lion, Lucerne

PENGUIN

	Length		
Inscribed: *Made in England.* (Sometimes missing).			
(a) Black trim around base, black feet, coloured beak	83mm	375.00	475.00
(b) Sandy base, no trim, white feet, black beak	83mm	375.00	475.00
(c) White base, no trim, black feet	83mm	375.00	475.00
(d) All white glazed	83mm	215.00	265.00

The strong Goss family connection with the Falkland
Islands probably prompted the appearance of this model.
Matching Arms: *FALKLAND ISLANDS*

PRINCE LLEWELLYN'S DOG - GELERT
Inscribed on plinth: *Prince Llewellyn's Dog "Gelert".*
This is an identical model to the DOG   Length 133mm   740.00†
listed above, but coloured.

RACEHORSE	Length 120mm	325.00	415.00

Inscribed: *Model of Racehorse* (sometimes missing).
Matching Arms: *NEWMARKET*

RHINOCEROS	Length 129mm	565.00	600.00

Matching Arms: *B.E.E. WEMBLEY*

SHEEP On Plinth	Length 147mm	185.00	220.00

Possible correct arms would be those of any sheep
farming areas, e.g. Tavistock. A First Period
variation of the sheep not on a plinth will be found
in 9C ORNAMENTAL AND DOMESTIC Chapter

SHETLAND PONY	Length 103mm	180.00	235.00

(Goss Record. 9th Edition: Page 36)
The model also appears with arms of places on
Dartmoor and Exmoor and was obviously sold in
these areas as a model of a local pony.
Matching Arms: *LERWICK*

Model	With any Arms £ p	With Matching Arms £ p

for SQUIRREL
see FIRST PERIOD 9C ORNAMENTAL AND DOMESTIC Chapter

for SWAN
see FIRST PERIOD 9C ORNAMENTAL AND DOMESTIC Chapter

TIGER on rocky base	(a) White	Length 170mm	750.00	
	(b) Coloured†	Length 170mm	1300.00	

WEMBLEY LION (Made for the British Empire Exhibition 1925)
Matching Arms:*BRITISH EMPIRE EXHIBITION 1924 OR 1925*   Length 100mm   130.00   200.00

Polar Bear

Bull

Calf

Cheshire Cat

Cow

Dog

Hippopotamus

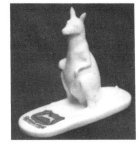

Kangaroo

Standing Lion

The Lion of Lucerne

Penguin

*Prince Llewellyn's Dog,
'Gelert'*

Racehorse

Rhinoceros

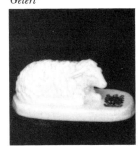

Sheep

Shetland Pony

Tiger on Rocky Base

Wembley Exhibition Lion

The Lion of Lucerne, brown unglazed with Latin wording and 7mm protruding spear

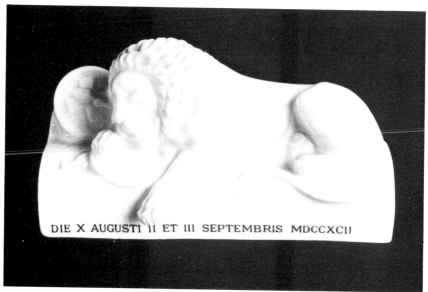

The Lion of Lucerne, white glazed with Latin wording and broken spear missing and glazed over

J Miniatures

The range of Goss miniatures was the result of experiments in the 1860's with eggshell porcelain which was chiefly made by Thomas Boden, a highly skilled craftsman. This range of tiny shapes included a variety of delicate jugs and matching bowls, and tea sets with tiny blue and gold butterfly handles on the cups, less than half an inch high! Yet they were so very strong that even now it is unusual to find a broken miniature.

Llewelynn Jewitt waxed lyrical over his friend's best eggshell porcelain in his *Ceramic Art of Great Britain*, hailing it as:

> Yet another achievement in the plastic art in which W H Goss stood pre-eminent. The pieces produced in this almost ethereal and very difficult ware are so light as to be devoid of gravity, and yet the body is of such extreme hardness and firmness to be as strong as thicker and more massive wares, of a finer and purer body than the Sèvres, thinner and far more translucent than Belleek, more delicate in tone than Worcester and more dainty to the touch than any other, the eggshell produced by Mr. Goss is an achievement in ceramics of which he may be justly proud. Lighter and more delicate than even the shell itself, and of perfect form down to the minutest detail, nature has in this instance been outdone by imitative art. The specimens of Mr. Goss's egg shell porcelain are worthy of a place in the choicest cabinets!

Most of the miniatures are First and Second Period and embrace a choice variety of decorations, the best known perhaps being forget-me-nots. Others include a jug decorated with blue and gold dots which pairs with a plain bowl, thistles, and The Trusty Servant. A later decoration was the Good Luck Shamrock with a horseshoe. Crested miniatures were Third Period and rather thicker and cruder in quality. The Second Period tea sets are particularly sought after. The lid of the tea pot, being so small, is never found factory marked, it being too small to carry the Goshawk.

KEY TO DECORATIONS

A   Forget-Me-Nots with a ring of blue and gold dots on Jugs and Tea Pots.
B   Blackpool or other Coat of Arms
C   No decoration (except blue and gold dots on Jugs and Tea Pots only)
D   Shamrock, Horseshoe and GOOD LUCK
E   Trusty Servant
F   Thistles
G   Shamrocks

Miniature Tea Service on oval tray
Comprising Oval Crinkle Tray, 165mm long, two or four cups and saucers, tea pot with lid, sugar basin and milk jug. Four 38mm Dia. plates can also be found, but are rare, as is the 60mm cake plate.

Miniature Tea Service on square tray

Comprising 70mm square tray, cup and saucer 35mm Dia.,
tea pot with lid, sugar basin and milk jug.
A Tea Pot lid, always unmarked is worth £17.50

Prices for each piece:

Decoration	Tea Pot and Lid Height 35mm	Cup and Saucer Height 16mm	Milk Jug Height 20mm	Sugar Basin Dia. 28mm	Tea Plate Dia. 38mm	Cake Plate Dia. 60mm	Square Tray Width 70mm	Oval Tray Length 165mm	Addition for Complete Set
A	40.00	40.00	34.50	34.50	75.00	110.00	30.00	40.00	40.00
B					30.00		10.00		
C	40.00	30.00	27.50	17.50	50.00				
D	50.00	40.00	23.00	30.00	65.00		25.00		30.00
E	75.00	47.50	40.00	40.00	110.00		30.00	40.00	30.00
F	56.50	56.50	40.00	40.00	110.00[1]		40.00	40.00	40.00

When the Trusty Servant decoration is found on a First Period tray, which is of heavier material, the Trusty Servant verse will be found on the base, but never on a Second Period tray.

Jug and Bowl Set

All sizes are the same price with the exception of the 20mm jug bearing decoration A.
Height of Jug 20mm Diameter of Bowl 35mm

25mm	40mm
30mm	45mm

Each item priced separately. No premium is to be added for a matched pair. The 20mm Jug doubles as the milk jug in tea services.

The large size Bowl can also be found produced from patterns in the Third Period. Such pieces are marked GOSS ENGLAND (See THIRD PERIOD 11S WARE Chapter).

Two very early First Period jugs have been seen. one 22mm, the other 28mm. Both are unglazed and have a floral decoration not previously seen by the author.

Decoration	Bowl £ p	20mm Jug only £ p	40mm & 45mm Jug only £ p
A	30.00	34.50	30.00
B	13.00[3]		
C	17.50	27.50	22.50
D	25.00	23.00	26.00
E	35.00	40.00	40.00
F	35.00	30.00	30.00
G	17.50	30.00	30.00

Miniature Tea Service on Oval Tray, Forget-me-nots

Oval Tray, Forget-me-nots

Miniature Beaker, Trusty Servant

Miniature Tea Service on Square Tray, Trusty Servant

Miniature Tea Plate, Forget-me-nots 38mm

Miniature Vase Two Handles, Shamrock, Horseshoe and Good Luck

Miniature Jug, Thistles

Miniature Bowl, plain

Cup and Saucer, Forget-me-nots

Milk Jug and Sugar Basin, Forget-me-nots

Jug and Bowl. Blue and Gold dots on Jug only.

Tea Pot and lid, Trusty Servant

Vase, Two handled All same price regardless of size   £   p
          20mm
          25mm
          30mm

		£ p
A	Forget-Me-Nots	35.00
B	Blackpool or other Coat of Arms	20.00 [3]
C	No decoration (except blue and gold dots)	26.00
D	Shamrock, Horseshoe and GOOD LUCK	30.00
E	Trusty Servant	40.00
F	Thistles	35.00
G	Shamrocks	30.00

Miniature Beaker

A		19mm	45.00
B		19mm	26.00
E		19mm	75.00

Bottle and Four-beaker set on 70mm square tray
E   325.00

A miniature is not known to have a particular decoration where no letter or price is given.

for Miniature Winchester Jack see
10E HISTORIC MODELS AND SPECIAL SHAPES

Miniature Winchester Jack Trusty Servant   *Miniature Vase, two handles, Forget-me-nots*   *Miniature tea service on oval tray, thistles*

An example of one of Adolphus Goss's travellers photographs with his own notes.

Another of Adolphus Goss's Travellers photographs. The uncrested pieces were his samples.

K Ornamental Articles

Many of the pieces in this section were made during both First and Second Periods. They most naturally fall in the Second Period and to avoid double listing are all shown here. Pieces also produced during the First Period are suffixed thus [1].

Rare group of ten Amphora Vases on circular moulded base with acanthus leaf pattern, height 200mm

Bag Vase 45mm

Frilled shallow Bowl 28mm

Cylinder Vase, Three Tiny Feet 40mm

Early Squat Vase 40mm

Cheese Dish and Cover, Miniature

Bagware Vase 70mm

Bowl, Narrow Base, 35mm

Bagware Tea Pot, Miniature

Club Vase 55mm

Cone Vase 56mm

Wide Taper Vase, vertical rim, Narrow Neck 50mm

Taper Vase, Rounded Base, wide neck 45mm

£   p

1   FAIRY SHAPES UP TO 60mm HIGH:

Bag Vase, Crinkle top	45mm	10.50
Ball Vase, Crinkle top	46mm	7.00
Beaker	40mm	5.50
Bowl, narrow base (identical to Holy Water Bowl page 313	Dia. 55mm Height 35mm	10.00
Bowl. Shallow frilled	28mm	5.50
Cylinder Vase, three small feet	40mm	5.50
Globe Vase, crinkle top [3]	36mm	7.50
Squat Vase, angular sides [1]	40mm	10.00
Squat Vase, angular sides [1]	Dia. 74mm Height 48mm	20.00
Taper Vase Rounded Base, wide neck	45mm	10.00
Taper Vase Rounded Base, small vertical rim	50mm	10.00
Miniature Cheese Dish and Cover (CHEDDAR could be considered matching)	Length 80mm Height 50mm	26.00
Miniature Taper Cup and Saucer	38mm	12.50
Miniature Bagware Tea Pot and lid	White cord 60mm	30.00

2   VASES 50mm TO 75mm HIGH:

Bag Vase with white or coloured cord	(a) White	70mm	15.50
	(b) Blue	70mm	20.50
	(c) Green	70mm	25.75
Ball Vase, crinkle top		55mm	7.50
		71mm	8.25
Ball Vase, crinkle top. With 2 handles		62mm	11.50
Ball Vase, crinkle top. With 3 handles		56mm	15.00
		67mm	25.00
Club Vase		55mm	5.50

Earlier varieties have slightly crinkled rims.

Conical Crinkle Vase, Flat Base 71mm

Conical Crinkle Vase, Rounded Base 70mm

Ball Vase, Crinkle Top 55mm

High-Lipped Ewer 72mm

Jar with Decoration in Relief, or Ali Baba Vase, 57mm

Narrow Taper Vase with Everted Rim 75mm

Thistle Vase, Two Handles 64mm

Trumpet Top Vase, Two Handles 75mm

Urn with Handle 70mm

Wide Taper Vase with Everted Rim 65mm

Ball Vase Two Handles 62mm

Ball Vase Three Handles 76mm

		£	p
Cone Vase	56mm		5.50
Conical Vase, top. Flat base	71mm		7.50
Conical Vase, top. Rounded base	70mm		7.50
High-Lipped Ewer	72mm		5.50
Jar, with decoration in relief. Sometimes called Ali Baba Vase	57mm		7.50
Taper Vase, Squat	64mm		10.00
Taper Vase, Wide, everted rim, wide neck	65mm		10.50
	74mm		10.50
Taper Vase, Narrow with everted rim	75mm		7.50
Thistle Vase. Two Handles	64mm		7.50
Trumpet-top Vase, Crinkle top, Two Handles	75mm		8.00
Urn, Two butterfly handles	70mm		35.00
Urn with or without handle	70mm		7.50

3   VASES 76mm TO 100mm HIGH:

		£	p
Amphora Jar	80mm		16.00
Amphora Vase mounted on three Blue Balls and Plinth	93mm		28.50
Amphora Vase on blue, orange or red coral legs	85mm		26.00
Amphora Vase, with 3 butterfly handles, on 3 coral legs	85mm		40.00
Bag Vase. Narrow	93mm		22.50
Bag Vase, with blue cord [1] Dia. (mouth) 50mm (body) 60mm Height	95mm		30.00
Bag Vase. Circular, wide mouth Dia. (top) 70mm (body) 95mm Height	100mm		35.00
Ball Vase. With two handles	76mm		16.50
Ball Vase. Crinkle top, with three handles	76mm		22.50

Amphora Vase with Three Butterfly Handles 85mm

Amphora Vase on three Blue Balls and plinth 93mm

Amphora Vase on Three Coral Feet 85mm

Amphora Vase, two Butterfly Handles 110mm

Urn with Two Butterfly Handles 85mm

Amphora Vase, two Butterfly Handles, flat base 120mm

Diamond Mouth Vase, with foot 80mm [1]

Diamond Mouthed Vase 80mm

Oviform Vase, Crinkle 80mm

Bulbous, Crinkle Top. Violet Vase curved base 76mm

Oviform Vase, Crinkle Top, Narrow Neck 80mm

Oviform Vase 80mm

		£	p
Bulbous vase, curved base, medium width crinkle top. Known as a Violet Vase by the factory.	76mm	18.00	
Diamond-mouthed Vase [1]	80mm	10.50	
Diamond Vase. Old pattern, with foot [1]	80mm	17.00	
Jar, Flat base, wide top	86mm	10.50	
Lozenge-shaped Vase. With moulded bows at neck. **Oval top** [1] decorated in relief, or flat	86mm	60.00	
Oviform Vase	80mm	9.00	
Oviform Vase, crinkle top, narrow 20mm neck	80mm	12.50	
Oviform Vase with crinkle top	80mm	10.50	
Oviform Vase. With crinkle top and two knobby handles surmounted by butterflies	88mm	45.00	
Oviform Vase. With plain rim and two knobby handles surmounted by butterflies	86mm	45.00	

Taper Vase, wide (a) vertical rim, narrow neck [1]   80mm   10.50
(b) everted rim, narrow neck [1]   80mm   10.50

Taper Vase, rounded base	83mm	9.00
Thistle Vase with pineapple moulding in relief	80mm	11.00
Urn, gourd shaped,with rectangles of dots in bas-relief	82mm	18.00
Urn with two butterfly handles [1]	85mm	40.00
Urn	96mm	7.50

4   VASES OVER 100mm HIGH:

Amphora Vase.   (a) No butterly handles   100mm   30.00
(b) Two butterfly handles   110mm and 120mm   56.50
(c) Three butterfly handles,
    flat base   110mm and 120mm   67.50

Vase, crinkle top, three blue butterfly handles, blue cord to base   110mm   47.50

Ball Vase, crinkle top (No handles)   105mm   40.00
114mm   40.00

Urn 70mm

*Early Lozenge-shaped Vase,
Oval Top 86mm*

*Taper Vase Rounded Base
83mm*

*Thistle Vase, Pineapple
moulding in relief 80mm*

Cone Specimen Vase 117mm

Jar 86mm

Crinkle Top Ball Vase 55mm

*Ball Vase Four Handles,
crinkle top 125mm*

Club Specimen Vase 114mm

Bag Vase Narrow 93mm

*Bag Vase, Blue Cord [1]
93mm*

*Bag Vase, Circular, Wide
Mouth 100mm*

		£	p
Ball Vase, crinkle top, two handles	115mm	40.00	
Ball Vase, crinkle top, four handles	125mm	80.00	
Circular sided Vase with oval top, blue wreath, and pink dot decoration to sides	(a) 118mm	85.00	
	White (b) 118mm	56.50	
Club Specimen Vase	114mm	9.00	
Cone Specimen Vase	117mm	9.00	
Cylindrical Vase, with everted rim Dia. 80mm Height 135mm	40.00	
Four Crinkle Top Vase group	114mm	100.00	
	146mm	125.00	

Ten Amphora Vase Group, crinkle tops, on flat circular base with
beading, and acanthus leaf pattern in relief around the lower base [1] 200mm   200.00

Classical shaped vase in orange lustre numbered 850.
   Dia. 32mm (neck) 90mm (shoulder) 45mm (base)   Height 160mm   70.00

Globe Vase, narrow neck	196mm	30.00
Globe Vase. With two small knurled handles, narrow neck	196mm	45.00
Globe Vase. With three small knurled handles, narrow neck	196mm	47.50
Goblet with central stem	168mm	75.00
Jar, curved base, narrow top	109mm	16.00
Jar, flat base, wide top	105mm	14.50
Lozenge-shaped Vase. Upright with diamond top [1]	139mm	80.00
May be found with bud stopper and cork	160mm	120.00

Oviform Vase, pedestal base, knobby blue handles
   surmounted by butterflies

(a) With 2 handles	115mm	65.00
(b) With 3 handles	115mm	75.00

**Pear Shaped Vase. Flat with rectangular top and
black trim** [1]

	106mm	30.00
	122mm	30.00
	130mm	40.00

Quadruple Amphora Group on Plinth 150mm

Bagware Sack Vase 110mm

Four Ball Group 114mm

Triple Amphora 110mm

Triple Bag and Shell Centrepiece 159mm

Vase, Bell-shaped on Socle Base 203mm

Bulbous Vase with Cup Top and Strap Handle [1] 176mm

Bulbous Vase, Cup Top and 2 Strap Handles [1] 176mm

Globular Vase, Two High Curved Handles 200mm

Taper Vase, 2 High Handles 172mm

Vase, Pear shaped, Balmoral transfer, green grapevine 132mm

Ball Vase, Crinkle Top 114mm

£   p

Pear Shaped Vase as above, with:
      (a) Green grapevine decoration overall with brown
         transfer of Balmoral Castle [1]   132mm   300.00
      (b) Orange grapevine decoration overall with brown
         transfer of Windsor Castle [1]   132mm   300.00

Pompeian Centrepiece On Plinth   125mm   56.50
(Illustrated. Goss Record. 8th Edition: Pages 4 and 75)   340mm   225.00

Pompeian Centrepiece. No plinth.   111mm   70.00

Quadruple Amphora Group. On plinth with intertwined blue
  trim decorated around trefoil base   150mm   125.00

Quadruple Centrepiece with four oval bag vases, central one
  elongated   200mm   200.00
  (Goss Record. 8th Edition: Page 4)

Sack. Bagware. Blue cord   110mm   47.50

Scent bottle-shaped Vase   115mm   11.50
(See also Scent Bottle Domestic 10. L.19 Miscellaneous)

Taper Vase   110mm   16.00

Taper Vase. Crinkle top (no handles) blue cord   107mm   22.50

Taper Vase. Crinkle top.(a) With two blue   (a) 115mm   40.00
  angular handles and blue cord around neck (b) 115mm   30.00
  (b) in white

Taper Vase. With two high angular handles, each
  incorporating a small circular finger grip, fluted,
  everted rim and base   172mm   40.00

Triple Amphora. Three joined vases   110mm   65.00

Triple Bag Vase and Shell Centrepiece. Having three glazed 159mm   200.00
  66mm bag vases fixed together with a cone-shaped
  shell held centrally

Vase   Dia. (base) 45mm (shoulder) 95mm Height 160mm   35.00

Vase. Bell-shaped on socle base. Rare. May also be   203mm   90.00
  found with two handles

Vase. Bulbous. With cup top and strap handle [1]   176mm   50.00
    218mm   65.00

Vase, cylindrical, everted rim 135mm

Taper Vase, Crinkle Top, 2 Blue Handles 115mm

Globe Vase 2 Small Knurled Handles, Narrow Neck

Goblet 168mm

Jar, Curved Base, Narrow Top 109mm

Early Lozenge-shaped Vase, Upright, Diamond Top 139mm

Pear shaped Vase 106mm [1]

Pompeian Centre Piece 340mm

Pompeian Centre Piece 125mm

Bass Basket small 64mm Blue Handles

Bass Basket Medium 80mm Blue Handles

Early, 94mm Bass Basket

		£ p
Vase. Bulbous with cup top and two strap handles [1]	176mm	55.00
	218mm	70.00
Vase, globular with two high handles and circular mouth	200mm	60.00
Vase, Oviform. numbered 849 Dia. 100mm Height	225mm	110.00

5   MISCELLANEOUS ITEMS:

Bass Basket.

The smallest 64mm size has pinched in sides at the centre of the top edges. The largest size is early and carries no arms. The two smaller sizes have turquoise blue handles.

64mm	13.50
80mm	16.00
94mm[1]	26.00

Buttons Circular with central hole

All found unmarked	(a) Unglazed	Dia.	15mm	17.50
	(b) Blue glazed one side	Dia.	15mm	26.00

Cameo Oval with bust of a lady in bas-relief

All found unmarked	White glazed	20mm	35.00

Cigarette Holder not marked, but several have been discovered in the factory spoil heap (See page 32)   Length 75mm   30.00

Disc, circular, probably originally mounted in a silver ring. Dia. 50mm   9.00
see also M - METALWARE

Limpet Shell, coral legs   Dia. 74mm Height 36mm   18.50
see also FIRST PERIOD 9C. ORNAMENTAL Chapter
  for the eggshell variety

Nautilus Shell

Glazed and crested with orange or dull yellow coral legs on white
glazed rocky base   150mm   170.00
See also FIRST PERIOD 9C. ORNAMENTAL Chapter for the
  smaller eggshell variety.

Scallop Shell.	(a)	3 short legs	Length	76mm	13.50
	(b)	on coral legs	Length	76mm	24.50
	(c)	on coral ring	Length	76mm	26.00
	(d)	on yellow coral ring base	Length	76mm	35.00
	(e)	3 short legs	Length	101mm	14.00
	(f)	3 short legs	Length	120mm	15.50
	(g)	no legs	Length	140mm	16.00
	(h)	3 short legs	Length	140mm	16.00

(See also Third Period for W H Goss
England same model as (a) above)

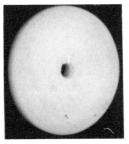

Circular Unglazed Button

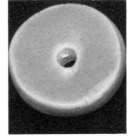

Circular Button. One side Blue Glazed

Oval Cameo

Circular Disc

Limpet Shell, Orange Coral Legs

Nautilus Shell, large 150mm

Scallop Shell on Coral Ring 76mm

Scallop Shell on Three Short Legs 76mm

Pot-pourri Bowl, small 40mm

Pot-pourri Bowl, large, curved top 80mm

Pot-pourri Bowl, large, flat top, gilded rim 80mm

Scarborough Flags Plate 105mm wide

    £   p

Picture Frame, rectangular, containing sepia transfer
of Romsey Abbey Crucifix, made all in one piece.
                     Height 170mm Width 137mm
(a) Wall hanging, with two pierced holes for cord hanging   200.00
(b) Free standing, the stand being 86mm in depth at base   200.00

Pot-pourri Bowl. Small, six holes   Dia. 98mm Height 40mm
        (a) No decoration   17.50
        (b) With central colourful star   30.00

**Pot-pourri Bowl or Rose Bowl. Large. With central
hole and 15 smaller holes.**
(a) With rim gilded around circumference and flat top, star
    decoration around centre hole   80mm   40.00
(b) As above but with no central star decoration   80mm   25.00
(c) Without rim with curved top and star decoration on top   80mm   40.00

Holy Water Bowl, used in a travelling communion
set, with **IHS** in red Gothic lettering on
the side.   (a) Dia. 52mm Height 35mm   20.00
      Also found without lettering   (b) Dia. 52mm Height 35mm   10.00

Travelling Font, white glazed, with **IHS** in gold Gothic lettering
on the side. The piece is similar in style to the Haddon Hall font,
and is found in a leather carrying case lined in blue silk, marked
as sold by *A.R. Mowbray & Co. Ltd. Oxford & London,* inside the
case lid.   Dia. 90mm Height 70mm   200.00

Salt Vase & Pestle so named in Gothic script on a
club vase.   Height 55mm   75.00

Toilet Salt Mortar so named in Gothic script on a circular dish;
an unnamed Roman Mortarium with inscription on base in
handwriting of W.H. Goss extolling the virtues of cleaning the
teeth with ground salt, as follows: Dia. 95mm   75.00
*The very best tooth-powder is table-salt, finely pounded to
prevent bleeding of the gums. It cleanses without scratching,
helps to check decay, and aids sweetness of breath. William H. Goss*

                Above two items priced as a pair   175.00

Salt Vase and Pestle 55mm

Wall Pocket, 75mm

*Flower Holder or Hair Tidy
Wall Pocket 122mm*

Toilet Salt Mortar

Largest Wall Pocket 173mm

Holy Water Stoup

*Toilet Salt Mortar, underside, with inscription in
handwriting of William H. Goss*

*Flower Holder, profile of
Shakespeare in bas-relief 122mm*

Slipper Wall Pocket

£   p

Scarborough Flags Plate. A three-quarter shaped plate,
specially commissioned by J.G. Nairn of Southport.
Having six flags (Japan, France, Russia, Belgium,
Serbia and Montenegro) around the perimeter, and the
Union Jack central. It bears two inscriptions:-

Up, Ye Sons of England, And Wreak Vengeance on the Baby-
Killers of Scarborough around the edge, and *We follow*
You In Our Daily Thoughts On Your Certain Road To Victory.
George R.I. Dec. 5th 1914 around the Union Jack.   Width   105mm   375.00
On reverse. Imprinted with The Royal Arms
and inscribed under: *No. 22794 - A.D. 1913*
Patentee
John Gordon Nairn
"Morland" 84, Promenade
Southport

Manufacturer
W.H. Goss
Stoke-on-Trent
Rd. Nos. 646416-7

The plate has been found with a special fitting metal stand which
appears to have been made for the special shape of the plate.
Curiously, the Nairn Patent No. is dated one year prior to the
outbreak of war. It is assumed that the special shape was on sale as
a display plate or plaque, with other than flags decorations, and
complete with the metal stand, which is probably the subject of the
patent. For the metal stand add £50.00 to the value of the flags
plate.

"SWABS" Plate, Specially Decorated, one of only twelve
produced in bagware, with coloured cartoon of army Medical
Officers, Major Embleton and Major Vernon Goss,
designed by Margaret Goss around 1920, and most of them
unmarked   Dia.   150mm   300.00

(See The Price Guide to Arms and Decorations on Goss China,
Section N.1, Margaret Goss Decorations, for detailed
explanation and description)

£   p

6   WALL POCKETS

Shield-shaped

			£ p
Usually inscribed: *HAIR TIDY*	(a)	60mm	8.50
With arms other than those overall below	(b)	75mm	11.00
	(c)	80mm	13.00
	(d)	92mm	15.50
	(e)	100mm	19.50
Inscribed *FLOWER HOLDER*	(f)	122mm	24.50
	(g)	173mm	45.00

Size (f) is square shield-shaped and inscribed *FLOWER HOLDER* on the back and Rd. No. 201914 which refers to the piece.
Size (g) bearing the crest **E Pluribus Unam** (USA) has been found marked **Emblematic T England,** in addition to the Goshawk mark.

Shield-shaped Wall-pockets or Posy-holders. With arms of Cambridge University, Eton College (with motto: *Floreat Etona)*, Harrow School (with motto: *Stet Fortuna Domus*), Oxford University or Harvard University, Boston, Mass. USA. (Motto: *Veritas*), fully covering piece (Goss Record. 8th Edition: Page 4 includes the Cambridge University and Eton College examples)   173mm   110.00

Slipper. To hang on wall as posy vase   Length   96mm   11.00

Flower Holder with profile of Shakespeare in bas-relief.
Glazed   122mm   170.00

See also 10E HISTORIC MODELS AND SPECIAL SHAPES for Durham Sanctuary Knocker Flowerholder

See also FIRST PERIOD 9C ORNAMENTAL for Humming Bird and House Martins nest Wall Vases

7   HOLY WATER STOUPS

	Height	With any arms	With I.H.S
These are found in five sizes, normally carrying the letters I.H.S. in red at the centre of the cross. This is the familiar monogram of the first three letters of the Greek word for Jesus IHℇOYℇ or the Latin, *Iesus Hominum Salvador.* Some examples carry normal coats of arms. The design comprises a shell-type water container surmounted by a cross pierced for wall-mounting.		£ p	£ p
(a) 124mm	40.00	56.50
(b) 142mm	47.50	65.00
(c) 190mm	52.50	65.00
(d) 219mm	60.00	82.50
(e) 256mm	65.00	90.00

L Domestic and Utility Wares

This section has been arranged into the various headings listed below. Ornamental ware will be found in Chapter K. As these pieces all date from the Second Period, the First or Third Periods should be checked when an item cannot be found. Pieces known to have also been produced during different periods are denoted thus: [1] or [3].

Whenever possible, given names for shapes have been taken from *The Goss Record*. Its compiler J J Jarvis, obtained information from the Goss factory between 1900 and 1921, so that in the absence of any official catalogues, these publications provide the only source of correct terminology. However, reference to the photographs and papers formerly belonging to Adolphus Goss have provided further information. Mugs and loving cups were known at the time of manufacture as ½ pint, pint, quart mugs etc. Domestic shapes too small for daily use have been catalogued in the Ornamental Section as Fairy Shapes, which is how the factory originally termed them.

*High Melon Cup and Saucer
Height 115mm*

*Bagware Cup and Saucer
Height 60mm*

*Low Melon Cup and Saucer
Height 44mm*

Taper Cup and Saucer 69mm

*Straight Sided cup and saucer
70mm [1]*

Coffee Can and Saucer 50mm

*Individual Morning Set
Cup on Platter*

*Octagonal Coffee Cup and
Saucer 62mm*

*Octagonal Sugar Basin
46mm*

*Octagonal Coffee Pot and
Lid 192mm*

Octagonal Milk Jug 77mm

*Cup, two square gilded
handles, 68mm [1]*

Table Ware

1 BAGWARE TEA SERVICE

£   p

This ware is in the form of a tied bag, gathered in by a blue cord
with gilded tassels and having a matching blue cord handle.
Some items have words in illuminated Gothic script emblazoned on the side or lid. Alternatively some cord and handles are
coloured green, orange or yellow; other cord can rarely be found
uncoloured, or red.

Cup and Saucer					50mm	19.50
					60mm	19.50
Cream Jug					60mm	24.50
With red cord Add £10.00					75mm	21.50
Milk Jug					105mm	35.00
					114mm	35.00
Sugar Basin	(a)	Dia. 70mm	Height	45mm	30.00
	(b)	Dia. 88mm	Height	40mm	30.00
	(c)	Dia. 97mm	Height	55mm	30.00
	(d)	Dia. 103mm	Height	47mm	30.00
Bowl	(a)	Dia. 110mm	Height	55mm	32.50
	(b)	Dia. 125mm	Height	70mm	32.50
	(c)	Dia. 140mm	Height	65mm	38.50
Jam Dish and Lid				86mm	33.50
Marmalade Dish and Lid				86mm	26.00
Preserve Jar and Lid		With word HONEY (a)	95mm	19.50
		(b)	105mm	19.50
		With Green Cord (c)	105mm	26.00
Tea Pot and lid				115mm	65.00
				140mm	65.00
				155mm	65.00

for **Miniature Tea Pot** see ORNAMENTAL ARTICLES
K.1 FAIRY SHAPES

Tankard Cream Jug Early, Angular Handle 67mm

Fluted Milk Jug 86mm

Welsh Lady Cream Jug 94mm

Large Frilled Cream Jug 57mm

Manx Legs Cream Jug 67mm

Big-lipped Cream Jug 67mm

Urn-Shaped Cream Jug, Early, Butterfly Handle 65mm

Ball Cream Jug 47mm

Shaped Low Melon Cream Jug 53mm

Shaped High Melon Milk Jug 100mm

Bagware Cream Jug 60mm

Bagware Milk Jug 114mm

		£ p
Tea Plate	Dia. 100mm	9.00
	Dia. 115mm	9.00
	Dia. 125mm	9.00
	Dia. 130mm	10.50
	Dia. 135mm	10.50
	Dia. 150mm	12.50

The 150mm size also appears with a 5mm blue band
around the edge with the gilding inset.   30.00

Cake Plate	Dia. 250mm	26.00

Add around £5.00 for each additional crest.

For Bagware Vases
see 10K ORNAMENTAL ARTICLES Chapter

2   TAPER TEA SERVICE

Cup and Saucer	69mm	8.50
	82mm	9.00

For Miniature Cup and Saucer
see 10 K.1 ORNAMENTAL ARTICLES Chapter

Cream Jug smaller rim	80mm	7.50
	87mm	8.50
	95mm	10.00

Milk Jug smaller rim	108mm	9.50
	124mm	12.50

Jug smaller rim	145mm	30.00
	159mm	30.00
	176mm	45.00

Hot Water Jug smaller rim	(a) with pewter flip lid	155mm	45.00
	(b) with lip and lid	176mm	50.00

Sugar basin smaller base	(a) Dia. 80mm Height	42mm	6.50
shaped, with everted rim	(b) Dia. 85mm Height	48mm	8.50

Slop Bowl smaller base	(a) Dia. 95mm Height	42mm	8.00
With periwinkles in relief	(b) Dia. 97mm Height	46mm	25.00
	(c) Dia. 93mm Height	60mm	9.00
	(d) Dia. 97mm Height	54mm	19.50
	(e) Dia. 125mm Height	60mm	19.50
	(f) Dia. 105mm Height	75mm	10.00

Tea Pot and lid smaller rim	112mm	30.00

Coffee Pot, often named Taper Coffee Pot and lid	118mm	30.00
smaller rim	160mm	45.00

Taper Milk Jug 124mm

Giant 176mm Taper Jug

Upright Cream Jug 100mm

Taper Sugar Basin 48mm

Taper Sugar Basin, everted rim 42mm

Fluted Sugar Basin 58mm

*Ball Sugar Basin
Dia. 88mm Height 55mm*

*Bagware Sugar Basin
Dia. 88mm Height 40mm*

*Bagware Sugar Basin
Dia. 70mm Height 45mm*

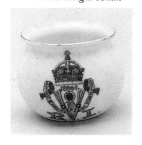

*Ball Sugar Basin
Dia. 72mm Height 55mm*

Taper Sugar Basin 48mm

*Bagware Bowl
Dia. 140mm Height 65mm*

£   p

3   MELON TEA SERVICE

The Melon saucer can be found with four flutes (rare)
instead of the normal nine

Low Melon Cup and Saucer		44mm	8.50
		52mm	10.00
Medium Melon cup and Saucer		55mm	10.00
		75mm	10.00
High Melon Cup and Saucer		70mm	8.50
		115mm	10.00
Low Melon Cream Jug		55mm	8.50
		60mm	9.50
		72mm	11.00
High Melon Milk Jug		87mm	9.50
		100mm	11.00
		118mm	15.00
Hot Water Jug		155mm	30.00
Hot Water Jug with thumb lip and lid		165mm	50.00
Slop Bowl	Dia. 78mm [1]	38mm	9.00
	Dia. 94mm	48mm	9.00
Sugar Basin		42mm	5.50
		54mm	9.00
Tea Pot and lid		93mm	30.00
		114mm	35.00
		140mm	50.00
Tea Plate	Dia.	100mm	7.00
	Dia.	130mm	7.00
	Dia.	150mm	7.00
	Dia.	155mm	7.50
	Dia.	160mm	8.50
Cake Plate	Dia.	250mm	20.00

Add around £5.00 for each additional crest

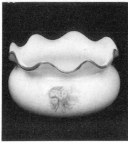

Large Frilled Sugar Basin 35mm

Melon Sugar Basin 42mm

Sugar Basin, Kneeling Manx Legs 67mm

Frilled Sugar Basin 35mm

Bagware Marmalade Dish and Lid 86mm

Circular Tea Pot Stand 102mm

Tea Pot, Globular, Three Small Feet 116mm [1]

Bagware Teapot 140mm

Taper Coffee Pot 160mm

Tea Pot, Kneeling Manz Legs and lid 110mm

Melon Teapot and Lid 114mm

Taper Tea Pot and Lid 112mm

                                                 £   p

4   OCTAGONAL COFFEE SERVICE
With heavily gilded rims and handles

		£ p
Cup and Saucer (See also Royal Buff version, Third Period T.3)	62mm	40.00
Milk Jug	77mm	40.00
Sugar Basin	46mm	40.00
Coffee Pot and lid (See also Royal Buff version, Third Period T.3)	192mm	75.00

5   OTHER CUPS AND SAUCERS
See also 11 S THIRD PERIOD for late examples.

Coffee Can and Saucer	50mm	9.00
Straight-sided Cup and Saucer, square handle [1]	70mm	14.50
Curved Cup and Saucer	70mm	9.50
Two-handled Straight-sided Cup and Saucer **with two blue or gold square handles** [1]	68mm	50.00
Moustache Cup and Saucer	98mm	50.00

6   CREAM AND MILK JUGS
See also 11 S THIRD PERIOD for late examples.

Ball	⅓ pint	45mm	5.50
	¼ pint	55mm	6.50
	½ pint	65mm	9.50
Ball Big-lipped		60mm	9.00
		75mm	11.00
Upright	¾ pint (a)	100mm	16.00
	with verse and crest (b)	100mm	24.50
Fluted angular handle. Sometimes found with blue, orange, pink or yellow handle. Add £10.00	½ pint	86mm	15.00
Frilled	(a) small frills	57mm	11.00
	(b) large frills	57mm	11.00
Kneeling-Manx legs and handle (a) blue or yellow [1] (Rd. No. 149157)	70mm	40.00
	(b) White	70mm	30.00
Tankard with everted rim, angular handle [1]	1/5 pint	67mm	12.00

Tea Plate 125mm [3]

Bagware Teaplate 115mm Dia.

Melon Tea Plate 100mm Dia.

Tea Plate Side View 125mm [3]

Bagware Tea Plate Side View 115mm

Melon Tea Plate Side View 100mm

Coupe Plate 230mm

Scallop Edge plate 112mm

Taper Plate 125mm

Coupe Plate Above 250mm Side View

Bagware Cake Plate 250mm

Child's Feeding Bowl Dia. 130mm

		£ p
Urn-shaped with butterfly handle [1]	65mm	35.00
Welsh Lady (Coloured) Black Hat. Plain or Plaid Red Bodice	94mm	45.00
Impressed on base rim: *Ychydig O Laeth*		

7   SUGAR BASINS

Ball		48mm	5.50
	Dia. 72mm Height	55mm	6.50
	Dia. 88mm Height	55mm	6.50
Curved sided		48mm	6.50
Fluted		58mm	9.00
Frilled	(a) small frills Dia. 85mm Height	35mm	6.50
	(b) large frills Dia. 75mm Height	35mm	6.50
Kneeling-Manx legs (Rd. No. 149157) in yellow		67mm	40.00

8   TEA POTS and lids

Kneeling Manx Legs in yellow, with a Manx leg as a handle to lid	110mm	75.00
Add 20.00 for Manx Coat of Arms		
Globular, having straight spout, curved handle, and 3 small feet [1]	116mm	70.00

9   JUG STANDS

	Dia. 82mm	7.50
	Dia. 102mm	9.00
	Dia. 110mm	9.00
	Dia. 120mm	10.50
	Dia. 144mm	11.50
	Dia. 160mm	14.00

TEA POT STANDS square		
With one Arms	144mm sq	20.00
With up to four Arms and verse	144mm sq	30.00

Bagware Preserve Jar and Lid 105mm

Preserve Jar and Lid, Plain, Crested 110mm

Preserve Jar and Lid, Floral, coloured knop 120mm

Small Preserve jar and Lid, Strawberry knop 100mm

Jar and Lid, Bees and Clover 110mm

Preserve Pot and Lid as Timbered Cottage 115mm

Cheese Dish and Cover with Dolphin Handle 90mm

Butter Dish, Four Fern Leaves, Dia. 143mm

Butter Dish, Waste Not Dia. 143mm

Invalid Feeding Cup 76mm

Jam Dish or Nut Tray Dia. 145mm

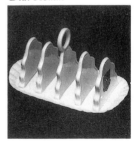

Toast Rack, Four section Length 170mm

£   p

10   PRESERVE JARS AND LIDS

As well as the normal crested variety, these can be
found decorated with colour transfers of the following
fruits, etc. and have either plain white or coloured
fruit knops on the lids.
Spoon cut outs are to be found on either the lid or
the base.

Cylindrical crested	Dia. 57mm	Height 100mm	25.00
	Dia. 72mm	Height 110mm	30.00

Price for either size decorated with:-

Apples (on a branch)	75.00
Blackberries	75.00
Californian Poppies (a) purple (b) yellow	100.00
Country Cottage Garden Scene	80.00
Cherries (on a branch)	75.00
Grapefruit	80.00
Grapes (red and white bunches)	80.00
Honey (bees and clover, clover as knop)	75.00
Lemons	80.00
Life Plant, Bermuda	100.00
Plums	80.00
Strawberries	75.00
Thistles, with thistle knop	80.00

For matching fruit knop: Add £10.00

Appropriately decorated base plates may be found for
the above.   Dia. 110mm   30.00

for Orange-shaped Preserve Jar and lid
See 11S THIRD PERIOD.

for Bagware Preserve Jar and Lid
See 10L I Domestic and Utility Wares

Preserve Jar and lid, green trim, acorn knop in green cup,
   four flat green oak leaves spaced on lid, four outpressed
   green oak leaves spaced around body Dia. 75mm   Height 120mm   100.00

Preserve Jar and lid in the shape of a timbered
   cottage with thatched, or tiled roof   115mm   75.00

Honey Section Dish - Square, decorated with bees and clover
   with bee as knop on lid, square [3]   145mm x 145mm   56.50

Napkin Ring 40mm

Oviform Cruet in Stand 100mm

Beaker 80mm

Taper Beaker with Handle 95mm

Mustard Pot and lid, one handle 60mm

Shaped Sugar Castor 115mm

Porcelain Spoon 150mm

Tea Infuser and Lid 35mm

Shaped Salt Castor 90mm

Trinket Tray small 230mm

Trinket Tray large 310mm

Shaped Pepper Castor 87mm

£   p

11 OTHER ITEMS OF TABLEWARE

			£	p
Beakers (or Tumblers) (For 44mm Fairy size	(a)	80mm	7.50	
see 10 K. 1 ORNAMENTAL	(b)	100mm	8.25	
Note: (a) (b) and (c) varieties occasionally	(c)	115mm	12.50	
found with handles, for which: Add £5.00	(d)	145mm	14.50	
Barrel-shaped	(e)	75mm	19.50	
Lincoln Imp in high relief	(f)	80mm	60.00	

Bowl, octagonal (sometimes in lustre)   Width 128mm   22.50

Bowl, soup or dessert   Dia. 185mm   13.00

Butter Dish WASTE NOT and ears of corn in relief   Dia. 143mm   23.00
on white unglazed rim; the centre dished and glazed.

Butter Dish, four fern leaves in relief,   Dia. 143mm   27.50
centre dished

Butter Dish, in carved wooden surround with   Dia. 150mm   40.00
BUTTER carved around rim. Also with BOURNEMOUTH

Butter Dish circular lid and dolphin   Height 85mm Dia. 140mm   32.50
handle with BUTTER in illuminated lettering

Cheese Dish circular lid and dolphin   Height 90mm Dia. 152mm   32.50
handle, with CHEESE in illuminated lettering

Cheese Dish. In carved wooden surround with
CHEESE carved around rim   Dia. 150mm   40.00

Child's Feeding Bowl   Dia. 130mm   16.50

Dinner Service:
Two 62-piece dinner services were made for the Goss agent in
Malta. Upon his death they passed to his two daughters living
in England. Made from earthenware, each piece carries the
arms of Malta and comprises:

One soup tureen and cover with base plate
Two vegetable dishes and covers with base plates
One meat platter
One gravy boat and stand
One cheese dish and cover
Twelve dinner plates
Twelve side plates
Twelve soup dishes
Twelve dessert bowls

Total value of set   450.00

Egg Cup, Cylindrical 60mm

Egg Cup, Goblet 50mm

Egg Cup on Plate 62mm

Egg Cup, Goblet 58mm [3]

Menu Holder 69mm

Square Tea Pot Stand 144mm square

Oval Crinkle Tray large frills Length 158mm

Round Dish Plain Rim Dia. 78mm

Square Pin Tray with Tassels 70mm [1]

Crinkle Edge Dish Dia. 70mm

Round Dish, with Turned Under Rim Dia. 82mm

Square Pin Tray, Plain, 70mm

		£ p
Dish Oval, fluted. When decorated	200mm	40.00
with strawberries: Add £50.00	250mm	40.00
Egg Cup, Cylindrical	60mm	16.00
Egg Cup, Goblet	50mm	19.50
Several patterns, one scalloped	58mm[3]	19.50
Egg Cup, Mounted on curved tea plate Dia. 100mm	62mm	23.00

for Fruit Basket.
see FIRST PERIOD 9C ORNAMENTAL

Individual Morning Set - Cup on elongated platter [1]	203mm	32.00
Invalid Feeding Cup	110mm	22.50
Jam Dish, twelve sided and crinkle edged Dia.	110mm	16.00
	145mm	16.00
Mustard pot with square handle and domed lid with spoon		
cut out	60mm	20.00
Napkin Ring	40mm	19.50

for Nut Tray - see Jam Dish

Oviform Mustard Pot and lid	60mm	11.50
Oviform Pepper Castor	60mm	11.50
Oviform Salt Castor	60mm	11.50
The above three items are found also in a stand		
with tall handle Price Complete:	100mm	82.50
Plate, crinkle edge	205mm	25.00
	230mm	25.00
Plate, cake, fluted octagonal 236mm x	263mm	25.00
Plate, plain rim	200mm	˙25.00
Plate, scallop edge	112mm	30.00
Plate, Dinner, curved or coupe shape [1]	240mm	19.50
	255mm	25.00

Plate, with violet pattern in relief around rim; in the centre the
arms of *Sir William Wallace.*
Inscribed: *Pub. by W. Middleton Wallace Memorial Stirling* [1]   Dia. 130mm   30.00

Puff Box and Lid 40mm

Pomade Box and Lid 50mm

Hairpin Box, Length 98mm

Candlestick Column 153mm

Candlestick Column 89mm

Candle Bracket 175mm

Tankard Mug, Angular Handle, Everted Rim 73mm

Tankard mug, Taper, Square Handle 85mm [1]

Tankard Mug, Angular Handle 75mm

Picture Frame, one piece, Romsey Abbey Crucifix sepia transfer 170mm

Hair Tidy, Taper and Lid 93mm [1]

Hair Tidy and Lid 93mm

			£ p
Pepper Castor, Shaped - *PEPPER* moulded in blue	87mm		14.50

Salt Castor, Shaped - *SALT* moulded in blue   90mm   14.50
Can be found with either one or several holes in top.   100mm   16.00

Sugar Castor, Shaped - *SUGAR* moulded in blue   115mm   16.00

Spoon, Coat of Arms in bowl   Length 150mm   155.00

for Tankard Mugs
see L.20 LOVING CUPS AND MUGS

Tea Infuser and lid   Dia. 82mm   Height   35mm   20.00
Inscribed on the outside of the bowl: *Tea Infuser Rd. No. 678890*

Toast Rack
  (a) Four section on fluted edge, oval base, with   Length 170mm   40.00
       central circular handle
  (b) Five section   Length 183mm   45.00

Tray elongated and heavy fluted   Length 345mm   40.00

12   TRINKET AND PIN TRAYS

Trinket Tray	(a)	One crest	Length 230mm	22.50
	(b)	Multi-crested		45.00
	(c)	One crest	Length 310mm	30.00
	(d)	Multi-crested		60.00

Oval Crinkle Tray	(a)	With large frills	Length 165mm	12.00
	(b)	With small frills	Length 165mm	12.00

Round Crinkle Dish   Dia.   70mm   5.50
Sometimes found with coral or blue legs   75mm   5.50
when £12.50 should be added   85mm   5.50
       95mm   7.50
       105mm   9.50

Round Dish. Plain rim [1]   Dia.   80mm   10.50

Round Dish. Heavy, with turned-under rim [1]   Dia.   80mm   10.50

Round Dish, very flat, shallow   Dia.   95mm   10.50

Square Tray. Plain   70mm sq   16.50
    See also 10 J MINIATURES

Square Tray. Heavy, with gilded tassel corners   70mm sq   22.50

Crinkle Edge Dish on Three Coral Legs Dia. 75mm

Ring Tree 62mm

Pin Cushion Diameter 78mm

Scent Bottle with Stopper 130mm

Vase, Identical to Scent Bottle 115mm

Shaving Mug 99mm

Lip Salve Pot and Lid, Cylinder 35mm

Lip Salve Pot and Lid, Ball, 33mm

Rectangular Stamp Box and Lid Length 52mm

Cylindrical Pot and Lid, Dia. 90mm

Hat Pin Holder shaped as Candlestick Column 92mm

Night-Light, Frilled base and Globe

£   p

**Square Tray. Heavy with gilded tassel corners, and
hollow base**   (Overall depth 17mm)   75mm sq   29.50

13   BOWLS AND BOXES WITH LIDS

Cylindrical pot [1]   Dia.   90mm   17.50

Lip Salve Box, Ball   Dia. 43mm Height   33mm   9.00

Lip Salve Pot, Cylinder   Dia. 43mm Height   35mm   9.00

Stamp Box, Rectangular
                        Length 52mm Width 40mm Height   18mm   11.00

Puff Box, domed lid   Dia. 82mm Height   40mm   9.00

Pomade Box with small knob on lid   Dia. 62mm Height   50mm   8.50

Rectangular Boxes with decorations in relief on lids
                        Length 98mm Width 52mm Height 35mm

(a)	Glazed, with Forget-me-nots	17.50
(b)	Unglazed	17.50
(c)	Word HAIR-PINS	40.00
(d)	Illustrated hairpins (one or two)	45.00
(e)	Word MATCHES	40.00
(f)	Illustrated matches	45.00

Powder Bowl. Large with shaped knob on lid.
Often found in lustre   Dia. 130mm Height 100mm   40.00

14   CANDLE HOLDERS AND NIGHT-LIGHTS

Candlestick Column   (a)   Plain   90mm   17.50
                                   (b)   Coloured band 127mm   26.00
                                   (c)   Coloured band 153mm   26.00

**Candlestick Column with tapered base and
splayed sconce over central oval decoration**   180mm   75.00

Candle Holder, flat, round, low frilled, with handle Length   110mm   19.50

Candle Holder, flat, oval, high frilled with handle   Length   120mm   19.50

Candle Holder, flat, oval, high frilled, with handle Length   120mm
as above with standing Lincoln Imp on sconce   Height   45mm   60.00

**Candle Holder. Flat, oval, frilled, with handle
and Snuffer**   Length   170mm   50.00

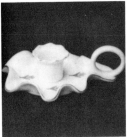

*Candle Holder, Round,
Frilled with Handle 110mm*

*Large Candle Holder and
Snuffer 170mm*

*Candle Holder with Lincoln
Imp 120mm*

*Candle Holder, Oval, Frilled
with Handle 120mm*

*Extinguisher Holder & Snuffer
Round, Frilled with Handle*

*Extinguisher Holder and
Cone Candlesnuffer*

Mitre Candlesnuffer 60mm

Monk Candlesnuffer 82mm

Nun Candlesnuffer 94mm

*Mr. Punch Candlesnuffer
92mm*

*Conical Shell Candlesnuffer
81mm*

*Welsh Lady Candlesnuffer,
white 95mm*

			£ p
Candle Bracket. Shield shaped (To hang on wall)	Height	175mm	55.00
Night-light. Base with handle and Ovoid			
Globe (in two parts) Length 105mm	Height	80mm	100.00
Night-light, Ovoid, Fluted base and Globe	Height	100mm	100.00

For Durham Abbey Knocker, Mary Queen of Scots,
  Windsor Round Tower and Yorick's Skull Night-lights
  see 10 E HISTORIC MODELS AND SPECIAL SHAPES

for Cottage Night-lights
see 10 F COTTAGES AND COLOURED BUILDINGS

15   CANDLESNUFFERS AND STANDS

Cone (round or waved edge)		53mm	10.00
Mitre		60mm	110.00
Monk		82mm	145.00
Nun		94mm	190.00
Mr. Punch		92mm	145.00
Conical Shell		81mm	95.00
Welsh Lady	(a) White glazed	95mm	50.00
	(b) Multi-coloured	95mm	82.50
Extinguisher Holder, on round crinkle dish **with cone candle snuffer**	Dia. 70mm		27.50
Extinguisher Holder, flat, round, frilled **with handle**	Length 110mm		25.00

16   INKWELLS

Inkwell, safety, tapered sides	57mm	19.50
Inkwell, crinkle top, glazed	80mm	22.50

17   MATCH HOLDERS AND TOBACCO JARS

Match Holder, ball-shaped, unglazed	67mm	12.50
	76mm	16.00
Match Holder, ball shaped with hallmarked silver rim, unglazed	68mm	60.00

Safety Inkwell 57mm

Crinkle Top Inkwell 76mm

Match Box Holder 46mm

Match Holder 76mm

Circular Ashtray Dia.115mm

Pipe Tray Length 112mm

Scallop-Edge Fern Pot 92mm (Jardiniére)

Taper Fern Pot on Base 78mm

Double Fern Pot, Two-piece 90mm

Barrel Shaped Mug 74mm [1]

Mug One Square Handle 68mm

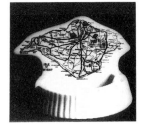

Ashtray with Map of Isle of Wight [3] 70mm

			£ p
Match-box Holder	Height 46mm Length	66mm	75.00
Tobacco jar with word **TOBACCO** on lid or side	(a) 80mm		26.00
	(b)115mm		40.00

18   ASHTRAYS AND PIPE TRAYS

**Ashtray with coloured map of the Isle of Wight standing
    on rear edge of the ribbed dish** [3]   70mm   125.00
Only found with Isle of Wight arms.

Ashtray. Circular, ribbed edge   Dia. 115mm   15.00

Ashtray. Oval with rests at each end
            (a) four thistle sprays in relief   Length 100mm   26.00
            (b) four fern sprays in relief   Length 110mm   26.00

Pipe Tray   Length 112mm   12.50

19   MISCELLANEOUS

Fern Pots
(a) Double Flower pot in circular base to hold water (2-piece)   90mm   30.00
(b) Scallop-edge (Jardinière)   92mm   21.50
(c) Taper, on flat, circular 95mm Dia. base,
    with hole in pot base **(2 piece)**   Height 78mm Dia. (top)   80mm   24.50

Flower Pot, taper   Height 78mm Dia. (top)   80mm   20.00

Flower Pot, taper, indented dots at the top,
no hole in pot base, circular base plate   Height: Pot 76mm Overall   79mm   20.00

Hair Tidy Inscribed: **HAIR TIDY** in blue, with either
forget-me-nots, pink roses, thistles, or leeks and shamrocks on lid
                        Straight Dia. 70mm Height   93mm   19.50
                        Taper Dia. 80mm Height   93mm[1]   19.50

Hat-Pin Holder in shape of candlestick column   92mm   22.50

Menu Holder [1] in shape of square tray with gilded corner
tassels, supported by a moulded back-stand   69mm   22.50

Pin Cushion. Small, squat, wide vase with circular hole in
centre to receive sawdust filling and velvet cover   Dia.   78mm   25.00
See also FIRST PERIOD 9C ORNAMENTAL

Ring Tree   62mm   24.50

*Loving Cup Three Handles
85mm*

*Loving Cup Two Handles
110mm*

*Loving Cup Three Handles
95mm*

*Loving Cup Three Handles
133mm*

*Loving Cup Three Handles
121mm*

*W.H. Goss Profile in High
Relief on Loving Cup 110mm*

One Handle Mug 68mm

*Mug Two Square Handles
76mm*

*Loving Cup Three Handles
95mm*

*Loving Cup Three Square
Handles 38mm*

Mug Two Handles 57mm

**Beaker, Barrel-shaped,
74mm [1]**

		£ p
Scent Bottle with porcelain and cork stopper	130mm	19.50
Shaving Mug	99mm	45.00

20 LOVING CUPS AND MUGS

See also POSTCARDS Chapter 5.

Loving Cups-Three Handled			
Fairy	(a)	38mm	11.00
	(b)	43mm	12.50
Toy	(c)	50mm	14.50
	(d)	57mm	17.50
⅓ Pint	(e)	70mm	19.50
	(f)	78mm	22.50
½ Pint	(g)	83mm	24.50
	(h)	95mm	30.00
Pint	(i)	121mm	56.50
Quart	(j)	133mm	87.50
Covered with separate lid	(k)	133mm	140.00

NOTE: As a variation, some of the above may have square handles for which add £5.00

A loving cup descriptive leaflet can be found and is worth £15.00

Mugs - Two Handled		
(a)	38mm	6.50
(b)	51mm	11.00
(c)	57mm	13.00
(d)	70mm	15.00
(e)	76mm	17.50
(f)	82mm	19.50
(g)	110mm	30.00
(h)	121mm	47.50

NOTE: As a variation, some of the above may have square handles for which add £5.00

Mugs - One handled		
(a)	38mm	5.50
(b)	51mm	8.50
(c)	57mm	9.50
(d)	68mm	11.50
(e)	76mm	12.50
(f)	82mm	17.50
(g)	121mm	35.00

NOTE: As a variation, some of the above may have square handles for which add £2.00

An early factory sales photograph showing part of the range of cream and milk jugs

Early 1880's Adolphus Goss photograph of Loving Cups

		£ p
Barrel-shaped mug, one square handle.	75mm	20.00
With blue handle: add £10.00		

| **Tankard Mug, taper, with everted rim and angular handle** | 73mm | 12.50 |

| **Tankard Mug, taper, no rim** (a) angular handle | 75mm | 12.50 |
| (b) square handle | 85mm | 12.50 |

N.B. See note on Minor Variations in Size. (Chapter 3 -
Notes for the Collector) The items in this section vary
considerably in size and the nearest height should
be taken.

21   MARGARET GOSS DECORATIONS

Normally identifiable by the monogrammed letters
M.G. and the date 1922, 1923, 1924 or 1925. Margaret
Goss was a grand-daughter of William Henry Goss and
daughter of William Huntley Goss. Margaret (known
as Peggy) designed a number of coloured scenes,
usually depicting humourous animal and nursery
rhyme themes for childrens' mugs and plates. See *The
Price Guide to Arms and Decorations on Goss China*, Section
N.1, for the detailed list and additional values.

22   DECORATIONS IN RELIEF

The following may be found on two or three-handled loving cups:

Profile in high relief of **W.H. Goss**
with the arms of W.H. Goss and Stoke Upon Trent   110mm 160.00
(Produced after his death in 1906)
Inscribed in the banner ribbon: *W.H. Goss F.G.S. F.R.MET.SOC.*

In bas-relief Profiles of:

King Edward VII	two handled	90mm	100.00
King Edward VII	three handled	90mm	110.00
King Edward VII	three handled	120mm	125.00
King George V	two handled	90mm	120.00
King George V	three handled	120mm	140.00

These are usually found with corresponding
commemorative devices.

The following decorations in relief may also be found and
details are given in the relevant chapters:-

Durham Abbey Knocker	10E
Mary Queen of Scots	10E
Stratford Sanctuary Knocker	10E
Shakespeare	10K.6
Lincoln Imp Beaker	10L.11

Silver Pin Box, hinged lid, height 45mm, porcelain insert with arms of Calcutta.

Goss Plated Spoon 120mm

Brass Holder 190mm, Porcelain Posy Vase

Copper and Porcelain Dish Dia. 110mm overall

Brass Pipe Rack, length 220mm, with Commemorative Porcelain insert

M   Metalware

A metal teaspoon was produced with the permission of W.H. Goss, bearing the name Goss in the bowl, and having a handle in the shape of the Portland Vase. On the handle was an enamelled coat of arms, usually that of London, but several others are known.

One example has the word SILVER clearly impressed into the shaft but the base metal is obviously nickel-silver, which takes on a dull yellowish hue unless kept regularly polished. Presumably these spoons were originally silver-plated, but time and wear have resulted in many losing the plating.

Production of the spoons is estimated to have taken place from about 1905 until the mid-1920s, and they were made in Birmingham by the firm of Arbuckle (no longer in existence). Arbuckles were large producers of such seaside souvenirs, and the Goss spoons would have represented only a very small portion of the firm's total output. They were retailed by many Goss agents at 1/- each with various coats of arms enamelled in correct colours. Retailers obtained their supplies from the sole wholesale agent, Henry Jones & Co. Ltd., St. Paul's Churchyard, London.

Length of Spoon 120mm   £47.50

See also 10L.11 DOMESTIC AND UTILITY WARES for porcelain spoon.

Brass ornaments, as listed hereunder, can be found with Goss porcelain inserts, usually bearing arms commemorating Queen Victoria's Diamond Jubilee, not of a design found elsewhere on Goss china. The combination of porcelain and brass was the idea of William Henry Goss himself. The brass manufacturer was Harcourt, and a registered number of 128998 is quoted, which indicates a date of 1889. Possibly Harcourts were anticipating the Golden Jubilee, but there are probably other examples with normal coats of arms. (Note: it is necessary to dismantle these items to find the Goshawk/ W.H. Goss mark. Sometimes the corners of the plaques have been trimmed to fit the brass holder by the manufacturer).

Inkstand, ornate, with hinged lid, and glass inkwell insert

160mm sq. Height 135mm   £300.00

Mantel Clock   £125.00

Pipe rack   Length 220mm Height 150mm   £125.00

Posy vase holder   Height 190mm   £100.00

For porcelain 78mm insert Add £22.50 per Metalwork item

In addition to the above brass ornaments, other metal surrounds are found fitted to Goss porcelain items with flat, circular bases, converting them to a variety of ashtrays, pin trays, or tea strainers, examples of which are as follows:-

    (a) Copper dish, raised rim, Flags of the Allies
        decoration. Porcelain fitting   Dia.   70mm
                                     Overall Dia. 110mm   £30.00
    (b) Silver, raised rim. Porcelain fitting decorated
        with coats of arms   £40.00
    (c) Silver pin box, hinged lid. Porcelain insert
        with arms of Calcutta on lid   Height   45mm   £70.00
    (d) Tea Strainer inside EPNS three-legged ring
        supporting EPNS strainer, produced for the
        Canadian market   Dia.   80mm   £25.00
    (e) Tea Strainer, metal, on surround as the top of
        a shallow porcelain dish   Dia.   75mm   £25.00

N Dolls

During the First World War, Huntley Goss manufactured dolls in an attempt to save his ailing factory. He thought that the Goss Factory could become the chief source of supply for porcelain dolls' heads, arms and legs because the German firms could no longer export their ware to Great Britain as trade with the enemy had been cut of since 1914.

It took much time and expense to buy the correct equipment and make the moulds, as well as organise the sales. Goss dolls, with their mohair and beautiful hand painted faces, had only just begun to capture the toy market, despite their high price, when the war ended in November 1918. In no time at all the German factories resumed their highly competitive exports and the English trade tailed off. Noel Goss, eldest son of Huntley, said that the firm did not manage to break even with this line and the extra losses only added to the firm's financial troubles. Manufacture had commenced in 1916 and no more were made after 1918.

Goss dolls can be identified by the word GOSS impressed into the base of the neck at the back, quite unlike any other Goss mark. Under this was a mould number, sometimes prefixed with the letter G. Each doll has an oval purple stamp on the back on the stuffed body incorporating the words TRADEMARK REGISTRATION APPLIED FOR or BRITISH TOY COMPANY around the word WARDOL.

Dolls were made for the British Toy Co., Wardol Works, Stoke-on-Trent, whose doll manufacturing was organised by Mrs. Ritner, wife of the local M.P. The heads were made by W.H. Goss, and the dolls themselves at the Wardol Works where W.H. Goss was also a director.

From head to toe, lengths varied from 160mm to 700mm, depending on whether they were baby, child or girl dolls. All left the Goss factory dressed in Edwardian style clothing with frilly petticoats and lacy outer garments.

Value is dependent on condition, a wig being preferable to moulded hair, and glass eyes more interesting then painted ones. If a doll has its original clothing, it is of higher value than one without.

The following dolls have been recorded to date. The publishers will be pleased to learn of any further varieties for inclusion in future editions of this guide.

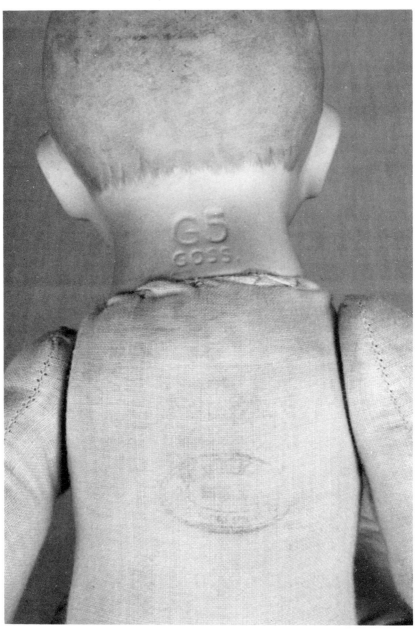

This photograph of the back of doll model G5 shows clearly the model number and factory name impressed into the nape of the neck. Note the oval purple trade mark which will be found on the back of every doll.

Model Number	Type	Length	Hair	Eyes	Arms	Legs
8	Child	700mm	mohair	painted	china	china
8	Child	700mm	mohair	painted	stuffed	stuffed
14	Child	340mm	mohair	painted	china	stuffed
15	Girl	400mm	real	glass	china	china
17	Girl	420mm	mohair	glass	china	china
18	Child	440mm	mohair	glass	china	china
19	Child	650mm	real	glass	china	china
21	Girl	560mm	real	glass	china hands	stuffed
23	Baby	160mm	mohair	glass	china	china
25	Child	440mm	mohair	glass	china	china
30	Child	400mm	mohair	glass	china	stuffed
31	Child	340mm	real	glass	china	china
32	Girl	620mm	real	glass	china	china
35	Child	340mm	real	glass	china	stuffed
36	Child	340mm	real	glass	china	stuffed
G4	Baby	350mm	painted	painted	china	stuffed
G5	Baby	330mm	painted	painted	china	stuffed
G7	Boy	325mm	real	painted	china	stuffed
G9	Child	400mm	mohair	painted	china	stuffed
G10	Child	500mm	mohair	painted	china	stuffed
G12	Child	400mm	mohair wig	painted	china hands	stuffed
G13	Young Boy	230mm	painted	painted	china	stuffed
G13	Baby	265mm	painted	painted	china	stuffed

N.B. The following G4 version does not carry the usual purple stamp, and is the only one found to date with the inscription:
Copyright As Act Directs. W.H. Goss. Stoke on Trent Dec. 1. 15

G4	Child	425mm	painted	painted	china	china

Values range between £450.00 and £650.00

Doll Model 23

Doll Model 15

Doll Model 30

Doll Model 35

Doll Model 31

Doll Model 31

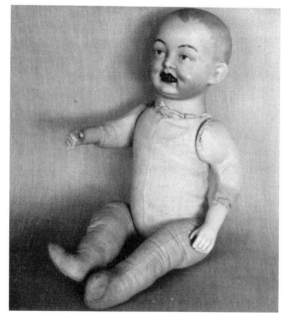

Doll Model G5, unclothed

11   The Third Period 1930-1939

INTRODUCTION
O   BUILDINGS AND MONUMENTS
P   FLOWER GIRLS
Q   TOBY JUGS
R   FIGURES AND ANIMALS
S   ORNAMENTAL ARTICLES AND DOMESTIC
    AND UTILITY WARE
    1. Ornamental Articles
    2. Domestic and Utility Ware
T   W H GOSS COTTAGE POTTERY
    ROYAL BUFF AND BASKET WEAVE
    1. Pieces in the shape of a coloured cottage
    2. Pieces decorated with a cottage scene
    3. Royal Buff
    4. Basket Weave Pottery
U   HAND PAINTED WARE
V   GODFREY WILLIAM GOSS WARE AND
    DECORATIONS

+---+
| **Period Symbols** |
| |
| Where a shape was known to have been made during more |
| than one period, the number in brackets after its entry|
| denotes the other period(s) during which it was |
| manufactured. |
| |
| **The First Period**   [1]   **1858-1887** |
| |
| **The Second Period**   [2]   **1881-1934** |
| |
| **The Third Period**   [3]   **1930-1939** |
+---+

Introduction

Armorial ware continued in production until 1934, and it has been listed as Second Period as the majority of pieces were produced between 1881 and 1929 during the family ownership of the pottery. After 1930, the new owner, Harold Taylor Robinson, renamed the firm The Goss China Co Ltd, and had control over many other crested china firms, including Arcadian, Coronet Ware, Swan, Robinson and Leadbeater, etc. (See *The Price Guide to Crested China* by Nicholas Pine for the full story). Moulds from these other potteries were used at the Goss Works, as well as original Goss moulds. Pieces made during this period include porcelain (glazed parian) and pottery. The latter were glazed on the base, making the Goshawk blacker and darker. This situation continued until 1934, although Robinson was made bankrupt in 1932. After May 1934 when he took over Willow Art, the Goshawk appeared on china from Willow Art moulds. The word ENGLAND appeared on most, but not all, of the factory marks, mainly after 1935. The pattern books of The Goss China Co Ltd were registered in the name of Messrs Allied English Potteries Ltd., and included the Royal Buff designs used on the beige earthenware tea services.

The sales of heraldic ware alone were not enough to keep the firm viable and production began to change to the brightly coloured toby jugs, comical figures and animals, Cottage Pottery tea sets, Royal Buff Ware, and earthenware Commemorative mugs and ashtrays, in an attempt to keep up with changing trends and fashions in the roaring twenties. During the thirties, trade was grinding to a halt and one ex-works manager said at that time, that the predominant products were the famous Goss flower girls, bowls of china flowers and the like, mostly for the American market. In 1939 the factory was closed.

The Goshawk was used during Robinson's ownership in preference to other factory names because Goss had always been the market leader and stood for quality and perfection. The cataloguing of the other factories' wares for the *Price Guide to Crested China* has shown which of the Third Period Goss, or Goss England as it was popularly known, originated from Arcadian, Willow Art etc., the most common ranges being white glazed buildings and black cats.

A large amount of domestic ware, difficult to describe and list, of the late period, is constantly coming to light. All of this is of relatively little value and the reader is advised to refer to the DOMESTIC AND ORNAMENTAL WARE Chapters and to take the value of a similar item for the piece in question.

It should be remembered that all prices in this book are for the *items* of Goss only and *not* for any decorations which may appear on them, details of which can be found in *The Price Guide to Arms and Decorations on Goss China* by Nicholas Pine (Milestone Publications).

Norwich Cathedral

Banbury Cross

Big Ben

Chesterfield Church

Tower Bridge

St. Paul's Cathedral

The Cenotaph, Whitehall

Westminster Abbey, West Front

Temple Bar

Norwich Edith Cavell Memorial

The Old Curiosity Shop

Windsor Round Tower

355

O   Buildings and Monuments

Except where noted, all these models were white-glazed, and
usually carried the appropriate coat of arms. Many of them
can also be found bearing the manufacturer's mark of an
associated company, usually Willow Art or Arcadian.

An Clachan Cottage - in full colour, produced solely
as a souvenir of the 1938 Scottish Empire Exhibition,
Glasgow, at which had been built a full size replica of
this cottage.   Length 100mm   875.00
Inscribed on back: *An Clachan Cottage* and the
Red Lion motif captioned *Empire Exhibition Scotland 1938*
on the base, with the *W H GOSS ENGLAND* mark.

A second version of the **An Clachan Cottage** can also be found
but it is, in fact, the small version of **Robert Burns' Cottage**
merely re-named and, on the example seen, displaying the
motif of the 1938 Exhibition and a W H GOSS ENGLAND mark
                                                        Length 62mm   700.00

Banbury Cross	(a) White with arms	127mm	82.50
	(b) Brown or Blue/Brown	127mm	220.00

Inscribed front plinth or above: *Banbury Cross.*
Inscribed left front plinth: *Ride a Cock Horse to Banbury Cross.*
Inscribed right front plinth: *To see a Fine Lady ride on a White Horse.*

Burns Statue
Seated with dog at feet   170mm   75.00

Bury St. Edmunds Abbey Gateway
(Same as Willow model, but inscribed: *W. H. Goss England)*   80mm   75.00

Big Ben with *Big Ben* inscribed on front of base	103mm	47.50
With some colouring	103mm	56.50
	134mm	52.50
	152mm	56.50
	170mm	65.00

Canterbury Cathedral   64mm   65.00

Cenotaph, Whitehall   90mm   30.00
Inscribed on plinth: *Model of Cenotaph*   145mm   43.50

Chesterfield Church   76mm   75.00

                                                          £   p

Clachan Empire Exhibition Tower and Stadium
Glazed, grey colour, green trimmed dished tray bearing late
colour transfer of the *Empire Exhibition The Clachan*.
Inscribed on base in red: *Empire Exhibition Scotland 1938* and motif.
Also usual Goshawk mark. This model may have been intended
for use as an ashtray.   Length 115mm   Height 135mm   205.00

Clifton Suspension Bridge   Length 170mm   Height   64mm   130.00

Dover Patrol Monument   130mm   65.00

Edith Cavell Monument   100mm   50.00
                                                      180mm   75.00
Inscribed left side: *Humanity*.
Inscribed right side: *Sacrifice*.
Inscribed reverse: *Edith Cavell Nurse Patriot and Martyr*.

(Ann) Hathaway's Cottage, fully coloured   Length   50mm   56.50
Inscribed: *Model of Ann Hathaway's Cottage*   63mm   56.50
Shottery near Stratford-on-Avon Rd. No. 208047.   78mm   56.50
                                                   110mm   70.00
                                                   133mm   82.50
         Cottage Pottery Version   Length 75mm   Height   55mm   100.00

Hindhead Sailor's Stone   95mm   82.50
Inscribed on front: *The Sailors Stone, Hindhead*.
Inscribed on reverse: '*Erected. In detestation of a barbarous
murder committed here on an unknown sailor, on Sept. 24th. 1786.
by Edward Lonegon, Michael Casey and Jas. Marshall, who
were all taken the same day and hung in chains near this place.*
    *"Who so sheddeth man's blood by man shall
    his blood be shed." Gen., Chap. 9 ver.6.'*

Houses of Parliament   64mm   82.50

for King Alfred's Statue
see SECOND PERIOD 10E HISTORIC MODELS AND
SPECIAL SHAPES

John Knox's House in full colour   102mm   375.00
Inscribed: *Model of the house in Edinburgh where John Knox
the Scottish Reformer died 24th Nov. 1572.*

Lighthouse on Rocks   95mm   30.00

Marble Arch, London (found with top glazed and unglazed)   40mm   40.00
                                                       57mm   45.00

Nelson's Column   100mm   82.50

Norwich Cathedral   Length   105mm   95.00

		£ p

Old Curiosity Shop — 46mm — 65.00

Rock of Ages with verses of hymn of the same name on the front. — 79mm — 40.00
Inscribed on side of base: *Model of The Great ROCK OF AGES,*
Burrington Coombe, Near Cheddar Som.

Rock of Gibraltar, menu holder, coloured — Length 160mm — 260.00

Rufus Stone — 100mm — 15.00
For inscription see SECOND PERIOD 10 E HISTORIC
MODELS AND SPECIAL SHAPES

St. Paul's Cathedral — 75mm — 60.00
Inscribed on front step: *St. Paul's Cathedral* — 90mm — 60.00
— 120mm — 65.00

Shakespeare's Birthplace in full colour — Length 40mm — 45.00
Inscribed: *Model of Shakespeare's House.* — 50mm — 56.50
Rd. No. 225833. — 67mm — 75.00
— 78mm — 75.00
— 102mm — 75.00
— 115mm — 80.00
— 130mm — 80.00

Temple Bar — 65mm — 60.00

Tower Bridge — 58mm — 75.00

Westminster Abbey, West Front — 52mm — 52.50
— 73mm — 56.50
— 133mm — 60.00

Westminster Abbey (West Front)
Standing on rear of rectangular ashtray. Gilding to edge of tray,
and tips of tower pinnacles.
Inscribed on rear: *Westminster Abbey* — 85mm — 60.00

"Windsor Round Tower" — 55mm — 55.00
— 76mm — 60.00

York Minster — 56mm — 75.00

Clachan Empire Exhibition Tower and Stadium [3]

An Clachan Cottage

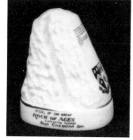

Rock of Ages

Shakespeare's Birthplace

*John Knox's House
Edinburgh*

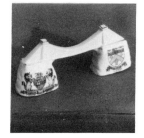

*Clifton Suspension Bridge,
Bristol*

*The Rock of Gibraltar
Menu Holder*

The Bride

The Bridegroom

The Best Man

The Mother-in-Law

The Parson

The Bridesmaid 99mm

P Flower Girls

The brightly coloured porcelain flower girls were the last successful series made by the Goss factory and spanned the 1930s. Several of these were made in two sizes and ranged between the tiny 68mm, often a cruet, and the more elegant 170mm.

All but one of the larger sizes of these ladies are named, the exception being the Bell lady. Small sizes were often unnamed, probably because of lack of room on the base to do so. They were all hand painted by paintresses who signed their initials in enamel on the base. No two flower girls are decorated the same and the range of colours includes purple, blue, pink, yellow, green and crimson, with great variation in colours used. The word ENGLAND appears on most, but not all, of the factory stamp marks.

			£	p
Annette		135mm	225.00	
"Annette" pink dress, black bonnet (not always named)		160mm	300.00	
Balloon Seller		90mm	130.00	
		137mm	250.00	
Barbara seated on settee		110mm	300.00	
Bell Lady		92mm	110.00	
Bridesmaid (see also The Wedding	(a)	90mm	110.00	
Group, this section)	(b)	150mm	200.00	
With variations to usual model	(c)	135mm	220.00	
Bunty			265.00	
Cruet two ladies in full colour, one salt, one pepper,				
(a) Bridesmaid and Granny	Each	68mm	110.00	
(b) Lorna and Peggy	Each	85mm	110.00	
(c) Bridesmaid and Granny				
(both painted brown base)	Each	87mm	125.00	
(d) Flower Girl pepper pot		90mm	110.00	
(e) Balloon Seller salt pot		90mm	110.00	
Daisy		120mm	215.00	
Daisy Flower Girls mounted on wooden bookends		Pair	450.00	
Doris		120mm	265.00	
Dutch Girl		87mm	200.00	
Edyth		140mm	225.00	
Granny		90mm	145.00	

Annette 135mm

"Annette" Pink Dress, Black Bonnet 160mm

The Balloon Seller 137mm

Bell Lady

Bridesmaid 140mm

Dutch Girl

Cruet Salt Granny

Cruet Pepper Bridesmaid

Edyth

One of a pair of Daisy Bookends

Daisy

Granny

		£	p
Gwenda	130mm	225.00	
Joan	130mm	205.00	
"June"	115mm	365.00	
Lady Beth		300.00	
Lady Betty	160mm	240.00	
Lady Freda		300.00	
Lady Marie	145mm	260.00	
Lady Rose	170mm	240.00	
Lorna	90mm	160.00	
Miss Julia	170mm	220.00	
Miss Prudence	135mm	250.00	
Mistress Ford	100mm	325.00	
Mistress Page	105mm	325.00	
Peggy	90mm	175.00	
	125mm	240.00	
Phyllis	95mm	300.00	

**A series of 6 figures entitled 'The Wedding Group'
modelled from the original designs of the American artist
C.H. Twelvetrees, were produced as follows:**

The Bride Inscribed: *God Bless Her*	95mm	220.00	
The Bridegroom Inscribed: *God Help Him*	100mm	220.00	
The Best Man Inscribed: *No Wedding Bells for Him*	95mm	300.00	
The Mother-in-Law Inscribed: *But a Very Nice One*	105mm	220.00	
The Parson Inscribed: *Solemn and Businesslike*	100mm	220.00	
The Bridesmaid (two moulds with variations) Inscribed: *"The Bridesmaid Sweet as a Rose" Rd. No. 804763*	99mm	240.00	

for Child kneeling on a cushion, at prayer 165mm,
fully coloured, see FIRST PERIOD 9B FIGURES

Gwenda

Lady Betty

Joan

Lady Marie

Lady Rose

Lorna

Miss Julia

Miss Prudence

Mistress Page

Peggy

Phyllis

Barbara

Child kneeling on a cushion, at prayer. The Third Period coloured variety is shown here.

Third Period Flower Girl Annette 135mm

Q Toby Jugs

Apart from the Stratford Toby Jug and basin and the Churchill Toby Jug, all Goss Toby Jugs are Third Period products and a wide selection of other crested china manufacturers' moulds were used. Sizes range from miniatures, little more than 30mm high, to larger sizes in the region of 160mm high. Female Toby Jugs were also made. The same jug is often found in a variety of colours. All handles are at the back unless otherwise stated.

		£	p
Churchill Toby Jug with blue or green coat. Inscribed on base: *COPYRIGHT 1927* and on top hat: *Any Odds - Bar one That's me who Kissed the Blarney Stone* [2]	164mm	175.00
Toby Jug British Sailor blue colouring	60mm	82.50
Toby Jug white glazed and crested	67mm	47.50
	80mm	56.50
Toby Jug miniature, circular base (a) Male	44mm	75.00
(b) Female	44mm	75.00
Toby Jug Standing with pint mug and pipe, tricorn hat high at front, multi-coloured, circular black base.	90mm	95.00
Toby Jug Lady in green bonnet with white ruff, yellow dress and orange spotted white apron, carrying yellow basket and holding black gamp. (a) White	70mm	52.50
(b) Multi-coloured	70mm	120.00
(c) Multi-coloured, with removable hat as cover, only found on circular base	80mm	160.00
Toby Jug sitting cross-legged, one arm forming the handle	85mm	95.00
Green jacket with black edging, orange knickerbockers,	110mm	125.00
black/yellow hat, brown circular base	170mm	145.00
Toby Jug Male in black tricorn hat, multi-coloured with pint pot and pipe, seated with crossed legs on brown circular base	100mm	125.00
Toby Jug Male in black tricorn hat, red, green or dark green jacket, red on blue knickerbockers, yellow hose, black boots, with pint pot and pipe, sitting on a plain white stool, or with the four corner legs in black or brown	65mm	75.00
Toby Jug Male in black tricorn hat, red, green, blue or dark green jacket, blue knickerbockers, yellow hose, black boots, with pint pot and pipe, sitting with feet on plinth	127mm	135.00
Inscribed on plinth front: *No tongue can tell*	160mm	145.00
No heart can think		
O how I love		
A drop to drink		
Welsh Lady with removable hat as cover, coloured (Found in blue or orange) (Rare)	85mm	220.00

for Stratford Toby Jug and **Stratford Toby Basin** see 10 E HISTORIC MODELS

Toby Jug 100mm cross legged on brown circular base

Toby Jug 60mm seated on stool

Toby Jug 85mm, one arm as handle, brown circular base

Toby Jug 90mm standing on black circular base

Toby Jug 160mm feet on plinth with verse

Toby Jug, Female, 68mm standing

Churchill Toby Jug [2]

Black Mammy in Bath, as ashtray

Two Babies on Tray

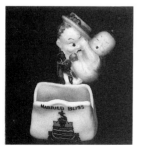

Father and Child Beside Open Bag, Married Bliss

*Gin and "It"
Two Ladies seated on Dish*

Two Coloured Children on Log

R Figures and Animals

Many figures were incorporated into ashtrays, cruets, posy-holders, and other domestic wares - while some appear to be purely ornamental. Ware in this section almost without exception originated from the Arcadian and Willow Art factories. For pieces not listed here, consult *The Price Guide to Crested China* where the model should be found. The prices will be similar.

		£	p
Babies (two) seated on Ashtray	70mm	75.00

One in a yellow romper suit, the other in blue
Inscribed: *That's the one Daddy told Nurse!*

Ballerina, Bust of   150mm   65.00
Holding fan as knop of lidded fluted pin box.
Made for *Empire Exhibition Scotland 1938*.
Yellow with green trim.

Black Baby as Pin Tray, red bow, green scarf
                    Length 90mm   Width 68mm   Height   68mm   125.00

Black Boy red and yellow hat, yellow trousers, holding
a white box as a match holder.
Inscribed: *Matches* or *Cigarettes*   100mm   125.00
                                also found in white 100mm   60.00

Black Boy and Girl seated on log   80mm   117.50

Black Boys, two seated on log   80mm   117.50

Black Cat in Boot   58mm   75.00

Black Cat on Dish   115mm x   70mm   65.00

Black Cat (seated) on Horse shoe-shaped Pin Box   70mm   65.00

Black Cat Playing Golf standing on Golf Ball   60mm   82.50

Black Cat on Pouffe blue handles   93mm   60.00
Inscribed: *Good Luck*

Black Cat Seated at Head of Horse shoe   Approx.   42mm   55.00
as Ashtray

Black Cheshire Cat identical to white variety   90mm   95.00

Black Mammy in Bath as Ashtray, multi coloured   40mm   120.00

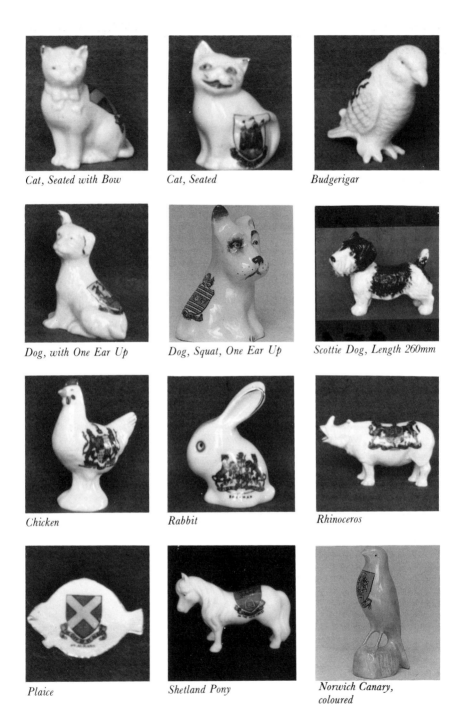

Cat, Seated with Bow

Cat, Seated

Budgerigar

Dog, with One Ear Up

Dog, Squat, One Ear Up

Scottie Dog, Length 260mm

Chicken

Rabbit

Rhinoceros

Plaice

Shetland Pony

Norwich Canary,
coloured

Black Moma as Ashtray holding skirts; found fully coloured
or partly coloured, with colour variations from version
to version   Length 90mm Height 68mm
                                             (a) Fully coloured   170.00
                                             (b) Partly coloured   110.00

Budgerigar   40.00

Burns, Bust square base   136mm   60.00

Burns, Bust socle plinth   136mm   60.00
                                                             145mm   55.00

Caddy, with Bag, standing on Golf Ball   75.00

Cheshire Cat (No base)   (a) coloured   65mm   40.00
(For coloured Add £20.00)   (b) white   98mm   40.00
                                (c) coloured   98mm   50.00

Cat, grotesque smiling, with bow   69mm   40.00

Cat, Seated, with White or Coloured Bow at Neck   60mm   40.00

Chicken White, or coloured (Add £20.00)   50mm   40.00

Cigarette Box (see Lady Reclining on box top page 373)

Comic Figure - a portly, bald, bespectacled dipsomaniac   80mm   85.00
clinging to the neck of a bottle   95mm   95.00

Crest Faced Man With coat of arms on flat face   80mm   50.00

Cruet. Punch (Salt), Judy (Pepper) and Toby (Mustard)
in full colour - all on tray.   (a) Punch 75mm (b) Others 65mm   200.00
NOTE: Items from the above set may be found
white glazed or in varying shades of lustre   Price Each   65.00

Dog and Whiskey Bottle on Ashtray
Inscribed: *His Master's Breath*   Some colouring Length 82mm   75.00

Dog, Scottie with blue Tam O'Shanter   60mm   47.50

Dog, Scottie, Black and White with glass eyes   Length 260mm   135.00

Dog, squat, one ear up, some colouring   90mm   65.00
Inscribed: *Daddy wouldn't buy me a bow*

Dog, with one ear up.   70mm   40.00
White, or Coloured (Add £10.00)

Black Cat in Boot

Black Cat on Horse Shoe Tray

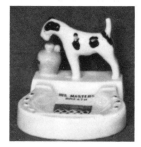

Dog and Whiskey Bottle on Ashtray

Falstaff

English Folksong Bride

Pixie on a Toadstool

White Boy Holding Open Matchbox

Scottish Lion on Ashtray

Punch and Judy Pepper and Salt

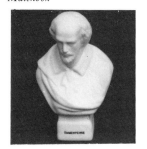

Shakespeare Bust

Gnome, carrying shells of produce under each arm

Golfer, standing on golf ball, holding clubs

			£ p
English Folksong Bride Standing beside ancient chest		93mm	75.00
Falstaff	(a) Coloured	100mm	195.00
	(b) Coloured	150mm	195.00
	(c) White	150mm	105.00
Fish, Plaice, two sizes	Length	78mm	35.00
		125mm	40.00

Flapper in Bath Tub
The top lifts off as a pin tray, coloured; both ends blue washed
with criss-cross pattern   Length 130mm Height   60mm   300.00

Frog		60mm	60.00
Gin and It Two seated ladies at side of dish, coloured Inscribed: *GIN AND "IT"*	100mm x 65mm		70.00
Golfer standing on golf ball, holding clubs		76mm	55.00
Golfer standing on golf ball, holding clubs - In centre of hexagonal dish	40mm x 75mm		65.00
Gnome standing, carrying a shell filled with produce under each arm, fully coloured		128mm	400.00
(Ann) Hathaway Bust, Coloured, unglazed	(a)	80mm	40.00
Inscribed, black printed, on plinth: *Ann Hathaway*	(b)	135mm	56.50
	White glazed (c)	140mm	40.00
Hippopotamus	Length	88mm	85.00
Jester On heart-shaped Ashtray, holding hearts	Coloured	65mm	100.00
for trumps, with heart-shaped handle	White	65mm	47.50

for Judy see Cruet

Lady in Bathing Costume and Cap on Ashtray base			110.00
Lady Godiva on Horseback. Small, glazed		80mm	65.00
Lady Reclining on Lid of Cigarette Box lady in colour	100mm x 85mm		435.00
Lifeboat Man		140mm	47.50
Man in the Moon (A face in a crescent-shaped moon) (Same as Willow Art version)		56mm	47.50

Frog

Owl

Royston Crow, coloured

Penguin on Ashtray

Scots Boy on thistle dish, holding heather, coloured

Lady on Cigarette Box Lid

Man in the Moon

Jester on Ashtray Hearts are Trumps

Three Welsh Ladies at Tea Table

Leaking Boot at Cleethorpes

Sergeant Major Pepper Pot

Toucan on Ashtray shaped as Bird's Foot

		£	p
Married Bliss Posy Vase, coloured			
(a) Girl, holding baby, with open bag in front	82mm	82.50	
(b) Man, holding baby, with open bag in front	82mm	82.50	
Inscribed: *Married Bliss*			

for Monkeys see Three Wise Monkeys

New Forest Pony	65mm	75.00
Norwich Canary coloured	102mm	110.00

Nude Female Seated on rock. Coloured with holes in base.
(For flower arrangement)   190mm   100.00

Owl one eye shut	95mm	65.00
Penguin	90mm	75.00
Penguin on Ashtray base	92mm	80.00
Pig	80mm	82.50

Inscribed: *Won't be Druv*

Pixie seated on toadstool, coloured	54mm	56.50
Policeman with raised hand.	94mm	75.00

Inscribed: *'Stop'*

for Mr. Punch see Cruet

Rabbit	75mm	47.50

Inscribed: *Isn't This Rabbit A Duck?*

Rabbit blue, yellow, green, brown, or Royal Buff	40mm	60.00
	50mm	56.50
	60mm	56.50
	80mm	56.50
	85mm	56.50
	100mm	56.50
Rabbit white	60mm	40.00
Racehorse and Jockey oval base, some colouring	108mm	240.00
Rhinoceros Length	90mm	87.50

Royston Crow almost always unmarked.	(a) Black	66mm	145.00
Inscribed: *Royston Crow* and additionally	(b) Coloured	66mm	250.00
Corvus Cornix on the plinth of the black model.			
Rd. No. 64718			

Basket containing six milk bottles

Bass Bottle and Glass on Tray

Bottle with cork, One Special Irish

Bowl, 85mm Dia., Matt Black or Lustre

Chess Pawn

Egyptian Canopic Jar with fixed Anubis Head

Coloured Lantern

Shoe, John Waterson's Clog

Square Vase 60mm

Weston-Super-Mare Floral Clock Surround

Whiskey Bottle, Soda Syphon and Glass on Ashtray

Two-piece Whiskey Bottle, Hip-flask

		£ p
		£ p

Sailor standing, vase, white   100mm   40.00

Scots Boy coloured, holding a bunch of heather on a thistle
shaped dish
The dish (a) White (crested) (b) grey lustre, or (c) coloured   90mm   80.00

Scottish Lion stylized, standing on square ashtray base.
Empire Exhibition Scotland 1938. Coloured, green trim   103mm   110.00

Sergeant Major Pepper Pot coloured   83mm   60.00

Shakespeare Bust
Inscribed black printed on plinth: *Shakespeare*
Impressed on back: *H & L.*
(Note: The exception is the bust on two books which
has no inscription)   (a) Coloured, unglazed   75mm   25.00
                       (b) White, unglazed on two books   75mm   40.00
                       (c) White, unglazed   80mm   26.00
                       (d) White, unglazed   110mm   30.00
                       (e) White, unglazed   135mm   35.00
                       (f) Bronzed   135mm   56.50
                       (g) Bronzed   165mm   65.00
                       (h) White, unglazed   165mm   35.00
                       (i) Bronzed   175mm   75.00

Shetland Pony (No base)   76mm   75.00

Swan   50mm   40.00

Three Wise Monkeys on a wall
Inscribed: *'I Speak No Evil'*
           'I See No Evil'
           'I Hear No Evil'
(Selfridge & Co. on base)   Length 50mm Height   70mm   40.00

Toff in Top Hat and Evening Dress on a Brown Bed
with scattered playing cards on the multi-coloured bedspread
covering the drunk, with cigarette in one hand.
Card holder.   Length 85mm Width   60mm   225.00

Trusty Servant coloured.   132mm   200.00
(Not to be confused with the early version)

Toucan Match holder on Ashtray shaped as a bird's foot
(Art Deco style) coloured. Colours can vary, for example:-
           (a) Blue/orange/yellow
           (b) Brown/orange/green   Length 90mm Height 61mm   100.00

Welsh Lady Bust, with some colouring   62mm   40.00

Welsh Ladies three at tea table on oval base   52mm   60.00

S.1   Ornamental Articles

£   p

Basket biscuit colour, with tiny flowers at base of handle	90mm x	75mm	60.00
Basket containing six milk bottles		50mm	45.00
Bass Bottle and Glass on Dish	60mm x	35mm	45.00
Bass Bottle and Silvered Tankard on Horse Shoe Dish	115mm x	70mm	45.00
Boot	70mm x	40mm	35.00
Bottle with Cork		70mm	30.00
Bottle with Cork Inscribed: *One Special Irish* or *One Special Scotch*		95mm	30.00
Bowl miniature, frilled edge similar to Second Period miniature	Dia.	47mm	10.00
Bowl. (a) Matt black inside and out.	Dia.	76mm	12.50
(b) Black lustre inside and out	Dia.	85mm	17.00
(c) Pearl lustre inside and out	Dia.	85mm	17.00
Bucket		55mm	22.50
Chamber Pot	(a) 52mm x	35mm	22.50
	(b) 55mm x	40mm	22.50
Chess Pawn		50mm	47.50
Chess Rook		50mm	40.00
Egg with Flapper's Head		38mm	40.00
Egyptian Canopic Jar with Anubis Head One-piece, fixed head		75mm	45.00

See also SECOND PERIOD 10E NAMED MODELS AND SPECIAL SHAPES
and THIRD PERIOD 11S DOMESTIC AND UTILITY WARE for other versions

Egyptian Mocha Cup bowl shaped (unnamed)		40mm	6.00
Fireplace with Kettle and Black Cat Inscribed: *There's No Place Like Home* or *Home Sweet Home*	90mm x	90mm	45.00
Jardinière		90mm	24.50

		£ p
Lantern coloured, hexagonal, with handle made for the *Empire Exhibition Scotland 1938*	200mm	240.00
Lavatory Pan brown seat. Inscribed: *Ashes*	60mm	30.00
Prime Cheddar Cheese, white glazed [2]	62mm	40.00
Puzzle Jug	70mm	40.00
Rose Bowl. Pink, with green foliage, with rose lid		
(a) rose knob	80mm x 50mm	47.50
(b) butterfly knob	60mm x 40mm	50.00

This piece is something of an anomaly in that it appears to be early yet bears a late mark.

Scallop Shell on three short legs See also SECOND PERIOD 10K5 ORNAMENTAL (same model)	Length 76mm	10.00
Shell, Cannon (Similar to Arcadian model)	70mm	20.00
Shoe - John Waterson's Clog in Arcadian Inscribed on side of heel: *Hawkshead The Early Home of Wordsworth the Poet*	Length 102mm	65.00
Slipper	38mm	35.00
Tankard, foaming over, with verse	55mm	30.00
Thimble	38mm	47.50
Thistle Vase	44mm	15.50
Thistle Vase coloured, no arms, with *Empire Exhibtion Scotland 1938*	65mm	30.00
Thistle Vase unglazed parian, green base, purple top, with *Empire Exhibition Scotland 1938* motif inside rim	67mm	30.00
Umbrella open	50mm x 35mm	35.00

		£ p
Vases. Various shapes and sizes under 70mm. including the following specific examples:-	Each around	5.50

(a) Ostend Vase Shape [2]	50mm	5.50
(b) Hexagonal mouth and bottom	55mm	5.50
(c) Pedestal, taper octagonal	58mm	5.50
(d) Letchworth Carinated Roman Vase shape, with stylized sunflowers decoration, black trim, numbered 27 [2]	60mm	60.00

Vase Art Deco (Clarice Cliff style), ribbed, brightly coloured	188mm	65.00

Welsh Hat plain crown, longest place-name *(Llanfair PG)* around brim. Inscribed underneath: *Made for Souvenir Shop Llangollen.*

Dia. 72mm Height	52mm	50.00

Welsh Hat, double rim		40.00

Welsh Leek (a) White	92mm	13.50
(b) Light green leaves	92mm	16.00

For inscription see SECOND PERIOD 10E HISTORIC MODELS AND SPECIAL SHAPES

Weston-super-Mare Coloured Floral Clock Surround
Can be found with original fitted clock, for which add £35.00

Length 230mm		130.00

Whiskey Bottle, Soda Syphon and Glass on

(a) Horse Shoe Ashtray	87mm	45.00
(b) Thistle Ashtray	87mm	45.00

Whiskey Bottle. Hip-flask type, two-piece	120mm	75.00

COLOURED AND LUSTRE ITEMS

Items such as coffee and tea cups and saucers, sugar basins, milk jugs, tea plates, pin trays, candle holders etc. appear in a variety of colours and lustres. Details of these are given in *The Price Guide to Arms and Decorations on Goss China*. Historic models appearing in lustre have thickly gilded handles and look most attractive.

S.2 Domestic and Utility Ware

				£	p
Ashtray.	Circular with three rests	(a) Dia.	70mm	12.50	
	With four rests	(b) Dia.	110mm	14.50	
		(c) Dia.	118mm	12.50	

Ashtray. Oval, with rests at each end — Length 100mm — 12.50

Ashtray. Rectangular with rests in each corner.
Length 135mm Width 103mm — 16.00

Ashtray. Square, card symbols in each corner — 60mm sq. — 30.00

Ashtray. Box-shaped. Thistle, spray of heather, Bust of
Burns transfer, Burns' cottage transfer and the
Empire Exhibition Scotland 1938 motif appear on this
and similar very late pieces — Length 120mm — 35.00

Ashtray. Shamrock shaped — Length 95mm — 24.50

Ashtray. Coronation, Crown, Flags, ER and
Edward VIII, Crowned May 12 1937 in bas-relief — Dia. 132mm — 35.00
(Various colours; pale blue, dark blue, green, pink, purple,
and yellow)

Bowl oval, deep fluted sides, green trim — Length 190mm — 12.50

Bowl with three floral sprays in relief around inside
rim and two coats of arms in centre — Dia. 128mm — 10.00
(Found numbered 27 with an 8 above)

Butter Dish in Wooden Surround with *Butter* carved
around rim — Dish Dia. 105mm. Overall Dia. 155mm — 17.00

Cake Plate, circular, with two moulded bow handles			
	(a) Width	220mm	19.50
	(b) Width	240mm	20.00
	(c) Width	248mm	20.00

Cake Plate, octagonal - with late colour transfer — Dia. 215mm — 30.00

Cake Plate, primrose-shaped - with late transfer — Width 265mm — 50.00

Cake Plate, square, with two ends shaped — Width 242mm — 18.50

Cake Plate, Burns, thistles, heather
Empire Exhibition Scotland 1938 — Width 250mm — 35.00

Cheese Dish, green — Length 165mm — 30.00

Ashtray, Edward VIII Dia.
132mm

Box Ashtray, Burns and
S.E.E. 1938 length 120mm

Circular Ashtray with Three
Rests Dia. 110mm

Ashtray, Rectangular,
135mm long

Hexagonal Cruet 65mm

Taper Cream Jug curved
handle 60mm

Cigarette Box rectangular,
domed lid

Cream Jug, Double Lip, No
Handle 40mm

Bulbous Milk Jug 100mm

Tea Pot and Lid
Length 180mm Height 90mm

Taper Cream Jug rope handle
97mm

Bulbous Milk Jug 100mm

			£	p

Cheese Dish   Width 160mm Length 200mm   15.00

Cigarette Box rectangular, domed lid, floral decoration   40.00

Coronation Mug *1937 George VI & Elizabeth*   80mm   40.00
This and any other item bearing this design would be worth
approximately the same.

Cream Jugs
  (a) Double lip, no handle   40mm   5.50
  (b) Taper, one lip, curved handle   60mm   7.50
  (c) Melon, black trim, stylized sunflowers decoration   85mm   50.00

Cruet (various) Salt and Pepper pairs:
  (a) Bulbous   Each   54mm   15.00
  (b) Hexagonal   Each   65mm   11.00
  (c) Octagonal   Each   85mm   12.50

Cruet. Trefoil dish, with combined salt tray, separate pepper,
and two-piece mustard   30.00

(See also Egyptian Canopic Jars with Anubis Heads adapted as cruet)

Cups and Saucers, various

	Saucer Dia.	Cup Height	
(a) Scalloped edged, plain	118mm	43mm	11.00
(b) Curved, loop handle	134mm	60mm	10.00
(c) Curved, plain, shaped handle	139mm	60mm	7.50
(d) Straight-sided, plain, slightly curved saucer, loop handle	135mm	68mm	10.00
(e) Curved, plain, loop handle	136mm	68mm	7.50
(f) Taper, everted rim, loop handle, double indentation rim to base of cup and inside saucer	135mm	70mm	10.00
(g) Curved, tall, cup on drip-free rim, loop handle	138mm	72mm	10.00
(h) Fluted, whorl pattern		70mm	12.00

N.B. With late cups and saucers, the saucers are usually plain,
with the arms/decorations on the cup, but sometimes on both.

Cylindrical Pot and lid with shaped knob
                    Overall Dia. 115mm Height   55mm   17.50

Dish quadrifoil   Length 143mm   10.00

Dish twelve-pointed oval   Length 145mm   15.00

Dish oval, with tapered sides, green trim and rose
decoration inside   35.00

*Cup and Saucer curved, loop
handle*

*Cup and Saucer curved, drip-
free rim*

*Cup and Saucer curved, loop
handle*

*Cup and Saucer curved, loop
handle*

*Cup and Saucer taper, loop
handle*

*Cup and Saucer curved, loop
handle*

*Cup and Saucer, straight,
everted rim*

*Cup and Saucer, Taper,
Shaped Handle*

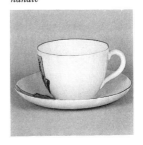

*Cup and Saucer curved, loop
handle*

*Cup and Saucer, taper everted
rim*

*Cup and Saucer, Scalloped
edge, ornate handle*

*Cup and Saucer, straight,
curved handle*

		£	p
Dish circular	Dia. 105mm	5.50

Dish circular Dia. 105mm 5.50

Dish oblong, fluted edges
Coronation George VI & Elizabeth 1937 130mm x 100mm 35.00

Dish circular, with pink roses transfer Dia. 140mm 35.00

Dish circular, rim deep-patterned with three panels of basket
weave and three wider panels of flower sprays, all in relief, with
colour transfer in bowl Dia. 145mm 10.00

Dish shaped, oval Length 142mm 10.00

Dish (for sweets or nuts) with bow tabs, maroon trim.
Empire Exhibition Scotland 1938 Length 145mm 30.00

Dish oval, tapered (scalloped sides) green trim,
floral centre Length 190mm Width 165mm 12.50

Egg cup beaker-shaped 40mm 18.50

Egg cup goblet-shaped 58mm 19.50

Egyptian Canopic Jar with Anubis Head

(a) **Pepper pot** in the form of the Anubis Head (Egyptian
Canopic Jar No. 1) with filling hole secured with metal-topped
cork plug in the bottom, and pouring holes on the Jackal's
snout; Blackpool arms; inscribed on the base: *Made in England.* 75mm 45.00

(b) **Salt Pot** in the form of the Anubis Head, as described for the
above pepper version, but with the pouring hole in the end of
the Jackal's snout. 75mm 45.00

(N.B. Both have fixed heads, unlike the named [2] model, but
with the same gilding line).

Honey section dish and cover square
(a) White with Bee knop [2] 35.00
(b) Coloured, Bees and Clovers 60.00
(c) Black trim, stylized poppies 70.00
Cover 115mm x 115mm
Dish 145mm x 145mm

Lip Salve Pot and lid, cylindrical Grey lustre
Dia. 43mm Height 35mm 15.00

Match Holder octagonal 45mm 13.00
Inscribed: *Matches*

Cake Plate square with two shaped ends 248mm

Cake Plate circular two moulded bow handles 240mm

Cake Plate coupe shaped 240mm

Cake Plate square with two shaped ends 248mm side view

Cake Plate circular two handles 240mm side view

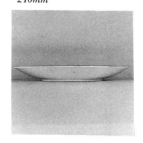

Cake Plate coupe shaped 240mm side view

Dish basket weave in relief pattern Dia. 145mm

Cake Plate circular two moulded bow handles 220mm

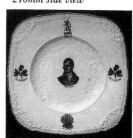

Cake Plate, Burns and S.E.E. 1938, 250mm

Soup Bowl, Octagonal

Butter Dish in Wooden Surround

Tea Plate, Dia. 150mm

				£	p
Milk Jug,	(a) Bulbous		90mm		7.50
	(b) Bulbous		100mm		7.50
	(c) Plain, rope handle		97mm		9.00
Mug with floral decoration, two handled			118mm		24.50
			133mm		24.50
Mug one handled			100mm		13.00
Mug, Little Red Riding Hood Scene, in relief (Also with *Empire Exhibition Scotland 1938)*			100mm		110.00
Pin Tray		Dia.	70mm		5.50
		Dia.	100mm		12.50
Pin Tray Spade-shaped Inscribed on rim: *Pin Tray*		85mm x	85mm		25.00
Pin Tray Heart-shaped with *Coronation George VI & Elizabeth 1937*		105mm x	112mm		30.00
Posy Rings and Holders blue, brown, or green					
	(a) Circular	Dia.	90mm		15.00
	(b) Circular	Dia.	155mm		15.00
	(c) Elliptical	Length	190mm		15.00
	(d) Horse Shoe	110mm x	115mm		16.00
	(d) Horse Shoe	160mm x	230mm		16.00
Preserve Jars and Lids					
	(a) Shaped		60mm		35.00
	(b) Orange shaped with peel pattern in				
	bas-relief, orange colour		90mm		60.00
	(c) Straight-sided, plain knop		100mm		20.00
	(d) Straight-sided, blackberry knop		100mm		30.00
	(e) With knop, and spoon cut-out		115mm		25.00
Powder Bowl and lid rose knop, yellow lustre		Dia.	130mm		40.00
Shaving Mug		(a)	100mm		57.50
	Ride a Cock Horse	(b)	100mm		65.00
Soup Bowl	(a) Two handles	Dia.	157mm		20.00
	(b) Octagonal	Dia.	150mm		20.00
Empire Exhibition Scotland 1938					
Sugar Basins and Bowls					
	(a) Octagonal	Dia.	70mm		10.50
			85mm		12.50
			100mm		15.50

Orange Preserve Pot and Lid

Sugar Basin circular 60mm

Taper Water Jug Potters Coil Pattern 235mm

Bowl, with 1938 Scottish Empire Exhibition motif

Mug 80mm

Green Posy Ring

Quadrifoil Dish

Octagonal Sugar Bowl

Welsh Lady Teapot

			£ p
(b) Shaped	Height 45mm Dia.	80mm	5.50
(c) Circular	Height 60mm Dia.	95mm	5.50
	Height 65mm Dia.	120mm	6.50
(d) Taper, pedestal base	Height 60mm Dia.	110mm	6.50
(e) Vertical flutes.	Height 60mm Dia.	80mm	30.00

Coronation George VI & Elizabeth 1937

Sweetmeat Dish green	Length 120mm	18.50
	165mm	18.50

Tankard shaped with curved handle. Huntsman with hounds and
fox in bas-relief. Coloured   95mm   90.00

Tea Plate, ribbed edge, dark red trim
Empire Exhibition Scotland 1938   140mm   22.50

Tea Plate, black trim, stylized sunflowers decoration   160mm   40.00

Tea Plates, various	125mm	6.00
	150mm	6.50
	160mm	6.50
	165mm	6.50
	175mm	8.50
	180mm	10.00

Tea Pot and Lid in form of Welsh Lady, coloured, her arms
forming handle and spout.
Inscribed on the front: *Cymmerwch Gwpaned O De*   152mm   85.00

Tea Pot and lid

(a) Length 180mm Height	90mm	35.00
With sunken lid (b) Length 205mm Height	100mm	30.00
Georgian style (c) Length 210mm Height	120mm	40.00

for Tea Strainer,
see M METALWORK chapter

Toast Rack green   Length 100mm   20.00

Tray shaped and multi-crested   Width 320mm Length 440mm   35.00

Water Jugs
  (a) Pedestal base, angular handle, coloured bandings around
      base, floral decoration on body   195mm   60.00
  (b) Potters Coil pattern, coloured   235mm   32.50

COLOURED AND LUSTRE ITEMS

Items such as coffee and tea cups and saucers, sugar basins,
milk jugs, tea plates, pin trays, candle holders etc, appear in a
variety of colours and lustres. Details of these are give in *The
Price Guide to Arms and Decorations on Goss China*. Historic models
appearing in lustre have thickly gilded handles and look most
attractive.

T W.H. GOSS COTTAGE POTTERY, ROYAL BUFF

AND BASKET WEAVE

There is a deal of inconsistency in the factory marks appearing on Cottage
Pottery and Royal Buff wares.

Cottage Pottery is pale yellow and usually, or should, carry the marks: W H
Goss Cottage Pottery, sometimes with the addition of ENGLAND under the
Goshawk.

Royal Buff is a darker, brown colour and tends to be thicker and usually, or
should, carry the mark: Royal Buff W H Goss ENGLAND. However, pieces of
apparently Cottage Pottery or Royal Buff can appear with either mark,
probably due to lack of care during manufacture.

The pieces have been listed in four groups in this section.

1. Cottage Shapes, which are pieces in the shape of a typical English thatched
   country cottage.
2. Cottage scene, where the items are decorated with an English country
   garden scene around a cottage.
3. Royal Buff, which is normally found decorated with crocuses, poppies or
   similar.
4. Basket weave, which is modelled in the shape of a woven basket, and
   variations thereof to suit the shape.

The reader should, therefore, look for the shape first under the above headings
and not be too concerned if the factory mark is apparently incorrect.

COTTAGE POTTERY - DOMESTIC WARE

1. PIECES IN THE SHAPE OF A COLOURED COTTAGE

			£ p
Biscuit Barrel and lid		150mm	65.00
Butter Dish and lid	Length 107mm Height	90mm	40.00
Butter Dish and lid, square		120mm	40.00
Cheese Dish and cover	Length 170mm Height	120mm	50.00
Egg Cup		35mm	22.50
Egg Cups, four		Set	95.00
	Add for circular tray Dia.	130mm	30.00
Milk Jug, square		56mm	45.00
		75mm	56.50
		98mm	60.00
		125mm	65.00
Mustard Pot and lid		50mm	30.00

		£ p
Pepper Shaker	50mm	30.00
Salt Shaker	50mm	30.00

The above three items can be found on a rectangular tray,
for which Add £35.00

Serviette holder	72mm	30.00
Sugar Basin and lid	70mm	35.00
Tea Pot and lid	150mm x 115mm	82.50
	190mm x 115mm	82.50
Toast Rack	(a) To hold two slices Length 70mm	30.00
	(b) To hold four slices Length 105mm	35.00

COTTAGE POTTERY - DOMESTIC WARE

2. PIECES DECORATED WITH A COTTAGE SCENE

for Advertising Stand
see 8. ADVERTISING WARE AND LEAFLETS Chapter

Cake Plate, circular	Dia. 240mm	35.00
Cake Plate, square, with handles	240mm	35.00

Cups and Saucers
(a) Curved, dark yellow, brown trim

	Saucer Dia. 134mm Cup height 66mm	15.00
(b) Taper, angular handle	70mm	18.00
(c) Taper, curved handle with thumb rest	75mm	18.00
Dish, two handles, cottage scene in relief	57mm	39.50
Dish, round, two twig handles	Dia. 157mm	40.00
Dish, oval	Length 125mm	40.00

Shakespearian Cottages Plate
Decorated with three coloured cottages, flower tubs, and trees.
Inscribed: *Famous Old English Cottages by W.H. Goss.*

Made in England	Dia. 230mm	40.00
Sugar Basin and lid	43mm	25.00
Tankard, Cottage decoration in relief	100mm	40.00
Tea Plate	Dia. 150mm	22.50

Cottage-shaped Tea Pot

Cottage-shaped Cheese Dish

Cottage-shaped 4-slice Toast Rack

Cottage-shaped Pepper Pot

Cottage-shaped Milk Jug

Cottage Scene on Oval Dish

Cottage Pottery Cup and Saucer curved

Royal Buff Pottery Beaker, 114mm

Cottage Pottery Cup and Saucer, taper

Cottage Pottery Plate Shakespearian Cottages

Royal Buff Honey Section Dish and Cover Bee Knob

Royal Buff Beehive Honey Pot and lid

£   p

3. ROYAL BUFF

Much late ware only appears with transfer printed pictorial views,
for which Add £15.00-£25.00

for Advertising Ashtray
see 8. ADVERTISING WARE AND LEAFLETS Chapter

Beaker, Taper, with or without handle		85mm	13.00
		105mm	16.00
		114mm	16.00
Beaker, King Cole and his Fiddlers Three on reverse, in relief, coloured		100mm	65.00
Butter Dish decorated with tulips or similar, in wooden surround carved with: *Take a little Butter*	Dia.	115mm	23.50
Coffee Pot and lid octagonal		200mm	65.00
Coffee Cup and Saucer octagonal		65mm	25.00
		90mm	25.00
Cup and Saucer	(a) Curved sided	65mm	15.00
	(b) Straight sided with everted rim	75mm	15.00
Fern Pot scallop edge		92mm	22.00
Honey Section Dish with Bee as knop [2]	Square 145mm x	145mm	35.00
Honey Pot and lid. Beehive shaped with Bee as knop on lid			
	(a) White	97mm	30.00
	(b) Coloured	97mm	60.00
Horse Shoe Posy ring		120mm	26.00
Jam Dish fluted	Dia.	150mm	18.00

Jugs

(a) Cream size	55mm	15.00
(b) Taper Tankard, diamond handle yellow, with transfer	75mm	20.00
(c) Bulbous, yellow, green trim	84mm	20.00
(d) Cylindrical	100mm	20.00
(e) Bulbous, Widdecombe Fair decoration	100mm	75.00
(f) Taper, green rim, sprays of pink roses: *Empire Exhibition Scotland 1938*	160mm	30.00
(g) Bulbous, striped horizontal decoration	300mm	35.00

Royal Buff Jug, taper

Royal Buff Jug, bulbous

Royal Buff Sugar Bowl, curved

The Little Brown Jug

Royal Buff Taper Milk Jug

Royal Buff Two-handled Cider Mug 100mm

Royal Buff Preserve Pot and Lid, with Proverb

Bulbous Jug, Widdecombe Fair Decoration

Royal Buff Tankard with Hunting Scene

Tankard, Cottage Decoration in relief

Cottage Pottery Teaplate

Tankard with Little Red Riding Hood Scene

		£	p

Little Brown Jug upright, with title, or verse, and sometimes also
a Black Cat decoration, or *From...*with resort name

	Sizes (various) 60mm to 110mm	40.00

Mug   80mm   11.00

Mug, twig handle, decoration in relief: *Ride a cock horse*
and on a milestone: *To Banbury Cross*   75mm   75.00
On reverse, a girl on a toy horse on wheels   90mm   75.00

Mug, decorated in low relief with Old King Cole and his Fiddlers
Inscribed: *Old King Cole was a Merry Old Soul*   100mm   75.00

Mug, Cider, two-handled, decorated with apples
Inscribed: *Yaa's tis thursty wurk 'ave a drop a' Zomerzet Zider*   100mm   75.00

Mug, peg handle, Widdecombe Fair scene in relief, with the   100mm   75.00
song words on reverse

Mug, one handle, Mary and Little Lamb scene in relief,   100mm   75.00
with rhyme and cottage scene in relief on reverse

Pepper and Salt Pots, oviform   Each   55mm   12.50

Pepper and Salt Castors, shaped   Each   90mm   12.50

Pepper Pot, Pixie, coloured   145mm   50.00

Pin Tray circular   Dia.   70mm   19.50

Plate   265mm x 230mm   45.00
Inscribed: *Education is Better than Wealth*

Preserve Pot and lid poppies decoration
Inscribed on pot: *East West Hame's Best* or other proverb, or verse.   110mm   30.00
Also found with Pixie Finial

for Rabbit see 11R FIGURES AND ANIMALS

Sugar Basin   (a) Octagonal   80mm   20.00
    (b) Taper, everted rim Dia. 85mm Height   50mm   15.00
    (c) Taper, everted rim Dia. 95mm Height   65mm   20.00

Sugar Bowl curved, green trim   Dia. 117mm Height   62mm   20.00

Tankard, Hunting scene in relief, coloured   75mm   75.00
Huntsman, hounds and fox   95mm   75.00

Tankard, shaped, one handle   95mm   16.00

Royal Buff Mug, with proverb

Royal Buff Beaker, taper, with handle

Royal Buff Horse Shoe Posy Ring

Royal Buff Mug, Mary and Lamb, in relief

Royal Buff Mug (reverse) Rhyme and Cottage, in relief

Basket Weave 2-slice Toast Rack and Preserve Dish

Basket Weave Cruet, Apple and Orange

Basket Weave 2-slice Toast Rack

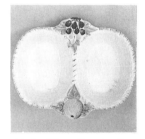

Basket Weave 2-section Jam Dish

Basket Weave Boat-shape Jam Dish

Basket Weave Jam Dish, Blue

Basket Weave taper Jam Dish and Lid

		£ p

Tankard, shaped, everted rim, Little Red Riding Hood　　100mm　110.00
Coloured scene in relief.
Also found with: *Empire Exhibition Scotland 1938*

Tea Plate green trim　　　　　　　　　　Dia. 166mm　　20.00

Tea Pot and lid taper　　　　　　　　　　115mm　　40.00

Tea Pot Stand　　　　　　　　　(a) Dia. 103mm　　20.00
　　　　　　　　　　　　　　　　(b) Dia. 145mm　　25.00

Toast Rack with coloured Pixie seated at each end　　80mm　　45.00

4. BASKET WEAVE POTTERY

Basket (see Cruet)

Beaker beige　　　　　　　　　　　　100mm　　20.00

Cruet
(a) Salt Castor, apple shaped, coloured　　　　　30mm　　35.00
(b) Pepper Castor, orange shaped, coloured　　　30mm　　35.00
(c) Basket, beige, holding (a) and (b)　　Length　80mm　　25.00
(d) The above three items as a set　　　　　　　　　115.00

Egg Cup taper, coloured, fruit in relief　　　　　　10.00

Egg Cups and Stands　　(a) Four egg cups (as above)　　35mm　　45.00
　　　　　　　　　　　　(b) Six egg cups (as above)　　　　60.00

Jam Dishes
(a) Taper, and lid with striped handle, fruit decoration on lid
　　Inscribed: *From*....(e.g. Lulworth)　　Height 75mm Dia. 110mm　　22.50
(b) Circular, with a single fruit on one side, and a bunch of small
　　fruits on the other side, both inside the rim　　Dia. 123mm　　15.00
(c) Oval, or Boat-shaped, beige, coloured orange at one end, and
　　coloured bunch of grapes at the other end
　　Inscribed: *from*....(e.g. Dymchurch)　　Length 160mm　　25.00
(d) Two-section, beige, joined by a coloured orange and leaves
　　on one side, and coloured grapes and leaves on the other side
　　　　　　　　　　　　　　　　　Length 160mm　　30.00
(e) As (d) in all one colour, e.g., pale green　　Length 160mm　　18.00

Nut Tray (see Jam Dish (c) version above)

Preserve Pot and lid cream, orange knop; pot decorated with
blue, mauve and yellow grapes　　　　　　115mm　　100.00

£ p

Tea Plate floral, and lady in period dress, in relief:
*Ride a Cock Horse to Banbury Cross To see a Fine Lady Upon a
White Horse*   Dia. 150mm   22.00

Toast Racks
(a) Two-slice; decorated with fruit at each end, and with
stripes matching the taper jam dish (a) above   Length 110mm   22.50
(b) Two-slice; the sections striped as above, and with two
dishes for marmalade or preserve, one at each end of
the rack   Length 175mm   35.00

U   Hand Painted Ware

As well as the normal W.H. GOSS ENGLAND trade mark, there is also a W.H.
Goss Hand Painted mark, usually found on domestic ware Royal Buff and
Cottage pottery (as opposed to porcelain). The hand painted ware covers a
large range of items, varying from a cottage-shaped tea set to the Little Brown
Jug versions, beakers, cups and saucers, and various other items of domestic
ware. These will be found in the preceding chapter T.

Obviously the original Goss moulds were still available during the Third
Period, and a number of shapes were used to carry a range of floral patterns
extending from delicate pastel shades to rather garish hand painted examples.

It is difficult to accurately list all Third Period ware as there are so many
variations. If a similar piece to one shown is found, then a price in the same
region will apply. The reader should also consult DOMESTIC AND
UTILITY WARES, ORNAMENTAL ARTICLES and the First Period after
checking all possibilities in Third Period Goss.

For full details and values of all decorations on Goss China, see *The Price Guide
to Arms and Decorations on Goss China* by Nicholas Pine (Milestone Publications).

V Godfrey William Goss Ware and Decorations

William Henry Goss's second son, Godfrey William, emigrated to America in 1882 and lived at Trenton, New Jersey. In the City Directory in the State Library, Godfrey is listed between 1885 and 1889 successively as decorator, kiln firer or potter. Little is known of his products while at Trenton, but a pierced cake basket made by him there is in the possession of the family in America. In 1886 he was joined by his betrothed, Alice Buckley, a paintress from his father's factory at Stoke-on-Trent. They married immediately upon her arrival in America, and moved straight to Godfrey's farm. By 1891 Godfrey's ambition to further pursue his pottery skills caused him to seek work at Peru, Indiana, where he set up his own factory and fired his first kiln. Alice then sold the farming stock and joined her husband, eventually moving on to Kokomo in Indiana, and employing at their factory two emigrants from the Staffordshire potteries, one a skilled kiln firer, the other a clay presser. For his enamelling, Godfrey used recipes received from his father at Stoke.

This brief foreword is intended to draw attention to some of Godfrey's pottery produced in America. Although his main line at the Kokomo factory was the production of electrical insulators, his pottery was never a viable proposition. Godfrey did, however, produce other pieces, decorated by Alice, of interest to Goss enthusiasts. They were not generally for sale commercially, apart from those listed hereunder, copies of which have appeared with increasing regularity in America, and which were definitely retailed there. In addition to the pieces listed, which have all appeared in Britain, it is understood that Godfrey also made floral crosses. His pottery activities had ceased by 1907 when he moved to Eldorado, Oklahoma, to farm, and where he helped to found the First State Bank of Eldorado before moving on to Raymondville, Texas, where he died in 1939, Alice having previously died there in 1936.

The full story of their lives in England and their adventures in America is told in the biography: **WILLIAM HENRY GOSS The story of the Staffordshire Family of Potters who invented Heraldic Porcelain** by Lynda and Nicholas Pine (Milestone Publications).

£   p

See the BIOGRAPHY page 127 for pictures of six GODFREY
items made in the USA

Comport moulded and mottled in relief,
plate top decorated with birds   Dia. 220mm Height   110mm   150.00

Cake Basket pierced, white   Dia.   220mm   150.00

Cat black lying down, legs forward, white paws, yellow eyes and
some white marks.   Length 225mm Height   120mm   150.00
Inscribed on base in manuscript: *Goss China*

Derringer hand painted reproduction of model circa 1840. Length   205mm   150.00
Inscribed on base: *Hand Painted Porcelain by Goss*

Duck as Posy Holder or Ashtray, with grooved tail as cigarette rest.
Inscribed in manuscript on base: *Hand Painted*
Underglaze Porcelain by Goss
     (a) White with pink/black/grey flowers
         Length 100mm Height   58mm   110.00
     (b) Mallard, male, natural colouring
         Length 135mm Height   80mm   110.00

Pheasant as Ashtray, coloured.   Length 220mm Width   65mm   175.00
Inscribed on base: *Hand Painted Underglaze Porcelain by Goss*

Powder Horn for wall hanging brown and white   150mm   100.00
Inscribed on base: *Hand Painted Porcelain* but no word Goss.

Plate multi-coloured, floral rim, tree, grasses and birds in centre.
Inscription hand written on base: *Alice Buckley paintress*
     Dia.   225mm   200.00

A dinner plate has been seen in the major U.S. collection produced
by American pottery Haviland and also marked *GDA*. The
decoration is of strawberries and leaves fully covering the piece and
signed GOSS, with pronounced serifs on all letters. This piece is
believed to have been decorated by Alice Goss.   Dia.   200mm   100.00

Tankard with brown handle in the form of a riding crop decorated
with black transfer of a horse and fence.   120mm   100.00
GOSS CHINA on black leaf mark.

Mark on base of Duck Ashtray

Leaf Mark on base of Black Cat

Leaf Mark on base of Tankard

Black Cat

Tankard Mug with Crop Handle

Duck Ashtray or Posy Holder

Multi-coloured floral plate decorated by Alice (Buckley) Goss

Comport modelled by Godfrey, height 110mm, width 220mm, with bird decoration in bas-relief

Reverse showing Alice's signature

Pierced cake basket, 220mm dia., made by Godfrey in Trenton, New Jersey

The Price Guide to Arms and Decorations on Goss China

Nicholas Pine

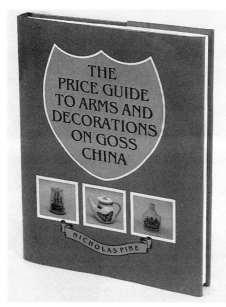

After ten years of research, Nicholas Pine and Editor Norman Pratten have produced a complete listing of all known **Goss arms and decorations** in a magnificent 320 page, large format Hardback book with full colour jacket.

The book provides a unique and comprehensive listing, with values, of the 10,000 plus coats of arms and decorations which adorned Goss China during its period of production spanning 80 years.

Also included are chapters on the Manufacture and Decoration of Goss China and a History of W H Goss and his factory.

The largest section, geographical place names, now contains 2,200 entries, only *one-third* of the number contained in the first (green cover) book of Arms and Decorations. The majority of those listed in this volume are now known *not* to be Goss First, Second or Third Period, but instead were introduced by Arkinstall & Son (Arcadian) when they took over the works in 1929. All these Arcadian place names, 4,400 in all, are listed in a special section of the new book so that collectors for the first time can ascertain the arms used only by the Goss factory.

The book comprises themes used by the factory including: Chapters on all Civic arms in the British Isles and overseas; Royal, Nobility and Personal; Educational, Medical and Ecclesiastical; Commemoratives and Exhibitions; Transfer Printed Pictorial Views and Enamelled Illustrations; Regimental Badges and Naval Crests; Flora and Fauna; Armour, Flags and Masonic, and late decorations known as Third Period.

The Guide contains over 2,000 illustrations, and every piece listed is priced or valued, sub-divided into over 100 easy-to-use sections.

The book has been designed for use in conjunction with **The Concise Encyclopaedia and Price Guide to Goss China** by the same author. Collectors and dealers who possess a copy of the price guide are strongly advised to acquire this new book so that accurate up-to-date values may be obtained for each piece, for, as often as not, the decoration on a particular piece is worth much more than the piece itself.

260mm x 215mm. 320 pages. 2000 illustrations. £19.95

William Henry Goss

The story of the Staffordshire family of Potters
who invented Heraldic Porcelain.
Lynda & Nicholas Pine

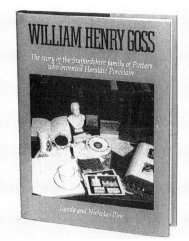

In this first ever biography of the man who is credited with inventing heraldic porcelain and his family who worked with him and at times against him, the authors tell the story of Goss china in fascinating detail.

From a promising start as a literary student, William Henry Goss used the important contacts he made in London to carve himself a career in the pottery industry in Stoke-on-Trent. At first he produced a limited, expensive range of Parian busts and figurines, but with the entry of his sons, Adolphus and later Victor and Huntley into the business, production switched to the small white models bearing colourful coats of arms for which the firm became famous.

The authors recount the stories of Godfrey, who ran away to New Jersey with a factory paintress, began a pottery there and founded the American branch of the family; the surprising Falkland Islands connection, still continuing today; why William refused to speak to his wife for the last twenty years of his life and how he came to have four homes all at the same time.

The history of the three periods of production is complemented by fascinating chapters on how the porcelain was both manufactured and sold through virtually every town in the country.

The book is illustrated with over 350 photographs and maps, includes much material not previously published and comprehensive family trees.

As the story unfolds you can discover:

- About the three periods of Goss manufacture and how the trade developed leading eventually to mass popularity nationwide.
- The amazing Falkland Islands connection, how Port Stanley and the Upland Goose Hotel came to be so-named and the exciting story of how the Goss family came to emigrate to those barren islands - and the dreadful fate that befell them.
- Why youngest daughter Florence married a bewiskered Bostonian millionaire older than her father.
- The truth about the rumour that second son Godfrey got a factory girl 'into trouble' and was banished to America. Why did Godfrey emigrate to America? and did he start a US Goss factory?

- The beginnings of William's potting career. Why did he decide to become a potter?
- How the romantic young William became an obstinate and pedantic father and eventually a near recluse.
- Why William did not speak to his wife for the last 20 years of his life - and how he came to have four homes all at the same time.
- His amazing generosity towards his friends and workforce and his unbelievable meanness and cruelty towards his wife and children.
- How William viewed his two sons Adolphus and Victor as rivals.
- Who *really* invented heraldic porcelain and how it was manufactured and marketed.

260mm x 217mm 350 Illustrations 5 Family Trees 256 pages. Bibliography and Glossary.
Casebound. £19.95

The Price Guide to Crested China

Nicholas Pine

The book, now in its fourth edition, lists, describes and prices every known piece of Crested China. It incorporates the history of every factory, where known, now numbering over 300, and over 500 marks. The author has now incorporated all information originally published in *Crested China* by Sandy Andrews, updated for 1992, resulting in a massive fount of information available in one book for the first time.

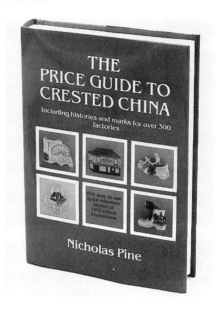

Particulars of over 10,000 pieces are given with their dimensions and relevant details where thought to be of interest. The Guide contains a complete listing of all the pieces made by every factory. The history of and all known information about over 300 factories is provided and a mass of other exciting facts answer all the questions that collectors ask such as 'Why does the same piece appear with a different factory mark?' 'Why do some pieces have no crest, factory mark or name?' 'Why are some pieces numbered?'; etc, etc.

In addition to all this information, over 500 line drawings of factory marks are shown to aid identification, the majority of which are not shown in any of the usual books on marks.

The story of Crested China, how the trade expanded and some of the colourful characters involved is also told.

Every item is priced at the current retail price charged by Goss and Crested China Ltd.

The Guide contains a special easy-to-use section of nearly 1000 illustrations, each described and priced, providing a quick reference for the expert, novice and dealer who want a quick visual guide to identification and price.

215mm x 155mm 500 pages. 1000+ illustrations. Casebound. £19.95

Crested China

Sandy Andrews

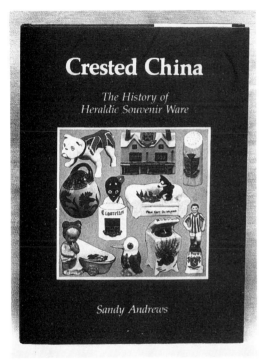

This title, first published in 1980, is the first and only serious and comprehensive work attempted on this subject - although written in a readable lighthearted style.

A large, lavish production with hard cover and coloured dust jacket, it contains 304 pages. Over 750 illustrations - 90 in full colour - are included, depicting over 1000 pieces from all factories and showing items from every possible theme with special emphasis on animals, buildings and Great War crested china.

The book is not a price guide, although indications of rare items are given, but a lasting, profusely illustrated reference work which is recommended to all crested china enthusiasts.

303mm x 220mm. 304 pages. Cased. 753 illustrations. £19.95

Available from bookshops everywhere or by post direct from Milestone Publications. Descriptive leaflets on this and all other titles connected with Goss and crested china are sent on request.

Goss & Crested China Ltd. are the leading dealers in Heraldic China.

We have been buying and selling for over 20 years and our experienced staff led by Lynda and Nicholas Pine will be able to answer your questions and assist you whether you are a novice or an experienced collector.

A constantly changing attractively priced stock of some 5,000 pieces may be viewed at the Goss & Crested China Centre in Horndean, including Goss cottages, fonts, crosses, shoes, lighthouses, models etc. and the full range of crested ware including military, animals, buildings etc. covering all the other manufacturers.

Visitors are welcome to call during business hours of 9.00 - 5.30 any day except Sunday. Those travelling long distances are advised to telephone in advance so that they may be sure of receiving personal attention upon arrival, but this is not essential.

Most of our business is by mail order and we publish *Goss & Crested China,* a monthly 32 page illustrated catalogue containing hundreds of pieces for sale from every theme and in every price range. The catalogue is available by annual subscription; please refer to the following page for details of this and the Goss and Crested China Club.

In addition, if you specialise, we will be pleased to offer your particular pieces or crests from time to time as suitable items become available. Please let us know your wants as with our ever-changing stock we will probably have something to suit.

Our service is personal and friendly and all orders and correspondence are dealt with by return. You will find us fair and straightforward to deal with, as we really care about crested china and this is reflected in our service.

Finally, we are just as keen to buy as to sell and offers of individual items or whole collections are always welcome. These will be dealt with by return and the very highest offers will be made.

Goss & Crested China Ltd,
62 Murray Road,
Horndean,
Waterlooville
Hampshire
PO8 9JL

Telephone: Horndean (0705) 597440
Facsimile: Horndean (0705) 591975

Would you like to join

The Goss & Crested China Club

Exclusively for collectors and customers of Goss & Crested China Ltd. Membership will provide answers to question such as:

How do I find the pieces I am looking for?

What is a fair price?

Where can I obtain information on Goss China and Goss collecting?

Where can I exchange or sell pieces I no longer require?

Join the Goss & Crested China Club without delay and receive the following benefits:

FREE Specially designed enamel membership badge.

FREE Membership card and number.

FREE Telephone and postal advice service.

FREE Information on books about heraldic china collecting.

FREE Especially favourable Club members part-exchange rates for pieces surplus to requirements.

FREE Without obligation search-and-offer service for any items and decorations that you seek.

FREE Invitations to Club open days.

EXCLUSIVE Valuation service for your collection

EXCLUSIVE Club Members only special offers announced regularly in Club members monthly catalogue *Goss & Crested China*.

Membership is free and is available to subscribers to Goss & Crested China the club's monthly catalogue of pieces for sale.

To join, just send £12.00 annual subscription* to The Goss & Crested China Club, 62 Murray Road, Horndean, Waterlooville, Hampshire PO8 9JL, and you will receive a membership application form with your first copy of the catalogue. Upon receipt of the completed form, you will be sent your enamel badge, membership card and full details of the club's special offers and services.

*For Airmail outside Europe add £8.00

Other titles available from

Milestone Publications

Please send for a full catalogue of these and other books about antique porcelain.

William Henry Goss. The Story of the Staffordshire Family of Potters who invented Heraldic Porcelain
Lynda and Nicholas Pine

The Price Guide to Arms and Decorations on Goss China
Nicholas Pine

The Concise Encyclopaedia and Price Guide to Goss China
Nicholas Pine

The Price Guide to Crested China
Nicholas Pine

Crested China. The History of Heraldic Souvenir Ware
Sandy Andrews

The Goss Record 8th and War Editions
J.J. Jarvis A facsimile reprint.

Goss and Other Crested China
Nicholas Pine

In Search of the Better 'Ole The Life, The Works and The Collectables of Bruce Bairnsfather
Tonie and Valmai Holt

Goss & Crested China. Illustrated monthly catalogues listing items for sale. Available by Annual Subscription. Details upon request from 62 Murray Road, Horndean, Waterlooville, Hants PO8 9JL.